GÜNTHER RALL

—A Memoir—

LUFTWAFFE ACE AND NATO GENERAL

GÜNTHER RALL

---A Memoir---

LUFTWAFFE ACE AND NATO GENERAL

The Authorized Biography

by
Jill Amadio

Library of Congress Cataloging-in-Publication Data

Amadio, Jill.
  Guenther Rall : a memoir : Luftwaffe ace and NATO general / by Jill Amadio.
    p. cm.
Includes bibliographical references and index.
  ISBN 0-9715533-0-0
      1. Rall, Guenther. 2. Fighter pilots–Germany–Biography. 3. World War,
      1939-1945–Aerial operations, German. 4. Generals–Germany–Biography.
      5. North Atlantic Treaty Organization–Armed Forces–Germany. I. Title.
  D787 .A52 2002
  940.54'4943'092--dc21
                    2002004372

Library of Congress Control Number: 2002004372
ISBN 0-9715533-0-0

First Edition   1 2 3 4 5 6 7 8 9 10

Published by
Tangmere Productions
A Virginia Bader Company
19531 Campus Dr. Ste 19
Santa Ana, CA 92707
949-263-1404

Designed by

creative
continuum

1213 Athens Avenue
Placentia, CA 92870
714-524-9566
www.creativecontinuum.com

Dedicated to my father
Pilot Officer John Philp, B.E.M., Royal Air Force
149 Squadron
Bomber Command

One of the Stirling Gardeners Who "Planted" Mines

Table of Contents

Introduction

by Günther Rall

I have lived, it seems, several lifetimes. I have packed into eighty-odd years so many careers, both military and civilian, and realized so many dreams I cannot count them.

First and foremost is my life as a husband to a perfect wife, Hertha, sadly no longer with me, and father to two exceptional daughters, Franziska and Felizitas. I continue to be blessed with their presence.

I have also had the honor to serve my country as best I could, flawed as it was with the rise to power of Adolf Hitler. My generation and the idealism we cherished was cheated and misused by the hypocrisy and fanaticism of one man and his system for an unrealistic and unreachable goal. The question of how this could happen is still unanswered. The fact that we did not explore the essence of the Nazi regime when it came to power is, of course, one of our great failings and what we learned piece by piece after the war of Hitler's atrocious crimes makes it still worse. So in this biography are included a few insights into the political situation that inspired me to become an officer, and that is one of my reasons for wanting my story told.

After World War II I served with the North Atlantic Treaty Organization, a gift to me in the aftermath of World War II that I would never have believed possible. To be invited to join this noble NATO alliance almost from its birth and to be able to contribute whatever I could has been a privilege that I fully appreciate.

I am also grateful to those who promote aviation, such as the National Air and Space Museum at the Smithsonian Institution in Washington, DC, the "Gathering of Eagles" symposiums and to those who have invited me to the United States on many occasions to participate in talks and debates with former opponents whom I have come to respect. It is gratifying to know that yesterday's enemies are now friends. I would also like to pay tribute to historian and military author Colonel Raymond F. Toliver (Ret.) for the books he has written with Trevor Constable that offer a permanent record of my fellow pilots of the Luftwaffe so that they not only be remembered but also accepted. I met Ray Toliver, a career officer and pilot, in 1956 while he was still on active duty. We in Germany are grateful to these two authors because they wrote in great detail about Germany's World War II fighter pilots, recording their stories so that they shall never be forgotten.

In the mid-1970s Virginia Bader also made a significant contribution to the aces of the air by pioneering and promoting aviation art in America. She also contributed to the bringing together of pilots from opposing World War II forces at her symposiums, particularly the first meeting, fifty years later, between the Russians and Germans since the end of the war. What Toliver and Constable did with their books, Virginia did with her fine arts gallery. For that, and her symposiums, we are all appreciative because the paintings and prints she sells are permanent records of that era, and both sides are able to meet and share experiences.

Telling my story through this biography affords me an even greater opportunity to consider what went before, to gather my thoughts, and in later chapters to present my honest assessment of where the world sits today.

Working with the author, Jill Amadio, who has respected my wishes to have my recollections written from my own personal viewpoint, may go against the premise of a scholarly biography but I am grateful for her understanding that I had a lot to say as she researched the book and I wanted it said my way. I believe she has captured the essence of the man who is Günther Rall, enabling readers to catch a rare glimpse into who I truly am.

Although this is the first time I have poured out my soul publicly, so to speak, my children and my four grandchildren have long known the many parts of my life and love me for all of them. This book is for my family and for those brave pilots on all sides who died during World War II and for those who survived.

Munich, Germany
2002

Author's Note

In 1999, fifty-four years after World War II ended, I sat with Lt. General Günther Rall in the salon of his country mansion high in the Bavarian Alps. At ease opposite me on a 17th century straight-backed chair was the 81-year old pilot of two hundred and seventy-five confirmed victories who was assured by his doctor, after shooting down thirty-six enemy aircraft, that he would never fly again. Yet he went on to become one of a very small group of renowned and remarkable German aces and marksmen who survived the lethal skies of aerial combat and were among the legends of their day despite Germany's ultimate defeat.

The Rall estate, established as a German hunting preserve for aristocrats during the 1600s, is extensive and the architecture of the main three-story residence, built in 1683 and classic Bavarian, is unusual. In 1890 it was fashionable to add onion-shaped cupolas and several of them adorn Rall's house. A tower crowns the steep, ribbed roof and the massive, arched oak front door, medieval in design, creaks on huge iron hinges.

Farther up the road is Berchtesgaden and Obersalzberg, the complex where Adolf Hitler had his headquarters and underground bunkers at the Berghof that nestles at the foot of Kehlstein Mountain. Higher up, at the crest, is the site of the Eagle's Nest with its panoramic view across hundreds of miles, where Hitler once took tea and socialized. Built by Martin

Bormann, the Eagle's Nest was given to the Führer for his 50th birthday. A few miles away is another mountain building, a restaurant whose dining room straddles Germany's border with Austria. Shortly after the war ended Rall's wife, Hertha, made a perilous journey to Vienna to visit her aged parents. Travel for Germans was prohibited by the Allies so she, like many others, entered the restaurant's front door, emerged out a secret back door and continued on her way.

Northwest of Günther Rall's house is Munich, and northeast, from the windows of his elegant salon the granite walls of Salzburg Castle glisten in the distance. The secluded and sumptuous home sits virtually on the German-Austrian border in one of the most magnificent settings in the region. The mountains rise steeply on either side, and a quiet, small lake hides beyond the woods. A much larger body of water, Lake Chiemsee, a popular tourist spot, is just seven miles away. Ironically, it is where Rall and several of his unit were taken prisoner by the American Eighth Army one spring morning in May 1945.

The longest living top German ace, Rall was born in 1918. He has lived through almost the entire 20th century. His war service began during the first few moments of World War II in France, continued with service on the Eastern Front and finished with his transfer back to Germany on the Western front to help protect the Third Reich against the advancing Allies. After a few years in civilian life he was called upon to serve his country once again with the new German Air Force.

Of a medium and athletic build, with the remains of fair hair tinged with gray, he could easily pass for a man of fifty-five thanks to a daily regimen of intense calisthenics and, he claims, a preferred diet of German sausages. Full of energy, vitality and an endless curiosity he impresses everyone as almost the same

Günther outside his home in the Bavarian Alps.

human dynamo, strong-willed and competitive fighter pilot who fought spectacularly in Greece, Crete, the Balkans, and Russia and in the home defense of Germany, ending the war as the third highest-scoring Luftwaffe ace.

Rall is a man of high intellect, exceptional intelligence, and possessed of a dry wit. He is quick to laugh, enjoys repartee, and is a lover of classical music. A compelling and eloquent debater, Günther discusses current world affairs with vigor, sometimes quoting from Shakespeare whose collective works in German, and other classics, line the walls of his second-floor library. As an avid student of history who follows global trends he is as fiercely passionate about the sequence of events of World War II as he was sixty years ago and punctuates his opinions by thumping on the table.

Remarkably, he has exceptional recall "because," he said, "so much of what happened then was so significant or horrendous, it is seared into my memory."

As a former chief of the new German Air Force he maintains contact with many of his old colleagues. They visit the affable host at his home where they gather for friendly, sometimes heated, exchange of views and a few very good drinks.

When talking of the war years at lectures and symposiums he keeps his audiences spellbound with vivid descriptions of aerial combat. Like most fighter pilots, he spreads his hands like wings to show the different positions of his plane and his enemy's aircraft, lifting arms and feet to demonstrate firing and evasive actions he took during dogfights. One hand, his left, is missing its thumb.

Rall lives simply, visited often by his daughters, Franziska and Felicitas, who each have two children. Clemens, who is an audio engineer, and Anna-Luise, an art student, live in Paris where their mother, Franziska, is an art restorer at the Louvre. Alexa and Carolina, both high school students and fine athletes, are in Munich with Felicitas, owner of an industrial graphic design studio.

There is nothing in any of the spacious home's rooms to remind the general of World War II and Hitler's futile fantasies except some precious photos kept in a bureau drawer. Instead, graceful pastel watercolors of Alpine flowers painted by his wife, Hertha, and architectural sketches by his daughter Franzi, hang on the walls and along the hallways.

On the south wall is a plaque inscribed with the poem, "High Flight," by Pilot Officer John Gillespie Magee, Jr, an American who flew the Supermarine Spitfire with the Royal Canadian Air Force in England during World War II. He was killed in a crash at the age of 19 over Tangmere, an RAF base in southern England, and is buried there.

Rall's tone as we met and reminisced was often somber, tinged with sadness. His passion he saved for angry diatribes against Hitler. Surrounded by photos of his family — Hertha who died in July, 1984, and his daughters — the former Luftwaffe fighter pilot also treasures the several albums of old, faded photos of the many airmen he flew with who gave their lives for their country. Some of their names, and their photos, are in this book. Here is III./JG 52 top ace Major Erich Hartmann, who scored an astounding 352 victories, standing with an arm around Rall's neck. Another photo shows Rall with Colonel Dietrich Hrabak, 125 victories, in Russia, and another is of Günther with Major Walter Krupinski, who shot down 197 enemy aircraft, congratulating Rall after his 200th victory.

"Of our 20,000 Luftwaffe pilots in World War II only one-tenth came home," he said, shaking his head. "Such a waste." Those memories are still with him, especially the sacrifices of fellow aces Hartmann, Walter Nowotny, Gerhard Barkhorn, Johannes Steinhoff, Otto Kittel, and many, many others.

Several books have been published on the lives of brave fighter pilots, both Axis and Allied, detailing their heroism. While Rall honors those in the stories and understands the interest in them, he has never considered himself a hero. He dislikes that description. He insists he was one among millions, thrust into giving of his very best because he respected the call to duty. As he talked about his life he was troubled most by Hitler's doomed World War II strategies, the immense betrayal Germans suffered at Hitler's hands, and, of course, the death camps.

"Later, after World War II, I became more concerned as an example of my generation that sought to shed a light on why

Germans were so eager to respond to Hitler's summons to serve, to adhere to the code of honor as an officer. This duty was sacred, there are no other words to describe it," said Rall. "In retrospect, it is easy to come to a critical judgement of that period. Why did we fight on with a dedication never seen before in our history? When did we lose our belief in victory and in Hitler? How could we have stayed so loyal?"

During the 1930s when the Führer and his party fanned the flames of patriotism as the German nation endured the full brunt of humiliation after its defeat in World War I, Rall and his peers were caught up in the fervor of getting back some semblance of national pride.

"We were beaten in World War I but we still had a German parliament and a Chancellor even though the country was in dire straits. The single and only hope for our future at that time was someone who played upon our emotions as Germans."

Germany was adrift and sought a savior, anyone with the will to rally its broken spirit. As Hitler's speeches struck more and more at the heart of German discontent a tremendous nationalism was reborn. In hindsight it is easy to understand how World War I set up the inevitability of World War II. In fact, from several points of view including Germany's the two were one war.

"I think we must have been desperate, longing for someone to give us a reason to have faith in our country once more." That "someone" promised to oust the French from their occupation of the German Rhineland's militarized zone and reunite it with its true country of origin.

"Hitler's decision to reclaim the Rhineland in 1936 made sense to us at the time," said Rall. "His promises to restore us to former glories stirred our hearts. We thought we were in need of a strong, passionate leader who said all the right words and gave us back our national confidence. Germany has always been a proud nation but under the shackles of the Versailles Treaty after World War I our pride, our economy, everything, even our culture, had been stripped away. Thus, we saw our future in Hitler and the Third Reich. Of course, those dreams and my words must seem weak now." The pain on the veteran pilot's face was palpable. He shook his head as he expressed his feelings with a heated anger he still feels five and a half decades after the collapse of Nazi Germany.

This biography of Lt. General Günther Rall, who held two commands at NATO, is the first to be written on the life of the third highest-scoring fighter ace in history and is a personal account of this modest man's distinguished military and civilian careers, his private thoughts, and his reflections upon the events that shaped him, his country, and the world. There are many finely written books that describe World War II, Germany, and its Luftwaffe. Of all the services, Germany's air force, its aircraft and its pilots have proven of continual interest to readers in dozens of countries, perhaps because all pilots, irrespective of nationality and allegiance, share a common bond and respect each other for their love of the skies and each other's skills, talents, and courage. This camaraderie has brought many of them together at symposiums as long as half a century later to relive their aerial battles when they flew and fought fiercely against one another.

The story of fighter pilot Rall covers as broad a canvas as other aviation biographies but with the advantage of Rall having ended the war not only as the Luftwaffe's third highest ace and later as Chief of Staff of the 4th Allied Tactical Air Force (ATAF) and Chief of the new German Air Force at NATO, but also as NATO's German Military Representative. In addition, not only was Rall called upon by the United States Air Force to offer his expertise and fly the legendary F-104 supersonic jet fighter as the first German test pilot of the pioneering aircraft, he was able to point out factors during different stages of its development that helped improve its performance and ensure its continuing service with the NATO countries.

While many of his fellow fighter pilots, whether they were Luftwaffe, Soviet, RAF or USAF, have already written their own stories of their exploits in World War II, most of them decades ago, Rall resisted putting pen to paper, or rather, voice to tape recorder until now for a number of reasons.

He wanted to make sure that his perspective was sufficiently removed from the devastating effects of Hitler's war and its consequences in order to allow a measured objectivity. He needed to examine from a distance the split feelings that he, like other Germans, experienced as they served Hitler only to discover later the Führer's betrayal of their idealism. Rall wished to weigh his viewpoint as a mature veteran. He also found himself engaged in activities that gave him the opportunity to work first-hand with world military leaders, and finally, he wanted to share the beliefs and opinions that a lifetime of public service has shaped.

The recollections in this book were related to me from Günther's personal experiences. He freely admits there may be a few lapses of memory and for these he and the author apologize although events, dates, and locations have been authenticated as accurately as possible. Research into Luftwaffe campaigns on the Eastern Front reveals that official accounts in reports and books vary quite widely, even between eye witnesses on identical occasions. Few official records remain. Many were destroyed or are in Russia's classified archives and unavailable.

Rall has lived almost entirely through arguably the most turbulent, progressive and, some say, the greatest century in history. He has personally seen his country rise, fall, rise and fall again through two world wars and watched Germany slashed into four foreign-occupied zones with one of them, East Germany, ruled for twenty-eight years by a brutal Communist puppet regime. These are among the reasons the highly-regarded Luftwaffe survivor has dedicated his life to one goal: to regain every nation's respect for his country.

"My decision in 1956 to help establish a new German Air Force, to work for NATO and its Allies was driven by my deep conviction that based on the experiences of the past only NATO could help lead Germany back to honor by joining with its democratic countries," he said. "No one can wipe out the heinous crimes Hitler committed." While ethnic cleansing, expulsions and genocide continue to horrify the world, most recently in the Balkans, Rall believes that Germany will pay for Hitler's actions for "a thousand years to come. If I could help to mitigate some of the damage he caused not only to other countries but to my own and the German people and if I could help to rehabilitate our reputation then I decided I would give the rest of my life to it." And indeed he has. Rall's post-war public service spanning forty years has been both challenging and hugely rewarding.

In his living room in Bavaria Rall summed up his life by saying, "I determined to do all in my power to understand what happened and to find a way to help Germany redeem itself. My later friendships with the Americans and other Allies helped to strengthen my efforts to do that and I am still trying."

And he picked up his harmonica and blew a tune.

Part I

Crash-landing

1
eins

"You will never fly again. Never."
The harried doctor made his pronouncement barely an hour after he had performed back surgery on his patient, looking pityingly down at the 23-year old pilot encased in a thick cast from neck to pelvis. The Bucharest hospital ward in war-time Romania, an Axis partner of Germany, overflowed in 1941 with such young airmen, many of them missing limbs, others fatally wounded, a few already breathing their last as the cold Christmas season wound down in the second year of World War II.

"I'm sorry," the doctor continued. "Your back is broken in three places. You are partially paralyzed on the right side. There's no hope, I'm afraid." At the grim words, the patient turned his intense blue eyes to look at the doctor full face. He wanted to be absolutely sure that when he spoke to him the doctor would understand him correctly.

"Doctor, I will fly again." The words were intoned quietly. The declaration was short. But it was said with such force and determination the doctor was startled. How could anyone who knew the extent of his injuries, and this pilot definitely did, hope to walk again, let alone climb back into a cockpit? The eighth and ninth thoracic vertebrae, and the fifth lumbar vertebra that controlled some of the leg nerves, were crushed. Because Rall had spent a week at a temporary field hospital without treatment, then fourteen days traveling on four different trains, the breaks in his back were already three weeks old before doctors could perform surgery.

No matter. Because he could feel a faint sensation in his right leg it was an indication that the nerve, albeit smashed, had not been severed. He knew with irrefutable certainty that it would not be the end of his flying career.

Promoted to squadron leader in the Luftwaffe's single-engine fighter wing JG 52 barely eleven months previously, he had been the youngest flier to hold the rank at the age of twenty-two and was already a hardened and brilliant fighter pilot with thirty-six victories.

The patient closed his eyes, wishing for the tenth time in as many minutes that the heavy plaster-of-Paris cast wouldn't cause his skin to itch so terribly. Nevertheless, there was a smile on the pilot's lips as he tried to sleep. He knew he'd fly again. And fight again. And claim more victories. Nothing would stop him. He was a fighter ace and ambitious.

As he drifted off he began to re-live the dogfight that resulted in the nightmare that sent him to a field hospital in Bucharest instead of back to his air base on the Eastern Front at Mamaia, near Constanta, Romania, and the ice fields of the Ukraine.

"Two I-16s dead ahead!"

"I see them!"

Rall and his wingman, 1st. Lt. Steffen, pulled on their sticks in unison to meet the Russian planes head-on, leveling off at 1,000 feet in their new Messerschmitt Bf 109Fs that III./JG 52 had been issued a few weeks earlier after a brutal battle for the island of Crete. The weather was bitterly cold, minus forty degrees, on a late afternoon on November 28, 1941 as the two pilots made a sweep of the area. The weak, wintry sun was beginning to slip below the horizon and snow covered everything on the ground.

"It was a complete white-out and it seemed we were flying through nothingness," recalled Rall. He and Steffen were in a *rotte*, a two-ship formation, near the Russian front between Taganrog and Rostov in the Ukraine to search for stray Russian aircraft to add to a successful day. Rall had already bagged a Russian fighter that morning and another the day before. As he and Steffen prepared to face the enemy aircraft the two went to full throttle against the Voyenno-vozdushnyye sily (VVS), the Red Air Fleet aircraft.

Rall knew exactly how to approach. Move in fast. Target the wheel well area, the most vulnerable part of the enemy fighter. Estimate deflection angle. Squeeze off three bursts. Watch for white flashes on the opponent aircraft showing impact. Pull away at high speed. "Each dogfight is distinct from any other," said Rall. "No two are the same. Once you decide how to approach, you can usually determine how the combat will develop, but not always." In this instance, Rall was in for a surprise as he sent a hail of bullets into the Russian fighter's fuselage.

"Got him!" In the twilight, however, the sudden blaze momentarily blinded Rall as he continued to watch the enemy's smoking plane plummet to the ground

"I was completely distracted by the fiery crash," remembered Rall. "and I lost my situational awareness. Instantly the other Russian fighter was on my tail. His gunfire pierced my engine, killing power. To maintain speed I had to descend. I went down fast with a windmilling propeller, spiraling under control towards the ground. I realized that a belly-landing–and I'd already experienced three of those–was my best bet. Fortunately, I knew I was facing fairly flat land, no trees, woods or mountains."

But by now night had fully fallen. Since it was pitch dark Rall couldn't judge how close he was to terra firma. He wasn't even sure he was back behind German lines because on the Russian Front there were no neat demarcations of troop movements on either side but instead jagged spearheads that changed almost daily.

"You never knew if you were on German-occupied or Russian soil at any given moment," said Rall. As it turned out he was just a little ahead of the German front line, which at that time was deep into Russian territory.

"My speed was much too fast and before I knew it, bang! I'd struck the ground and bounced straight up again!"

He rebounded into the air but as luck would have it the initial impact point was close to a deep, wide ravine. By now the airborne Bf 109 was stalled again.

"This was a first for me and it was truly frightening. I could see the outline of the ravine's slope as I rushed towards it. I thought for sure this was the end. I crashed head-on into the side of the ravine. It was like hitting a brick wall. The impact threw my head against the canopy lever and I blacked out."

Rall's plane disintegrated with the force of the collision. The right wing was torn off, the nose crumpled, and the engine was thrown into the air, landing 130 feet away.

Steffen, the wingman, circled to pinpoint Rall's position. Fifteen minutes later a German tank whose commander had observed the crash arrived on the scene. The tank was in the area as part of the many vanguards the German panzer divisions had established but were now forced to abandon as the Red Army advanced. The crew could see Günther inside the plane but they couldn't open the cockpit to get him out. Finally, they managed to knock it open.

The soldiers found Rall slumped over, barely breathing. Because he was bleeding profusely from the head and in fact had been scalped by the canopy lever with the entire left side of his skin ripped from his skull Rall's rescuers assumed that cranium injuries were the extent of the damages. The panzer crew cut through the 109's wreckage and dragged him out, not realizing that any pressure on his back, broken in three places, was excruciating. They patched him up as best they could with their medical kit and radioed for help.

Among those who assisted Rall was young Luftwaffe Non-Commissioned Officer Rossman, who fifty-eight years later wrote a letter to Günther: "I am sure you won't remember me because when we pulled you from your plane you were more dead than alive. I helped to carry your stretcher. But you survived. I know that the experience was difficult. I, myself, was a prisoner for six and a half years in the worst Soviet POW camp in Moscow, worse even than Lubyanka. It was hell. But we are both still here. We are almost the same age and it is still a wonder to me that we are alive." Several weeks after Rall's crash Rossman was captured by the Russians after he went out on an early morning reconnaissance mission to scout weather and battle conditions and was shot down. Günther was touched by the letter because Rossman had spent years trying to locate him.

An hour after Rall was rescued an army transport rolled up and he was loaded onto its bare boards. The soldiers kept trying to sit him up still unaware of his back injuries. As the transport bumped over the frozen, rutted fields to the nearest German field hospital the jarring over the rough terrain was so acute it constantly sent Rall into unconsciousness then raised him back to agonizing awareness. Then he'd faint again from pain. During a lucid moment, he implored "Stop! I can't stand it!" The driver called for his unit to send out another truck, this time one with the bed lined with straw.

"It was midnight and unbelievably cold, I remember that," said Rall. Frozen blood covered his leather flight jacket like a sheet of crimson glass. A medical orderly traveling with Rall helped to keep Günther's spirits up by telling him aerial combat stories all night until they finally reached their destination. The truck left Rall at a makeshift first-aid station established temporarily in the cellar of a burned-out school building in Taganrog, on the edge of the Black Sea.

"The cellar was littered with the wounded. The doctor cut off my hair and sewed up my head wound. That's all he could do. But he was aware that my back was killing me." The German army's emergency doctors had no X-ray equipment or facilities for treating severe injuries so they flew Rall to Mariupol, Romania, in a four-seat Ju 88 bomber. One of its canopy panels was missing so a pilot who was awaiting a replacement for his crashed 109 sat with his back to it to protect his squadron commander from the cold air blowing through. Rall was always touched by such kind gestures and has never forgotten them.

On arrival in Mariupol, Rall and residents of the town were greeted by a raid by Russian bombers. In spite of the ensuing inferno Rall made his connecting flight to a hospital in Bucharest. Here, he was diagnosed with a broken back, wrapped in a cement-like body cast made of yards of bandages coated with gypsum, and told by his doctor that his combat career was over. A few days after Christmas, 1941 the medical staff decided to transfer Rall to the city hospital in Vienna because his case was complicated and he needed treatment by a spinal cord specialist.

"But I never despaired," said Rall. "I knew with one hundred percent confidence I could and would rejoin my unit as a fighter pilot once more." On a stretcher, with his name, diagnosis and destination scribbled in large black block letters in the middle of his plaster cast he was taken to Vienna in a Red Cross train filled with hundreds of German war wounded. The journey took seven days to travel from Bucharest in Romania, through the entire breadth of Hungary and Austria, traversing the Carpathian Mountains.

"The snow was deep and our progress so slow," he said. "Everyone was suffering." Once at the hospital in Vienna the iron-willed and impatient Rall launched an all-out campaign to rehabilitate his shattered back, especially since the station doctor was an elegant, petite, pretty young Austrian named Hertha Schön.

"I felt like a wild animal after living under the brutal conditions we endured in Russia both while fighting and at the makeshift field hospital so I made an extra effort to make a good impression on her," said Rall.

Hertha's determination to help patients regain their active lives matched Günther's own quest to heal. The two became firm friends as Rall's treatments progressed. At one point, it was she who broke the news to Günther, on January 19, 1942, that his father, Rudolf, had died at the age of sixty-six, which served to spur Günther on to his goal and resume his life as a fighter pilot. Hertha's gentleness in telling Rall of Rudolf's unexpected death served to establish a special, trusting relationship between them, a bond that was to deepen over time. But Günther's first priority was to get back on his feet and into a cockpit.

"I awoke every morning willing my body back to health. I spent every day exercising as I lay in bed, which mostly meant just tensing different muscles for a few seconds. If I couldn't feel the muscle, then I would envision it responding."

Within five months of his hospital stay Günther's cumbersome cast was removed. "That was terrifying, almost as bad as the crash," he remembers, with a wry grin. "Hertha and the nurses took this awfully big saw, the kind you'd use for sawing wood. There were no electric medical saws in those days so they had to depend on brute strength. As they started sawing through the cast I was afraid that sooner or later they'd slip or get tired and buzz straight through my ribs to my heart!"

Finally removing the last clumps of plaster-of-Paris that broke into pieces like small white rocks the nurses completed their job. It had taken two hours. Once free, Rall increased his rehabilitation hours, exercising ten times as often as the doctors recommended. Gradually, he felt movement returning to his wasted limbs and finally he was able to walk again, first on crutches, then with a cane.

"It was hard work. I sweated bullets and had to endure painful electrical treatments. But there was a war going on without me. My squadron was waiting. I didn't want to waste even one more minute than was necessary," he said, his words tumbling fast and furious as he recalled the drive he put into his recovery.

His efforts did not go unnoticed by his fellow patients. Rall's companions in the two other beds in his ward were army doctors, Austrians, with severe leg injuries.

"They saw me trying to walk and I think it gave them the encouragement to try, too."

Now mobile the pilot turned his sights on flying again. First he'd have to prove to his doctors as well as his Luftwaffe superiors that he was fit and able to handle the cockpit controls. That meant picking a test plane that was easy to fly, probably an older model. Rall called his pal Baron Alexander von Winterfeld. A World War I commander and now head of a fighter leader school in Vienna he was a frequent visitor to Rall's ward, usually hauling a keg of beer with him. Two weeks before Rall's appointment for flight testing, however, the Baron was killed in a plane crash, failing to come out of a roll. Nevertheless, Rall, accompanied by Hertha whom he was now courting, went out to the school to find the adjutant.

"You know, the commander told me I can take a plane," said Rall.

The adjutant waved him towards a hangar. "Help yourself."

Directing Hertha to observe so she could make her report back to the hospital doctors for her patient's release, Rall went inside. He taxied out in a Bücher Jungmeister stunt bi-plane that was certainly far from the medical staff's idea of a safe test flight. For the young pilot, it was paradise. He flew loops and rolls, steep and shallow dives, stalls, and split-Ss.

"If a patient wanted to try a test like that today, it would be impossible. The hospital would never allow it. But during the war years we improvised a little bit," said Rall in one of his frequent understatements. Then he became serious. "I needed to put G forces onto my body to test the reaction, and see if everything worked – arms, hands, legs, heart, and brain. And yes, thank God, everything coordinated with everything else. I was elated."

Hertha reported to the head physician, Professor Schönbauer, that Günther Rall was ready to be discharged. One week later he went back to his squadron just before the massive German attack in the Caucasus began. It would be a year before Günther was given the opportunity to return to the hospital in Vienna to marry his doctor.

Günther Rall's Early Years
1918-1938

2
zwei

War, and its aftermath, was a constant presence in Günther Rall's early life. He was born on March 10, 1918 during the last year of World War I, to Rudolf Rall and Minna Heinzelmann who already had a four-year old daughter, Lotte.

The Great War began in 1914 and pitted Germany, Austria-Hungary, and their allies against Britain, France, Russia, and the US. Although Germany surrendered and an armistice was accepted in November 1918, the formal end to the war was June 28, 1919 when the Versailles Treaty was signed. Highly punitive, the agreement carved up parts of defeated Germany and ceded various areas and colonies to the Allies which included France, newly-created Poland, Belgium, Denmark, Czechoslovakia, Lithuania, and Japan. German rearmament was restricted by the treaty and the nation was forced to pay devastatingly harsh reparations to the victors.

Rudolf Rall was serving on the Western Front in France in the rank and file of the German Army's signal corps at the time of his son's birth. He didn't see him until he returned home in November, when Günther was six months old.

Günther Rall's birthplace was the small town of Gaggenau in the Baden-Württemberg region on the edge of the Black Forest. The area is part of the Rhine Valley. In 1922, the family moved to Stuttgart which Günther has since considered his hometown. Rudolf re-established himself as a merchant after the war and the Ralls lived a middle-class family life but like most Germans they experienced economic hardship.

"Because of the Versailles Treaty there was much suffering," said Rall. "Our nation was broke. We had high unemployment. I remember as a boy people talking about inflation, tremendous inflation. Our political situation was shaky and Germany was in a state of flux." The Weimar Republic, named for the town where its constitution was drawn up, had reluctantly been established by the German National Assembly and was unpopular with a varying percentage of the population. Thus, the nation quickly became a hotbed of political intrigue and conspiracies, particularly by groups determined to re-establish the monarchy which could have provided stability, and by Communists. Indeed, the new republic served to create a base upon which radicals and activists flourished within a country that felt it had been unfairly forced to surrender all of its liberties and rights.

As Günther's parents celebrated their son's first birthday, a young Austrian-born army officer, Adolf Hitler, was serving in Munich and protesting against Communists, Jews, and the Versailles Treaty with its huge debt. Hitler's protests drew support. Over the next few years Germany fell so far behind in its reparations payments, leading to even greater political unrest, that in 1929 the United States sought to fix a final settlement amount for the debt to be retired. Germany agreed to the terms but considered them still harsh. Hitler, who by now had a following as leader of the National Socialist German Workers' Party, objected loudly to the terms, earning him nationwide fame.

In the Rall household, despite the tumultuous times, Minna and Rudolf were determined to give their children as many advantages as possible in preparation for adulthood. Günther credits those efforts for the principles and values he carries to this day. Three of them formed the young Rall's character.

The first factor was his family. The Ralls were a stable, close-knit unit. "My upbringing was loving but very disciplined," said Rall. His parents attended a Protestant church, typifying that segment of German society that was considered traditional conservative. Rudolf was not ideologically committed to the Nazi Party. He was nationalist only in the best sense of the word: religious and conservative with a sense of justice and a love and deep awareness of duty towards his country. During the rise of Hitler such traditionalists found themselves caught in the middle because Hitler and the Nazis came to power legitimately, winning an election. Once the Nazis revealed their true character, Hitler's agenda put a great burden upon the Rall family's segment of society and diminishing options became their subject of discussion. They found themselves serving a regime that was the antithesis of their principles. Yet patriotism was ingrained and young Günther always knew where his loyalties lay. He was raised during a time when terms such as honor and duty were drilled into German minds from a very young age. Obedience, orderliness, conformity, and regimentation were the order of the day even in the context of the Weimar Republic with all of its economic woes.

The second factor that had an influence on Rall during his youth was athletics. School sports taught him the value of teamwork, the joys of successful competition and the satisfaction of winning. He excelled at track and field, especially broad jump, and won honors as a sprinter in track meets. The third factor was education. Rall senior and junior both knew that education was a proven route to a professional career and prosperity.

Many ten-year old boys joined the Christian Boy Scouts and in 1928 Günther was enrolled. He learned the importance of integrity and respect. He also reveled in learning outdoor survival skills. His Scout leader was Wilhelm Lutz, who had traveled to Japan, and served as director of an orphanage in Palestine. His stories of far-off lands engendered in Rall a yearning for adventure.

In 1933 Chancellor Adolf Hitler launched the Third Reich. It followed two previous empires, the Second Reich, which lasted from 1871 under Chancellor Otto von Bismarck to 1918 when it collapsed with Germany's Great War defeat, and the medieval First Reich, the Holy Roman Empire of which Germany was a part and which was ended in 1806 by Napoleon. Hitler's lofty aim was to liquidate the democratic but chaotic Weimar Republic which lasted from 1919 to 1933. He saw himself as Germany's sole savior who would not only restore it to greatness but also establish a new world order under his Third Reich.

By the mid-to-late 1930s Hitler had accomplished some of his goals. Civilian life was becoming more and more comfortable. He had stimulated the broken economy in part by requiring industries to step up the manufacture of hard goods, most of which were oriented towards military ends and funded in part since the late 1920s by multinational investors, according to Professor Antony C. Sutton in his book, *Wall Street and the Rise of Hitler*. The steel mills in Essen, in the North Rhine, were one of the recipients of such financial aid from affiliates or subsidiaries of US firms eager to participate in Germany's revival.

Economists, aware of the fact that once money begins circulating an economy begins to feed on itself, know it will thereafter grow at an ever-increasing rate. This was especially true in Germany during the initial stages of the Third Reich because

Hitler's National Socialist party, a totalitarian dictatorship, was able to control not only the means of industrial production but also the cost of production by regulating salaries and benefits to employees as well as the return on investment.

When Hitler tore up the Versailles Treaty with the Western Allies in 1934 Rudolf Rall was appalled by the Führer's actions. A conservative nationalist, Rudolf believed that Hitler was a low-life opportunist destined to destroy Germany. He saw the Nazi party as radical, part of a fascist movement. Conservatives like Rall senior were nationalists but many did not embrace the aggressive and racial doctrines of the Nazis.

"Many well-known people supported Hitler in the beginning, but not my father," said Günther. "He refused to attend any rallies or meetings. My best friend's father was a member of parliament and believed that this passionate new leader would make Germany a glorious nation once more and get us out of the miserable situation the Versailles Treaty had put us in. However, when he learned of the direction Hitler was taking he joined the resistance, protested, and was summarily hanged, as were others who opposed the policies of the Third Reich."

In 1934 the Gleichschaltung, the agency of political conformity enforcement under the Nazi Party whose Führer was now Chancellor of Germany, converted the Scouts into the *Deutsches Jungvolk*, one of Hitler's youth organizations. To the young Rall it simply meant a change in the color of the uniform from a gray shirt to brown.

Hitler had been quick to institute the draft for all able-bodied young Germans but a combat German air force was still officially prohibited. This restriction was not to Hitler's liking. He surreptitiously began to resurrect the Luftwaffe as an arm of the military under Reichsmarschall Hermann Göring, turning it into a fighting rather than a civil unit.

The Austrian-born Führer next made plans to unify Germany and Austria and occupy Czechoslovakia and Poland in order to bring all ethnic Germans under his rule. There was only one option open to accomplish this. Invasion.

Soon, hundreds of new tanks and other armaments were paraded before the German people as marches were held in Hitler's honor. Spectacular events demonstrating great military power became commonplace. Their effect wasn't lost on Germany's youth.

After grade school Rall attended the Gymnasium, a combined junior college and high school. Rall's studies included nine years of Latin, five years of Greek and three years of English in addition to social studies and the humanities. The variety of subjects, the foreign languages, world history, the sciences, mathematics, and literature were all elements that shaped him, fueled his curiosity and provided him with a lifelong love of learning. A year before he was to graduate at eighteen young Rall decided to seek a career in the German army, part of the newly-created Wehrmacht, which would eventually also include the Luftwaffe. To increase his chances of acceptance in the armed forces he spent his final school year at the Nationalpolitische Erzehungsanlstalt (National Socialistic School) in Backnang, near Stuttgart. Founded as a state institution it was headed by the Minister of Culture and Education. Again, Günther would be taught Greek by a well-traveled teacher, Dr. Herlinger, whose descriptions of Greece fascinated Rall, who kept in touch with his Greek teacher for decades. Religion was also taught and students wore civilian clothes but two years after Rall left the school was taken over by the SchutzStaffeln, the SS, and its studies and activities followed a far more militaristic direction.

Günther applied to join Infantry Regiment No. 13. Although disabled by a sports injury, having dislocated his arm during a long jump contest, he passed the rigid entrance exam requirements but discovered that only four places were open to the seventy-four hopefuls. Not surprisingly considering his forceful personality, Rall was one of the four selected to join the regiment in Ludwigsburg on December 4, 1936. By that same month and year the Luftwaffe had been publicly unveiled.

Günther looked forward to a lifetime career in the army.

"In the 1930s an officer in the Wehrmacht was considered elite. It was many a young man's noble ambition and, believe me, I was more ambitious than most," said Rall. His Scouting days had also given him a romantic as well as a patriotic view of life. His favorite authors at the time were essayist and novelist Ernst Junger, a World War I army officer, and writer Count Felix von Luckner, famous for his wild escapades as a Naval officer in World War I, earning him the name Sea Devil, and for his hobby as a magician. Both also served in World War II.

Within the Rall family, however, there was little appetite for talk of war experiences. Rudolf had been conscripted at the ripe age of forty to fight in World War I (in 1943 Hitler was to conscript men in their fifties) and he was anxious to put those unhappy days behind him. So was his wife, Minna, whose younger brother Ernst, a budding architect, was killed in 1916 serving as a company commander in the horrendous Battle of Verdun in France. It had become folklore in Germany that a member of every German family living at the time suffered at least one such loss at Verdun.

After a year's training with Regiment 13 Rall was sent as a non-commissioned officer to the *Kriegschule* (War Academy) in

Dresden and assigned to an exclusive unit that was given special duties to perform with the cavalry in addition to standard training. By now, Germany was officially permitted to create an army with a limit of one hundred thousand men. In the early 1930s the German Republic had a small group of troops training secretly in Russia with artillery and tanks and when Hitler became chancellor the troops returned and joined his army to form a signal corps, a tank corps and an engineering division.

"I was so proud to be in the infantry," remembers Rall. "I tried to excel at everything. We learned horseback riding. Every day we were awakened at 5 a.m. and had to clean out the stables, then saddle the horses and take them into the ring for formal equestrian training. I loved it. Our uniforms set us apart and we were tremendously respectful of the fact we were training for service to our country. We believed Hitler's speeches. He knew how to appeal to our emotions. In 1936 he had marched into the demilitarized zone of the Rhineland, re-occupying it and stationing ours troops there, over French protests. We were bursting with pride over that bold accomplishment."

At the end of his training, during the summer of 1938, Rall was rated as "Fairly Good" in the final officer exam. Colonel von Bünau, his course commander, testified to Günther's "pleasant and open character, intellect, a quick grasp [of subjects], and independent thinking," traits that would stand him in good stead as a successful fighter pilot. He was also evaluated as having "blameless conduct off-duty, and was very popular among his comrades because of his lively and humorous nature." He was tactful towards his superiors and handled his finances in a well-ordered manner. These results qualified him to join the ranks of army officers.

But Rall was soon to change his priorities. The fun-loving

Günther had many friends. Among them was a boyhood school chum from his hometown who had joined the German Air Force and was training nearby at the Air Force Academy in Dresden. "Whenever we got together on Saturdays, he'd regale me with tales of his flight training. He'd describe flying over towns and rivers, and aerial stunts. It sounded thrilling," said Rall. "Here I was in one place and he was flying all over the country. Finally I couldn't resist wanting to experience the same excitement."

Rall asked for a transfer, took the exam at the Academy and was accepted for pilot training on September 1, 1938 at the Neubiberg Flying School just outside Munich, under Major Günther Lützow, a Spanish Civil War ace. In early 1939 Rall transferred to Werneuchen, north-east of Berlin, for training as a fighter pilot. Among his instructors were Major General Theo Osterkamp and other veterans of the Condor Legion who fought in the Spanish Civil War.

The freedom of the skies and the new dimension it added to his thirst for adventure opened a new chapter for young Rall although the Luftwaffe was not yet the deadly machine that bombarded England during the Battle of Britain two years later. Not until its build-up and training of fighter pilots was complete would Günther Rall take the path that would write his name and exploits into the annals of Germany's aviation history.

Rall Earns His Wings
September 1938

The Third Reich's draftees were now a million-man army. Tanks, guns, and other military necessities were produced in factories working around the clock to feed Hitler's military machine as the rest of Europe looked the other way. In the 1930s appeasement was the order of the day. No one wanted to rock the boat, England's prime minister, Neville Chamberlain, least of all. The British took a conciliatory attitude towards Hitler's threatening and warlike movements because of the terrible toll World War I had taken on its young men and Chamberlain was anxious to avoid even the smell of yet another war. Thus, even though Britain had a guarantee with the Czechs to protect them, Chamberlain acquiesced to Hitler's plan to invade Czechoslovakia during a fateful 1938 meeting in Munich. Hitler reasoned that since the Czech Sudenten was home to three million Germans, he would appropriate it as a protectorate of Germany. Adding to the equation was the fact that Chamberlain knew England's land forces were not ready for battle to prevent the plan, nor was the Royal Air Force, which at the time had no modern aircraft.

Again and again during the late 1930s Chamberlain had sought to pacify the German Chancellor, finally coming triumphantly home from Munich in September with a signed "friendship" document from Hitler that Chamberlain declared to the

British people promised "peace for our time." He was almost immediately betrayed by the Führer.

The German army had stockpiled masses of armaments and trained its troops. The Kriegsmarine, the German navy, was building up its fleet. All that was missing was a viable combat air force but while German bombers and fighter planes were quickly developed and built there were few qualified pilots to fly them. The Versailles Treaty expressly forbade the creation of a fighting arm within the German air force. While German army and navy training maneuvers were acceptable to the Allies nothing could disguise the training of combat pilots in Germany. But Hitler had already found the solution to this dilemma several years earlier, in Spain.

In 1936 he and Italy's fascist dictator, Benito Mussolini, volunteered to support Spain's Generalissimo Francisco Franco's side in the Spanish Civil War, which lasted from 1936 to 1939. In 1934 Adolf Galland, who was to become one of the Luftwaffe's most famous aces, and other pilots, had already taken combat training in secret in Italy. But flying the little Breda planes in mock battles was a poor substitute for actual war for their fighter pilots so when the opportunity to fight for Franco was upon them, many young German pilots were transferred south to Spain.

The German aviation presence in Spain was named the Condor Legion under the command first of General Hugo Sperrle, then General Wolfram von Richthofen. The small unit was equipped with a Junkers 52 bomber squadron, a Heinkel 51 fighter squadron, and a handful of reconnaissance planes. By the time Bf 109, He 111 and Do 17 aircraft had been added the Luftwaffe's fighting units were no longer a secret.

In spite of the fact that the Condor Legion, which embraced

Bf 109s.

army and navy personnel in addition to fliers, was active in the defense of Franco's cause in 1937 there was little aerial combat between the Legion's He 51s and the Spanish Republic's air force equipped with Soviet-made monoplane fighter, the I-16 "Rata."

29

Günther Rall knew little of the early days of the Condor Legion although some of its pilots later became his instructors and would have a direct effect on his life and times. It was in Spain that one of them, Germany's top ace at the time, Lt. (later Colonel) Werner Mölders, replaced Galland when his tour of duty was up and Galland was transferred back to Germany.

Mölders brought some Bf 109s to the Condor Legion and together with Major Günther Lützow developed the brilliant flight tactic of the four-ship formation, the *schwarm,* that consisted of two *rotten,* or dual two-ship teams. Each *rotte* was piloted by a leader and a wingman that flew in pairs with the wingmen flying just behind and to the side of their leaders so each could cover the other's blind side and whose flexibility allowed for either defense or offense. The *schwarm* was spread out equally, like the fingers of a hand, over a 600-1,000 foot area. During aerial combat the two *rotten* could split up into two separate teams.

"The most important effect of the *schwarm* and *rotten* formations is to give the pilot freedom, he is not bound to stay in one position, and the wingman has the flexibility to move around," said Rall.

The tactic, specifically designed for high-speed aircraft, was first admired then adopted by the British and later by the Russians on the Eastern Front and was to prove immensely successful for Rall's III./JG 52 fighter unit. The earlier three-ship V-formation flying wing-tip to wing-tip was not practical because it was much too constricted. In the V-formation, the leader flew slightly in front of the wingmen positioned to his rear right and left. The wingman had to concentrate on holding a tight formation and could not search for enemy planes. If the flight leader suddenly had to change direction it could mean a disastrous collision. US pilots, too, switched to the German *schwarm* tactic and found that it was particularly ideal for inexperienced recruits because of its simplicity.

At the flying school Rall was now training in all types of "beautiful aircraft," mostly open cockpit, two-seat bi-planes.

"It was exhilarating to pilot them. The first plane I flew was a Focke-Wulf 44 Stieglitz and then others that included a Heinkel He 82 B Kadet."

These small single-engine training aircraft had maximum speeds of 95-115 miles an hour, half the speed of the Bf 109E that Rall would soon fly, although the training planes' wing spans and overall lengths were almost identical to the Bf 109's. A later twin-engined, single-wing bomber version, the Heinkel He 111 B had gone into service with the Condor Legion in 1936. Used as a trainer in Germany until 1938, it was a far cry from its 1939 model, the Heinkel He 111 bomber that was equipped with six machine guns and could carry 5,500 lbs. of bombs. The He 111 achieved a maximum speed of 252 miles an hour from its two Junkers engines that pumped out 1,100 horsepower each. The small Stieglitz bi-plane, named after the goldfinch, that Rall enjoyed flying so much was built with a steel-tube fuselage and wooden wings covered in fabric and was among the most popular primary aircraft for teaching pilots to fly.

As soon as his training ended, on September 1, 1938, Rall was promoted to Second Lieutenant and awarded his pilot's wings that included a license in acrobatics, night flying and instrument flying. After graduation each pilot was given the choice of which career path they preferred to follow: bomber or fighter pilot. It took barely a second for Rall to make his decision known. With his bold, devil-may-care courage and a calm but fearless, risk-taking temperament, there was no doubt he possessed all the characteristics of the classic fighter pilot.

"I had always enjoyed the challenge of competition," he said. "I also loved acrobatics, treating your plane as if you wore its wings yourself. This type of nose up, nose down, banking, diving, lazy-eight flying suited my temperament much more than the steady, straight flight path that bombers must maintain."

After Rall was ordered to his first flying unit near Stuttgart, in the summer of 1939, he was even more pleased to discover that the pilots were taking instruction in an experimental small aircraft built by Willy Messerschmitt called a Bf 109 and used in Spain.

"I loved the old planes but it was the easy-handling Bf 109 with its powerful engine that I enjoyed the most. You could go fast and become one with the plane. We had trained pre-war in close, three-ship formations in open cockpit bi-planes but in the Bf 109s we flew in looser, four-ship formations. What a difference it made!" His favorite Messerschmitt was the Bf 109G, affectionately nicknamed Gustav because of its model designation. The E model was known as Emil, and the F model, Friedrich.

The Luftwaffe of Rall's service was organized into a number of tactical units called Geschwader, from fighters (Jagdgeschwader), to bombers (Kampfgeschwader), and reconnaissance, (Aufklärungschwader). The Jagdgeschwader, or JG, usually comprised of approximately a hundred and forty fighters that were divided into three Groups. Each Group designated by a Roman numeral, comprised twelve aircraft in each of three or four Staffeln, or Squadrons, which in turn were divided into three *schwarm* of four fighters each. Thus, III./JG 52 indicated that

Günther flew with the third group of fighter wing 52.

During the months of July and August 1939 Rall underwent more intense fighter pilot training at Werneuchen, northeast of Berlin. Using the sky as a backdrop as an artist uses his canvas, Rall quickly mastered the maneuvers that preparing for an aerial war demanded. He became adept at air-to-air target practice, scrambling for take-offs, and unconventional landings.

Later, as World War II progressed, his superiors were to discover he had a talent for deflection shooting, an unerring, intuitive and instinctive natural-born skill for figuring out the speed of his target and firing sufficiently ahead at the correct tangent so that he struck the enemy plane at the coinciding coordinates. Deflection was to become his trademark over the next several years and keep him alive. First among the admirers of Rall's deflection talent was one of Germany's greatest fighter pilots, Heinz Baer, who described Rall as the best deflection marksman he had ever seen. Friedrich Obleser who later served with Rall as his wingman on the Eastern Front agreed.

"Günther could hit his target from all angles, during turns, and from any distance," remarked Obleser. "It was amazing. He was tremendously talented at anticipating where the enemy was going, and be able to aim ahead and hit him."

Rall credited his deflection skills to a very fortunate gift.

"I really had no system of shooting, I just had a feeling for the right place to aim and the right amount of lead to use." He pointed out that his deflection skills would be useless today since modern jet fighters use computers to analyze and set up their targets. He conceded, however, that some input is necessary.

Pushing the envelope during dogfights in World War II would become another renowned feature of Rall's fighter tactics, admired for his keen eye that pinpointed the targets, instantly deciding upon the superior position from which to attack, and advancing farther inside Russian territory than any other Luftwaffe pilot to seek his prey.

Even though the three-ship formation became the favorite device of Baron Wolfram von Richthofen, cousin of World War I ace Baron Manfred von Richthofen, the more modern Mölders tactic proved far more effective.

During the final days of Rall's peacetime training at Werneuchen, in August, 1939, Hitler edged closer to a second world war. Rall, at twenty-one years old, was now a fully-fledged fighter pilot. Recognizing his potential the Luftwaffe posted him in January, 1940, to 4th Squadron Fighter, Group II, Wing 52 based at Böblingen, near Stuttgart where he added advanced radio communications and map-reading to his training. JG 52 was to become the most famous fighter wing of World War II. With more victories tallied, over two thousand, than any other unit by legendary aces Erich Hartmann, Gerhard Barkhorn, Walter Krupinski, Friedrich Obleser, Johannes Steinhoff, Günther Rall, and others, it was destined to enter the annals of aviation history like no other. In addition, no fewer than three of its pilots, Steinhoff, Rall and Obleser, would, years later, successively become Chief of Air Staff of the new German Air Force.

The Young Pilot at War

As August, 1939 drew to a close Rall and his fellow pilots knew the political situation was escalating. Germany had made a reluctant but expedient pact with Russia, although there was mistrust on both sides, while the British and the French had guaranteed support for Czechoslovakia against invasion. But when the British, French, and Italians had signed the Munich Agreement and forced Czechoslovakia to cede its Sudetenland region to Germany and become its protectorate, Hitler believed he could also take Poland, attacking on 1 September, 1939, without precipitating war with France and Great Britain. US President Franklin D. Roosevelt attempted to mediate but it was too late.

With Hitler already in Czechoslovakia, the Third and Fourth Army groups invaded Poland from the north and the Eighth, Tenth and Fourteenth Army groups invaded from the west and south. The armies coordinated their military effort, with Russia invading from the east sixteen days later. The Germans were so swift to penetrate Poland, the tanks initially had to wait for the infantry to catch up.

"Yet there was a general feeling of unease at this victory," remembers Rall, "not only at our base but, as I learned later, in all three services. Although we answered the call to duty readily our whole nation was upset that war had officially been declared in Europe once more."

By the time England and France declared war on Germany, on September 3, 1939, the Luftwaffe had amassed one thousand bombers and fifteen hundred fighter aircraft. The RAF had barely one hundred bombers, a substantial number of Hurricanes, and a few dozen barely operational Spitfires.

The invasion of Poland was the first of several serious mistakes Hitler was to make. Because of faulty information from Ambassador Ribbentrop and others he miscalculated the consequences of the invasion, which forced the British and French, two days later, to declare war on Germany. Nonetheless, the quick victory in the final days of September, 1939 saw the Third Reich and the Russians, having signed their pact before the invasion of Poland, divvying up their spoils, with Germany taking Warsaw and the western half of Poland, and Russia the remainder.

Günther Rall soon adjusted to his new unit, whose orders were to patrol the Rhine River.

"It was amusing," said Rall, "because we were directed not to cross the river but to fly up and down its eastern bank. The Armee d l'Air, the French Air Force, we learned, had been ordered to do the same along the western bank. So here we were, flying opposite each other barely a quarter of a mile apart, with no contact. This exercise seemed pretty silly considering we were now at war. It was boring, too, what the French call *drole de guerre*, and here was a classic definition of that expression."

Only reconnaissance planes and Heinkel He 111 bombers were permitted to cross the Rhine, which made easy targets for the French to shoot down. Although the missions were innocuous for the fighter pilots Rall and his fellow officers sensed the build-up of tension.

May, 1940 in France. Lt. Decker, Squadron Commander First Lt. Ehrlych, Lt. Rall

In January, 1940 Rall was promoted to First Lieutenant and part of a newly-formed III Group, the 8th Squadron, near Berlin. He was to stay with the group for the next three years, moving from one theater of operations to another and from country to country as the war progressed.

The pilots were equipped with the Bf 109E, which they were to fly until 1942 when a newer model was supplied. The 109Es weren't that easy on take-offs and landings because the landing gear was too close together and the strong prop torque could

41

cause the plane to veer off course. It was common knowledge that the aircraft was prone to ground-loops that could result in shearing off the landing gear. The French Air Force deployed mostly their own Dewoitine D.520s, Bloch MB-152s, and Morane-Saulnier M.S. 406s, as well as Curtiss Hawk 75 fighter planes, an export US Army Air Corps P-36 version they purchased from the US in 1939.

"Although it had effective tactics," said Rall, "the French air force seemed to have no punch and functioned as a subsidiary to the French army. Their fighter aircraft numbered very few according to army intelligence, and until their factories could increase production there were hardly any fighters we could take on. Many of the French aircraft were later captured by the Germans and given to their Axis comrades-in-arms: Romania, Italy and Bulgaria."

The French concentrated on protecting their Maginot Line, a fortification system that included a series of tunnels, bunkers and concrete pylons that snaked north along the French-German border from Basel, Switzerland to the Grand Duchy of Luxembourg. When in 1940 Germany invaded Belgium, their army was able to bypass the strongest sections of the Maginot Line and outflank it.

Convinced nothing could stop his relentless seizure of foreign soil, the Führer next targeted closer neighbors. With common borders to eight other countries, it wasn't far or difficult for Hitler's war machine to march north, south, east or west if he chose in his strategic campaign to conquer Europe. In April, 1940 some Luftwaffe units flew support for Germany's preemptive strikes in Scandinavia against Norway and Denmark, although Norway's small air force was considered insufficient to merit a large Luftwaffe engagement.

Typ	Datum	Uhrzeit	Ort	Höhe	Zeugen		Bemerkungen
tiss P36	18.5.40	18,40	S Metz				
B 3	24.6.41	07,25	O Konstanza	6000	Oblt.Lössnitz	8.St	ins Meer gestürzt
B 2	25.6.41	17,40	SO Konstanza	4800	Oblt.Lössnitz	8.St	ins Meer gestürzt
B 3	26.6.41	05,10	NO Konstanza	4000	Ogefr.Wachowiak	8. "	ins Meer gestürzt
16	4.8.41	05,47	Kiew	3000	Fw.Gottwald	8. "	abmontiert
16	4.8.41	05,53	Kiew	15000	Uffz.Köppen	8. "	brennend aufgeschlag
16	4.8.41	06,10	Kiew	1500	Uffz.Rossmann	7. "	Aufschlagbrand
16	6.8.41	10,05	SO Kiew	2000	Uffz.Köppen	8. "	"
B 2	9.8.41	05,35	SO Kiew	2000	Uffz.Köppen	8. "	"
g 3	11.8.41	14,28	O Kanew	2300	Lt.Graf	9. "	senkrechter Absturz
16	13.8.41	10,52	NW Kanew	1500	Uffz.Wachowiak	8. "	Aufschlagbrand
16	14.8.41	10,39	NW Kanew	1500	Lt.Kuttenberger	7. "	"
15	17.8.41	13,32	O Kanew	50	Lt.Burk	8. "	"
DB 3 A	30.8.41	15,15	O Dneprope-trowsk	3200	Uffz.Wachowiak	8. "	"
10	6.9.41	12,57	N Derijewka	300	Uffz.Kirscheblohr	8. "	zur Landung gezwungen
g 3	17.9.41	10,53	SO Kiew	1000	Uffz.Rossmann	7. "	Bodenaufschlag
26	25.9.41	07,40	W Charkow	1500	Uffz.Wachowiak	8. "	Aufschlagbrand
11	2.10.41	12,17	NO Poltawa	7000	Fw.Gottwald	8. "	"
10	4.10.41	12,35	SW Walki	1200	Fw.Köppen	8. "	"

Pages from Günther's logbook listing his first victory.

On May 10, 1940, Germany invaded France, passing unchecked through Belgium, Luxembourg and the Netherlands. Rall and his unit moved onto an airfield in occupied France that same month. Their mission was to fly bomber escort, an unpopular one for the pilots.

"We were fighter pilots," said Rall. "We were frustrated and bored flying at low speeds to fly direct escort over the Channel shackled to the bomber fleets. In the cockpit it felt like the Bf 109 was constantly stalling. Because we had to give up speed and maneuverability we were sitting ducks for the British Spitfires waiting above us. All they had to do was pounce."

It was a mistake also committed by the US Eighth Air Force

in early missions. When General James Doolittle took over command of the USAF in 1942 one of his first orders would be to release the Allied fighters to take on the Luftwaffe. The mission went from protecting the bombers to destroying enemy fighters. That turned the tide so that American warbirds could range free and go after the Germans.

On May 18th, as Hitler's forces continued to run rampant through France, Rall chalked up his first victory. A clear day, it was 4 p.m. before his unit was ordered to take to the skies from their provisional base in Trier, Germany, which was close to the border with Luxembourg.

"We were sitting around chatting in the tent. We knew we had a mission that afternoon to meet up with one of our reconnaissance planes, a modified version of the Heinkel 111 bomber, and escort it from Nancy, in France, safely back to Germany. At the appointed time we took off and picked up the He 111 in the air over the rendezvous point."

But Rall's eagle eyesight also picked out several tiny dots in full pursuit behind it and closing fast.

"We recognized them as French air force Curtiss P-36 Hawks single-seat fighters." The export version of the P-36 played a significant part in the beginning of World War II. In 1938 France ordered one thousand but by the beginning of World War II had taken delivery of less than three hundred. Some of the remaining P-36s ended up with the RAF and were re-designated Mohawks.

"When we saw the enemy aircraft we knew it was time to arrange ourselves into the classic Mölders attack formation." The twenty-two year old pilot who had never flown a plane before his eighteenth birthday was about to begin his meteoric rise to the top of the Luftwaffe's list of living aces.

"It was our first contact with the enemy. We were tremendously excited. The voices on our headsets were all talking at once. As we approached them we immediately forgot everything we'd learned. Tactics went out the window. I was soaked in sweat. We were a little bit higher in altitude than the French fighters because they were chasing the He 111 below us. There were twelve of them and ten of us. We jumped on them. I was the flight leader of the second *schwarm*. My squadron commander turned in towards the first and I took on the other one. It was a hectic engagement."

Everyone tangled with everyone else, with the German pilots shooting frantically at the enemy. At one point Rall found his plane stalling because it snapped after a rough turn. Then, as he tried to turn in to an adversary Rall's aircraft was hit. Bullets had punctured the belly of the Bf 109 but he was able to maintain altitude and fly it back to the area of his base west of Mannheim.

"The plane felt as heavy as lead. I lost my orientation but soon regained it. I was worried I'd run out of fuel and it took me forever to finally find a landmark I could recognize. When I landed at a base near Mannheim where we had been stationed months before, my wingman followed me down. Then I refueled and managed to fly my fighter the short distance back to my own base at Trier. The He 111 got home safely, too. It was never touched because of our engagement but we lost one of our planes."

Rall was debriefed. His report detailed the encounter but made no mention of the downed enemy plane, only that it was hit. When Günther's wingman made his own report, however, it told a different story. Rall was surprised to learn that he had indeed claimed his first victory, a P-36, at 1840 hours near the town of Metz, east of Verdun, in France. The official witness to Rall's victory, as required for the Luftwaffe's records, was Lt. Lossnitz, who would later be killed in Romania.

In a strange twist of fate another witness was to emerge several decades later. At home in Bavaria in the late 1990s Günther was surprised to find a letter with a Czech postmark in his mail. It was from a historian who lived in Prague. The letter read in part: "General, I can confirm your first victory. I have studied the archives but what you don't know, I will now tell you. The pilot of the Curtiss you shot down was a Czech non-commissioned officer serving with the French Air Force. Although his aircraft was in flames he was able to bail out. When the Germans moved into France, he went to England and flew with the Royal Air Force as

The point of the sword: a Bf 109

a member of the RAF's Czech Squadron."

The letter writer went on to relate that the pilot had the misfortune to again bail out, this time from a Hurricane. He parachuted into the mouth of a river but he was killed.

Günther's first aerial dogfight and quick victory gave him enormous confidence. He knew he was a winner.

"A fighter pilot's first contact is psychologically vitally important. It gives you the assurance you can fight and be successful. You can believe in yourself as a fighter pilot. For me, it was a marvelous feeling, one almost of relief that I had engaged the enemy, fought, and won. I had proved myself. When you are training you always wonder how you will react in actual combat. You never know until it happens. And remember, you are not killing a pilot, you are shooting down a plane. That's all you want to do, down that plane. It is machine against machine with men at the controls. We weren't taught to hate our enemy, we were taught how to remove his weapon, his plane, from the skies. Whoever maneuvered well and successfully enough to hit the target, won."

Rall's jubilation after his victory was tempered when he saw the bullet holes in his Bf 109 as he and Lt. Otto Decker, one of his closest friends who would be shot down in the Battle of Stalingrad, inspected the damage.

"Aerial combat can be both a victory and a warning: It is easy to be shot down. Next time you could be the loser. That's why it is so important to survive your initial missions, because you learn so much. Those French pilots were good and we had respect for them but their air force itself was not very effective. I am not blaming the French but they proved their military strength was on the ground, with the army, not in the air. Some of their planes were behind the times." French pilots claimed three hundred and eleven German planes in May, 1940. In spite of the victories aerial combat with the French convinced the Germans that the Curtiss posed little danger to the Luftwaffe.

III./JG 52 scored three victories that day but one of Rall's fellow pilots, Sergeant Adolf Walter, a non-commissioned officer whom he admired, failed to return. Just after midnight, Günther received a telephone call from the missing airman.

"He told me he'd be back tomorrow," said Rall. "He'd belly-landed, jumped out of the cockpit and was crawling across a field towards the forest when a German army sergeant yelled at him, 'Get down! Get down!' There were explosions all over the place. He'd landed in a mine field. But he was safe." In 1983, Rall was asked by former RAF Wing Commander Philip "Laddie" Lucas, Sir Douglas Bader's brother-in-law and a distinguished fighter pilot, to write an article about the incident.

"My fortunate NCO Walter, I wrote, was not an ace but he was a reliable man," recalls Rall. "He had three times the number of guardian angels than anyone else. He bailed out again later on, in Constanta, in the Black Sea. It was hazy, we were at 19,000 feet and pestering some Russian bombers. His plane was hit and he jumped. But because of the haze he couldn't judge his altitude, he had no depth perception, and nor could he see the horizon. Just before he reached the water, at 190 feet he punched the quick release for his parachute."

The airman was picked up but suffered heavy injuries. His recovery was lengthy but eventually he was able to fly again, only to be killed later in Russia.

"One trick pilots use over the sea, if they can," said Rall, "is to remove a shoe while parachuting down and let it drop. If they hear a splash they know they are close enough to pull the ring. We went out to get Walter with a lifeboat and picked him up but he was injured quite seriously and was *hors de combat* for three or four months. When he did come back, he went out on a mission and never returned. He was a fine, fine man. You could trust him to stick by you, no matter what."

New Posting Following
the French Defeat
1940-1941

5
fünf

In June, 1940, after Paris fell, France signed an armistice with Germany. To humiliate the French the agreement was consummated in the same railway carriage, kept as a museum, where Germany had surrendered to France's Marshal Ferdinand Foch at the end of World War I.

In July, 1940 III./JG 52 was pulled back from its French base to train in sea rescues from a base in Jever, west of Hamburg and close to Germany's border with Holland. Rall's Bf 109 trainers were now modified to accommodate dinghies so that the Wing could practice ocean-survival skills, navigating over water, reading compass headings, and air-sea rescue over the Zuider Zee inlet and the open waters of the North Sea.

"When we were issued life jackets and dinghies as part of our aircraft equipment and sent on training missions over the sea it was the first sign to us that Germany was about to cross the English Channel and enter into battle against Britain and the RAF's formidable Spitfires and Hurricanes." The Luftwaffe considered these aircraft their top competition in the early stages of World War II.

"The elliptical wings on the Spitfires had fantastic characteristics, great lift. They were very maneuverable. We couldn't catch them in a steep climb," said Rall. "On the other hand they could stall during inverted maneuvers, cutting off the fuel lines because the force of gravity prevented the flow of fuel. But they were still a highly respected enemy. In contrast, our Bf 109s had shortcomings. I didn't like the slats and our cockpits were very narrow, with restricted rear visibility. Fighter pilots need a good all-round field of vision and we didn't have it." The pilots of these small fighter aircraft earned the Germans' utmost respect.

"Most were just like us, the same breed. We all tried to act as gentlemen towards each other both in the air and on the ground. Post-war it is easy to sentimentalize this adversary relationship but it is indeed true that both the British and the Germans were sometimes known to hover above the planes they'd shot down hoping to see that the pilot had bailed out successfully. It also wasn't uncommon for enemy pilots to salute each other after a battle as they both turned away to go home. Once, one of our pilots escorted a damaged P-38 plane that had been hit over Germany, leading it to a German base so it could land safely."

With their sea training exercises complete Rall's unit was sent to Coquelles, near the port of Calais, to a temporary airfield on a local farmer's land. The farmer was ordered to harvest his half-grown grain, which he did under loud protest, just half an hour before the first Bf 109s landed. There were no buildings or hangars and the crew slept in a barn, while the planes were parked under the trees.

The pilots of III./JG 52 continued their escort missions, encountering Spitfires and Hurricanes, but two weeks after his victory Rall's squadron received the order to move to another base near Arras in northern France, about fifty miles from Dunkirk. Here, III./JG 52's missions were mundane, humdrum. There was little activity for the unit. It was understandable. As far as the Germans were concerned, the enemy was already beaten.

"The most excitement I had during that tour of duty was

Bf 109s in occupied France, 1940

landing near a wheatfield full of craters. I had returned from a mission and my wingman and I were looking for an open space to land in. It was May. The farmers couldn't cut the grass because of the craters. The grass was waist high and I was trying to dodge the deep holes as we came down. I came to a stop and opened the canopy. Achoo! Achoo! Our mechanic came over and he started sneezing too. We were suffering from hay fever! The rotation of our propellers had cut the wheat and stirred up all the pollen." Knowing that he would be forbidden to fly if he admitted to hay fever Rall swore the mechanic to secrecy.

One other incident a few days later, as a result of the landing in the field of pollen, was also hushed up. "When we returned from missions we always flew very high for safety reasons. On approach to the airfield we went down in a steep dive. But a week after our hay fever episode this pattern didn't work for me. The leader went down first and I followed but I began my dive too steeply. Suddenly, I felt a terrible pain in my nose as if someone had hit me with a hammer. I pulled up. I radioed my wingman: 'You go down very quickly and I will follow very slowly.' As I heard him laughing I leveled off. This time I came in for the landing very cautiously, on a flat trajectory. When I raised the canopy, got out of the cockpit, and took off my oxygen mask it was full of blood."

Because Günther was still suffering the effects of hay fever his sinuses had swollen, shutting down his air passages. This meant there could be no exchange of pressure in his sinuses, causing one of the veins in the right side of Rall's nose to burst.

"The lesson for me was: if you have hay fever and want to land, pay attention!"

Again, Rall told no one of the problem. The matter was closed.

With panzer divisions and ground troops deployed close to the shortest distance between Calais in France and Dover in England – a matter of a mere twenty-two miles across the Channel – the German invasion of Great Britain appeared imminent.

"Our practice games were over, it seemed," said Rall. "Now it was time for us to tackle the real thing. There was great anticipation, even anxiety at times, because we were still relatively unproven in battle. Although we'd racked up some early victories, we had no lengthy experience in aerial combat."

Hitler had been planning Operation Sea Lion for weeks and all Luftwaffe wings had been unofficially on alert since June, 1940. In early July, the Luftwaffe was sent to French and Belgian airfields and on July 10 the Battle of Britain began with German planes attacking the British fleet in the Channel and raids on the south coast of England. Hitler then planned a second bombing wave to wipe out the Royal Air Force because domination of the skies was essential for a successful troop landing on Britain's shores. Winston Churchill was in complete agreement with this precept. "Our fate now depended upon victory in the air... For the actual crossings and landings, complete mastery of the air over the transports and beaches was the decisive condition," wrote Churchill in his memoirs.

In August, while participating in the Battle of Britain, twenty-two year old Lt. Rall was promoted to squadron commander, a rank he was to hold for three years in several theaters, but he was sad at the way he earned it. Günther's group commander, Major von Houwald, was shot down over the Channel, bailing out but never reappearing, giving Rall an opportunity to move up.

"We endured heavy losses at that time due to the tactics we were forced to use," said Rall. "One week, in just three missions, our group lost its commander, adjutant and squadron commander, in addition to other commanders."

With his new rank Rall felt the increased tension as the war rolled forward. He was convinced his unit would be even more seriously engaging the British.

Certain aspects of III./JG 52's missions from its base in Coquelles, France, puzzled as well as frustrated the German pilots. Their fast Bf 109s were assigned only to direct, close escort for the heavy, bomb-laden Ju 87 Stukas as they strafed British harbors and British Naval convoys in the Channel.

"We had to stay with the bombers," said Rall, "making us easy targets for the Spitfires and Hurricanes."

Acknowledging the futility of the raids and the heavy attrition rate during the Battle of Britain Hitler's High Command, accepting Germany's first defeat, ordered the Luftwaffe to be pulled back to rebuild. In October Hitler would decide to postpone Operation Sea Lion for at least six months.

"We had observed the preparations for invasion and saw many of our large ships in Dutch and French harbors." Hitler had ordered almost two thousand landing barges to be ready at various French ports on the Channel for the invasion. But when many were sunk or damaged by Allied aircraft and with the Luftwaffe failing to achieve air superiority Hitler turned his attention to completing plans and readying forces for his ill-fated attack in the opposite direction: Russia.

In retrospect, historians theorize that had Hitler invaded England it would have been as big a blunder as his later one, the invasion of Russia, code-named Operation Barbarossa.

"You cannot make such an invasion without a strategic air force," argued Rall. "Germany didn't have one during the Battle of Britain. We had the He 111 and the Ju 88 but our fighters were short-range and therefore restricted. We could only cover one-tenth of the British Isles. Our Bf 109s could make it to London but only spend a few minutes there before risking running out of fuel for the return to our base. Plus, we had no strategic bomber. The idea that we would soften up the British with these bombing raids was completely wrong. Any subsequent dogfights were senseless because of the terrible losses we sustained."

The Luftwaffe lost almost twenty-five percent of its aircraft

8th Squadron in Coquelles, France, 1940, with Rall, center

during the Battle of Britain that had begun in 1940 with bomber attacks on shipping in the English Channel, progressed to raids on British airfields and aircraft factories, and continued with the bombardment of London.

In the meantime, Hitler and Mussolini, who had invaded Greece, met in Florence, Italy, where the Führer assured the Italian dictator of any necessary ground troop support to keep the British out of Greece, as well as away from Romania's precious oil supplies that were currently fueling the Italian forces. Hitler's agreement directly affected Rall and III./JG 52.

Transfer to Romania

6
sechs

On the move again and supplied with new pilots and planes during a short stay near Berlin, III./JG 52 was sent to an airbase south of the Neusiedler See, not far from Vienna. Once in Austria, the squadrons were surprised to be informed by their commanders that their current operation was highly classified. Provided with special maps of Hungary and Romania, the airmen were even more mystified.

A week after they'd settled into their new quarters, III./JG 52 was abruptly ordered to Arad in eastern Romania. To reach it they had to refuel en route in Kecskemet in the heart of Hungary, where the pilots were treated to their first taste of authentic and very spicy goulash before they had to take off again. The fuel stop was necessarily brief because the Hungarian hosts knew the Germans were on their way to Romania. Romania and Hungary were at odds because by treaty Hungary was given a region of Romania and the political situation between the two countries was tense. Any friends of Romania, such as the Germans, were not too welcome in Hungary, even though Hungary fought on the German side in World War I and would soon support Hitler's invasion of Russia.

After refueling in Arad, Rall's unit was directed to make any further aircraft repairs and then head farther east and south, to Bucharest.

Leaving for Romania in the fall of 1940. 1st Lt. Rall is third from right.

"We couldn't understand the order to move east because the enemy was to the west," said Rall.

By now Russia, Germany's ally, had already conquered the Baltic states of Lithuania, Estonia and Latvia, and Hitler's other ally, Italy, had made an attempt to invade Greece. General Ion Antonescu of Romania had assumed command of the fascist Iron Guard and on October 7 he invited German troops to maintain their advance into Romania, ostensibly to assist that country into reorganizing its forces. Officially, because of Romania's neutrality, the Romanian forces were posted as guards for the country's oilfields, refineries and derricks rather than supporters and trainees of the Wehrmacht.

In addition to German ground personnel the Luftwaffe also took up residence. Rall's entire Wing was transferred to the outskirts of Bucharest, in southern Romania. Here, the pilots finally learned their mission: to protect the crucial Romanian oil port of Constanta and the oil fields of Ploesti. The fuel was essential to Hitler's plan to invade Russia.

Rall's squadron was also ordered to protect a pontoon bridge across the Danube River at Galati, Romania. The Danube flowed for almost 1,800 miles from its source in Germany, through Vienna, Budapest, and Belgrade, and finally into the Black Sea. The pontoon bridge that spanned its banks was a vital link for troops crossing from Bulgaria into Greece.

The port of Constanta, once home to the exiled Roman poet Ovid, was the lifeline for the region's oil resources which were connected to the port's refineries along miles of pipelines.

The pontoon bridge over the Danube River

Did Rall lose a bet?

Enjoying a smoke and reflection. Rall, center foreground, in Romania, June 1941

Constanta was also prized for its shipbuilding yards and food processing factories. Its possession was crucial to both sides of the conflict.

Rall's duties included training a squadron of Romanian pilots who were supplied with Bf 109s. This move to Pipera, outside Bucharest, the capital of Romania, was almost a homecoming for the Luftwaffe.

"It was a very interesting development," said Rall, "because although the kingdom of Romania was a neutral country, it had a large German population that had originally settled there in the middle of the 16th century, so there was a lot of sympathy for our side."

Rall in Romania, June 1941

Much like neutral Lisbon, in Portugal, Bucharest was a hub of secret agents, military high commands, diplomats, and representatives from several Allied and Axis nations – occupied or free. The city itself simmered with underground intrigue.

One winter evening, around midnight, a few days after attending a parade for Romania's King Michael as honored guests, Rall and his wingman, Otto Decker, dined at a local restaurant then set off to return to their hotel on Bucharest's Boulevard Elisabeth at around 1 a.m.

"In those days we all wore military uniform, even off-duty. For many of us it was our only clothing. Most of the uniforms of

JG 52 on parade in Romania as Air Force Commander General Speidel reviews the troops

the different nations were similar in style and neutral, drab colors. It was snowing. As we opened the door to the hotel, glad to be in from the cold, we heard six loud reports from the next door cafe that sounded like pistol shots. We rushed back to the street and saw what we thought was a German officer collapsed on the ground. A civilian in a black overcoat was running off, so we gave chase." As Otto and Günther got closer to him the man threw a gun into the snow. Günther retrieved the pistol and he and Otto apprehended the man and handed him over to the German military police who were stationed at the hotel.

Investigators alleged that the man, who entered Romania

from Turkey, was working for a Secret Service organization. He had a commission to assassinate Commanding General Hansen, chief of the German Army Staff in Romania. The hit man had been told the German general would be identifiable by red insignia stripes. However, the assassin mistook a German general staff officer's uniform for General Hansen's uniform because the red stripes on their trousers were of a similar hue.

Soon afterwards, the Romanian Iron Guards of Horia Sima mounted a successful revolution against their country's military dictator, Antonescu.

"These Iron Guards were pro-German," said Rall. "Each morning, as we drove out to the airport where our Bf 109s were hangared, the Guards saluted us. But when German troops truly occupied Romania it all changed, of course."

Romanian General Antonescu and his army conquered the Iron Guards and assumed power in the name of then King Michael, who signed an Axis pact with Germany in November, 1940.

The Battle of Crete 1941

7
sieben

In April, 1941 Hitler invaded Greece and Yugoslavia. The Greek port of Piraeus came under attack when German bombers blew up the British ammunition ship, the *Clan Fraser*. Although Italy had taken up arms against Greece with an invasion, Mussolini's incursion had proved a failure. Hitler was forced to come to the rescue of its ally, signaling the start of the Greek campaign.

Soon sent packing from Greece by the Third Reich, the British sought refuge in Crete, the largest of the Greek islands in the east Mediterranean Sea that was to become an important strategic military base. But their new sanctuary was doomed. While the Battle of Britain was in its last stages on the Western Front and several Luftwaffe units were withdrawn for transferal to the Balkans, Hitler ordered his Eastern Front forces to begin an airborne assault on Crete.

III./JG 52 was among the Luftwaffe units to join the massive raid, whose strategy was to soften up the Allies in preparation for the unleashing of a full-scale air invasion on the island by German army forces on May 20.

"We were stationed in Molai, on the southern tip of the Peloponnese peninsula. From there we struck against Crete for the next four days, flying at dawn each day."

The three-thousand square-mile island was held by British

April, 1941. A view over Athens, Greece, from a Bf 109

Commonwealth troops who included New Zealanders, Royal Marines, and Australians, and by Greeks.

Günther's mission focused on air support for the German paratroopers. III./JG 52 protected the assault along almost the entire length of the northern coast from Suda Bay to Mirabella Bay using air to ground fire. More than eighty DFS 230 assault transport gliders and almost five hundred Ju 52 transport aircraft accommodating eighteen troops each, comprised the initial assault on the Allies' base at Maleme on the northern coast of Crete.

"Maleme was our prime objective and we struck hard be-

The airfield at Molaia, Greece

fore landing there," said Rall.

Along with the first wave of paratroopers, the Ju 52s dropped containers with rations and equipment. Included in each container was a red and black swastika flag that was to be used to mark the German front line and guide subsequent paratroopers to landing spots. However, the New Zealanders grabbed the canisters, emptied their contents, and displayed the German flags inside their own lines. The Luftwaffe's 1st Parachute Regiment and army mountain troop units saw the flags and headed directly for them, landing in the arms of the enemy.

"Everyone was running around trying to figure out who was

Crash-landing at Molaia

Bombs, fuel, an
Bf 109s at Mol

who. It sounds funny now but then it was awful. We were flying low over the area at high speed and found it very difficult to identify our opponents' troops. There was heavy artillery fire and communication was completely lost. Many of our gliders crashed into the mountains."

Another huge mistake was to drop the paratroopers from a height of 2,600 feet, much too high. This careless planning gave the Allies plenty of time to take aim. Hundreds of men were shot as they descended. The olive orchards were laden with dead bodies, their leaves dripping the lifeblood of Germany's airborne troops.

"It was tragic. Most of the 1st Regiment were killed except for Colonel Neumann, a medical officer, who then took over the command."

In spite of the setback, the Germans managed to rout the Allies from one of the major airfields and rushed in reinforce-

*Battle of Crete, 1941. A sunken
British destroyer in Sudha Bay.*

ments. Their position thus secured at one end of the island the Germans flew in hundreds more troops. With the invaders now laying claim to a large portion of the island, III./JG 52 was able to set up shop at Maleme. The base had come under heavy bombardment by Lord Louis Mountbatten's 5th Destroyer Flotilla which was then pulled back by the British Navy, which lost two ships to German fire as it left. By the end of May the Battle of Crete was over. Many of the vanquished were evacuated under cover of darkness by the Allied Mediterranean fleet. Commonwealth soldiers remaining on the island were taken prisoner. Rall was surprised to learn that the King of Greece was in residence on the island during the first two days of fighting. The king managed to escape by ship and sailed to Egypt.

Germany's casualties in the Battle of Crete numbered close to seven thousand. Almost three hundred Ju 52 aircraft were shot down by anti-aircraft fire. Records show that this outcome

·s of German paratroopers bur-
· the island of Crete, in front of a
Zealand anti-aircraft weapon at
·nes airfield.

convinced Hitler to curtail plans for any future large-scale airborne attacks, a decision that was to restrict paratroop commander General Kurt Student's and other generals' actions in the field in other theaters of war.

"Thereafter Ju 52s were allocated to ferrying only logistical supplies for the Luftwaffe. But in the end there were far too few and this factor had a direct effect on our war effort on the Eastern Front," said Rall.

Rall's squadron returned to Romania later that same month, its job to help secure Crete a success. In addition to raids on the island the Luftwaffe had also attacked cruisers and destroyers lying offshore but it was time to return to the mainland and receive new orders and new aircraft.

Now based in the gypsy village of Mizil, north of Bucharest at the foot of the Carpathian Mountains, the unit took delivery of the Bf 109F, considered by Rall to be the best version ever of the Bf 109 although the G version remains his favorite. Two thirds of the fighter units would receive the improved model.

The most noticeable differences from the previous generation were the redesigned engine cowling, the unbraced horizontal stabilizer, and rounded-off rather than square wingtips, all of which provided a smoother, more aerodynamic effect. Like its predecessor E model, the 109F had a Daimler-Benz DB 601 engine. But the new version was armed with only three guns, one of which was an engine-mounted cannon, compared to the earlier version that had two machine guns and two cannons.

The planes had originally been delivered to the Luftwaffe's Headquarters in Germany in the fall of 1940 and saw action in October, 1940, with the first one off the line piloted by Werner

Two worthy Allied opponents have given up the fight over Crete, at Malemes. The British insignia may have been stripped from the planes by souvenir hunters.

Mölders. III./JG 52 received a few in the New Year, 1941, and all three of the wing's groups were supplied with the new aircraft on June 1, 1941.

By the beginning of summer 1941, Hitler controlled the Balkans. Günther's opinion was that Hitler had come as far east as he intended. But during their time at the base in Mizil, west of Mamaia, the men of III./JG 52 observed a sudden build-up of German forces ranged along the Russian front that bordered Romania.

"What the hell's going on here?" wondered Rall. The discussions back at base were spirited. How far did the Third Reich plan to advance? Into Russia? To China?

Operation Barbarossa

8
acht

In the book *Ostfront: Hitler's War on Russia 1941-45* author Charles Winchester states that Hitler planned nothing less than a war of extermination in the East, eliminating the "Communist regime, [and] Jews. The conquered territories would become German colonies with new German cities linked to the Reich by thousands of miles of new highways and railroads, the Russian steppe dotted with German soldier-colonists establishing (like the Roman legionnaires of old) brave outposts of civilization in a barbarous land."

The rumors of a second front had spread rapidly through III./JG 52 in early June and were confirmed days later. Hitler set in motion Operation Barbarossa, invading the Soviet Union on June 22. "An army officer came to our base in Mizil and told us we were going to war against Russia," said Rall. "We were dumbfounded. It seemed the height of folly. How could we fight a war on two such vast fronts? No one could believe it. It was against every strategic rule: you don't open another war when the war on the first front isn't finished."

Even more bizarre was the fact that Germany had a ten-year non-aggression pact with Russia. The Soviets were part of the Axis alliance.

"This was an unbelievable situation," said Rall.

Hitler's unexpected offensive against his pact partner, Joseph

Stalin, who had pledged support for the Third Reich's war in Europe, stunned German civilians and military men alike. But Hitler and the generals had been planning the assault for a year.

Germany's High Command developed various strategies before deciding on the capture of Leningrad, on the northern coast on the Baltic Sea, and a three-pronged invasion that included Moscow. There was a theory floated that Stalin had planned his own invasion of his pact partner, Germany, switching his forces from defensive to offensive and the Soviets was almost ready to roll but Hitler pre-empted that strike by two weeks.

Germany calculated that its June invasion would secure Russia well before winter set in. Thus, Hitler would control the oil fields, tin mines and other resources. He planned to irrigate the wastelands and resettle German farmers in the Ukraine, making it the primary grain depot to supply all of the future Nazi-controlled Western and Eastern Europe.

While the army massed its forces Luftwaffe units were ordered airborne. Hitler wanted the Soviet Air Force targeted in air raids as Operation Barbarossa's first victim. Almost three thousand bombers delivered an air assault so devastating it all but obliterated the Voyenno-vozdushnyye sily, or VVS, the Red Air Force, in one fell swoop. Directive No. 21 that had been issued from Führer Headquarters on December 18, 1940 read in part: "The Luftwaffe will have to make available for this Eastern campaign supporting forces of such strength that the Army will be able to bring land operations to a speedy conclusion and that eastern Germany will be as little damaged as possible by enemy air attack. This build-up of a focal point in the East will be limited only by the need to protect from air attack the whole combat and arsenal area which we control, and to ensure that attacks on England, and especially upon her imports, are not allowed to lapse."

Supplied with intelligence reports that the Soviets had ten vulnerable airfields well within the range of German bombers, the Luftwaffe launched a massive strike before dawn on June 22, 1941. Heinkels He 111s, Junkers Ju 88s, and Dornier Do 17s pounded the VVS planes parked on the ground, followed by another assault that began at daybreak with five hundred additional bombers, two hundred and seventy dive bombers, and four hundred and eighty fighters.

Historian Von Hardesty writes that German Army General Franz Halder notes in his diary for the day of June 22 that eight hundred Soviet aircraft were destroyed with the loss of only ten Luftwaffe aircraft. However, Hardesty points out that the estimates were conservative and that in all probability the Soviets lost one thousand four hundred planes destroyed on the ground and three hundred in the air that day and another nine thousand by the fall of 1941, although no precise figures are available.

It didn't take long for the German armies to make their mark as they rushed triumphantly over Soviet soil. On June 28, Germany captured the northern industrial city of Minsk. Eight days later the city of Smolensk, on the Dnieper River, fell.

On July 3 Stalin declared that he was committing his country to a scorched earth policy, vowing to destroy Russia's own crops and everything that might be of use to the enemy. Anxious to leave no supplies for the advancing Germans, Stalin's new policy included destruction of the oil harbor in Constanta with its major oil production facilities, and the Ploesti oil fields further north.

On the heels of these Russian raids, III./JG 52 was ordered east, to Mamaia, to take on the VVS. "In those days the air base at Mamaia was practically an empty field, no radar, a single telephone. Otherwise, nothing. Every evening Ju 52s flew over and dropped barrels of fuel for us. We had to hand-pump it into the aircraft tanks. Our mission was to halt the Russian DB-3 attacks on Constanta." These three-seat, twin-engined medium VVS bombers were flown as strategic, tactical and reconnaissance planes and were also the first to be sent by the Soviets to bomb Berlin that year.

German troops had anti-aircraft weapons at Constanta but they were ineffectual and the Russian pilots had become used to little resistance from ground artillery. The Russian bombers took off from their air fields in the Crimean Peninsula that jutted out into the Black Sea. "We needed to attack them before they could reach the coastline and drop their bombs on Constanta and Ploesti. They had no fighter escort, but one time they changed direction and approached from the west over the Carpathian Mountains, not from the east, as we had expected. Three Pe-2 bombers flew really low in order not to be detected by radar, although they didn't know we had no radar. They got through and hit us."

At dawn each day Rall sent two aircraft to seek out the enemy on their way to Constanta. "We were on cockpit alert and as soon as the reconnaissance flight returned and told me, 'They're coming!' The entire 8th Squadron scrambled and we attacked them before they reached land. From the beach you could watch their planes crash into the water and see the impact on the sea with smoke, flames, oil, and debris. It was horrendous."

While the Soviet aggressors were persistent and those who evaded the Luftwaffe's eagle eyes were able to zero in on the harbor, pounding it with bombs and artillery, Rall's unit kept fully engaged, successfully fending off most of the aerial attacks by continuing to anticipate their arrival over the Black Sea and downing the bombers before they could reach their target.

Rall and his squadron quickly racked up victories, often as many as four or five a day due in part to the fact that the VVS bombers flew without fighter escort. In addition to DB-3s, Rall and his squadron downed the more modern bomber, the Pe-2, which became Russia's most widely-used aircraft. The twin-engined multi-role bomber carried up to four machine guns. During one instance, however, when the Bf 109s of III./JG 52 were busy over the Black Sea attacking incoming DB-3 bombers, three Pe-2 ground-attack bombers flew over Mamaia and hit Rall's base. The Soviets destroyed a number of grounded German fighters that were awaiting repairs. Rall lost at least forty of his men in the raid. The chief technical sergeant, a Viennese, had one of his legs blown off. Days later he died.

"As we returned from our mission we could see the fires raging on the ground at our base. It was a horrible loss, all those guys."

After two weeks the Russian attacks on Constanta abruptly ceased and never resumed. Rall's squadron had added fifty-two Russian bombers to its score, prompting an award to the entire unit for the defense of Romania's oil port. General Antonescu, the pro-German prime minister, presented III./JG 52 with the Romanian Order of Merit.

"The general was tremendously grateful to our entire III./JG 52 unit that we were able to stop the Russian bombers," said Rall. In addition to the medal, he and his crew received a case of caviar. None of the pilots liked caviar so Günther enjoyed it every day for weeks, rationing it out to himself with the tip of a knife.

From the day of the June invasion, when Hitler began his undeclared war against Russia with Operation Barbarossa, until

A Bf 109 parked at one of JG 52's temporary airstrips during the Russian campaign

the end of the year, Rall shot down a total of thirty-five Russian fighters and bombers that included Mikoyan MiGs, Polikarpov I-16 Ratas, Yakovlev Yak-1s, Lavochkins LaGGs, and Petliakov Pe-2 dive bombers, according to his *Leistungsbuch*, or logbook. The pilots usually referred to all Lavochkin aircraft as LaGGs even though some were LaGG-3s, La-5s, or La-7s.

The logbook recorded each of Rall's subsequent total of 275 victories: 273 kills on the Eastern Front and two on the Western Front, between May 18, 1940 and April 17, 1944. The type of aircraft he shot down, date, time of day, altitude, location, position, witness name, and explanation — demolished, exploded on impact, burst into flames — were all meticulously documented.

"We filled out a long questionnaire each night with all these facts as well as how much ammunition was used. This was important because it showed the ratio of bullets to victories." One of Günther's greatest heroes was the brilliant Luftwaffe ace Hans-Joachim Marseille, who shot down an unprecedented seventeen Allied fighters in one day in 1942. "He only needed a fraction of the ammunition all the rest of us fired and flew unbelievable missions, chasing aircraft all over the sky." Marseille was killed in North Africa after his wingman saw clouds of smoke spewing from the cockpit. The ace shouted over the radio, "I can't stand it! I can't breathe!" On the ground his wing commander and close friend, Eduard Neumann, frantically tried to find out the reason for the problem but received no reply.

The pilot managed to bail out but his back hit the Bf 109's tail as he jumped, slicing into his torso. He made no attempt to open his parachute and apparently died as he dropped to earth. Marseille is buried where he fell, in the sandy desert near El Alamein. His grave is a pyramid-styled tomb which notes he was twenty-three years old.

Missing from Rall's logbook are five additional enemy aircraft he destroyed in ground attacks over Greece and the island of Crete during April and May 1941, as well as a P-38 and a P-47 demolished in the same manner after he was recalled to the Western Front in 1944 to assist in the battle against the Allies. Aircraft destroyed on the ground are neither counted nor recorded as part of an ace's total yet these incidents are considered far more dangerous than aerial combat since the attacking planes come under fire from tanks, ground troops and anti-aircraft artillery. "I felt a bit of heat during those moments," said Rall in one of his characteristic understatements.

Summer and Fall 1941

9
neun

From Mamaia Rall's unit received the order to move to Mizil where he was given the order to move into Russia. III./JG 52 joined the Wehrmacht's advance from Belajacerkov, the unit's first base on Russian soil, on August 16 1941, the day the German army took Nikolayev, one of Russia's most important naval ports.

"Belajacerkov was abandoned by the Russian air force when it was still under construction and was our first base to have a concrete runway. It was clean and organized, and we were delighted with everything. We lived in tents but it was summertime and the war on the Eastern Front seemed to be proceeding as planned."

In early September, 1941 the Germans prepared their assault on Kiev, the capital of Ukraine and the third largest city of the USSR, that had been founded in the fifth century by the Vikings. III./JG 52 moved further south, to Skalewaja, to provide air support. One of their missions was to escort Ju 87 Stukas in their dive-bombing raids against the Russian tank divisions that were attempting to protect Kiev against the encircling German army and provide air support for the ground troops in the south, pushing towards the Crimean Peninsula under the command of Colonel Mölders.

Mölders formed a tactical group. He'd fly to the front lines in his Fieseler Fi 156 Storch, a tactical observation aircraft, assess the situation, land and then issue orders from the ground, directing the combat missions as a kind of forward controller.

"He acted as a traffic controller, I would venture to say. He'd radio to us, 'They are coming here and here, turn, turn.' It was relatively simple because we were fighting for a very narrow piece of territory, a land bridge between the Crimean Peninsula and southern Ukraine, so the battle was concentrated basically in one small spot. Mölders truly was the first great fighter pilot in France and in the Battle of Britain. But now he was grounded because he was so valuable. The Luftwaffe was anxious not to lose him in the aerial combat that marked that period of time He was a marvelous tactician. My admiration for him was boundless."

Rall met Mölders in France where they were attached to different wings.

"He had a great wit and a great personality. He was the most highly-principled man I ever met. He was a strong character and he became a father to the Wing. That's why his men called him Papa Mölders."

The triumphant German army rolled across Russia almost with impunity. In one day alone it covered more than fifty miles with their tanks and troops.

"Everything was going our way, according to the dispatches we received."

Technically and tactically the Red Army was considered inferior while the Red Air Force flew obsolete aircraft, among them planes from the Spanish Civil War, including the Rata, Russia's first monoplane fighter. It was a tough, reliable little aircraft whose blunt nose, cantilever wings, retractable landing gear and

One of JG 52's bunkers in Russia

thick fuselage was at its most effective in air-to-air combat. In later versions it excelled in ground attacks as well as dogfights. The I-153 bi-plane was a single-seat, single-engine fighter with a retractable undercarriage and one of Russia's oldest aircraft still in service, with over three thousand operational during World War II. "They certainly weren't up to modern standards during that first year of war on the Eastern Front," said Rall.

For a six-week period during August and September, 1941 the Germans engaged the Soviets in fierce fighting around Kiev, Russia's third largest city, finally taking it on September 19. III./ JG 52 was one of three groups flying support of the battle and

Rall in Russia, after receiving the Knight's Cross

were based in the steppe wastelands of the Crimean Peninsula, along with those led by Colonel Gothard Handrick, the 1936 Olympic five-sport pentathlon champion, and Werner Mölders.

"It was a big tank battle and we were escorting Stukas. We met up with them at the rendezvous point south of Kiev and

1ˢᵗ Lt. Rall in Russia, decorated with his Iron Cross

when they swooped down on the Soviet T-34 tanks we stayed right with them. The Russian fighters came in as soon as the Ju 87's pulled up after dropping their bombs. This was the Russian tactic, to get them after they'd dropped their bombs and were on the upswing. But we went down with them and fended them off at a low altitude."

As III./JG 52 entered into aerial combat with Soviet fighter pilots Rall initially found them inexperienced and unskilled. "In the early days they had no tactics. They came in loosely, all over the place, usually in circles, with no disciplined formation. They'd swing around looking for targets and appear right in front of your nose. At first we were able to pick them off quite easily." But that didn't mean there was no danger, either from the air or the ground.

On one of his quick climbs in a dogfight during the battle of Kiev Rall's wingman signaled his squadron leader. "You're trailing oil and smoke!" was the urgent message. Günther's oil cooler under the nose had been pierced by ground fire. The puncture sent the oil pouring out in one, long dark stream.

"The wind sent it over my front windshield, covering it with the black film. I couldn't see a darned thing forward. I knew I was flying low and the battle on the ground was fierce. It was the last place I wanted to land. And I had no idea if I was behind the German lines or not. I knew if I landed among the Russians I'd be massacred." Guided by his wingman and trying to see through the side of the cockpit canopy Günther headed for the Dniejper River. The two assumed it was the dividing line between German and Russian troop movements.

The pilots' radio exchange was terse.

"Heading for the river."

"Good luck."

As the aircraft approached the other side of the water a thick

Bathing in the Ukraine. Rall is at right.

forest loomed.

"Just what I need," mumbled Rall, his head leaning as far to the right as possible to see out the side window. Then he noticed a cut in the trees. Hoping it was a fire-lane Rall prepared to land. The opening was only about ten feet wider than the Bf 109's 32½-foot wingspan. Could he make it? It would be like threading the eye of a needle. Rall lined up his sights. It was going to be tight. Very tight. If he clipped a wing, it could be all over. If the fire-lane extended only a few yards or curved – he

103

had no clear sight where it led – the 109 was in big trouble.

Günther maneuvered the plane, corrected a couple of times, aimed at the center of the fire-lane and went in. He set the 109 down perfectly. Once landed he jumped out, sweating but unharmed. When his wingman, who had been circling above, saw his squadron commander was uninjured, he waggled his wings a couple of times and took off for III./JG 52's field base.

"Then I heard shots. Bang! Bang! Was I on the Russian side or the German? I had no idea. I ran like hell into the shelter of the trees. The artillery continued all around me. I still didn't know which side was firing. I knew fighting on the Eastern Front was totally different from the Western Front. Here, chivalry was dead. Here, there was no gentleman's agreement on the treatment of prisoners. Caught, you die. Savagely."

Hearing a crackle of leaves behind him Rall whirled. Facing him a few yards away was a man in a long brown leather coat, military cap, and a star on his collar.

"He just stood there with his hands in his pockets. I saw no rifle or weapon but that didn't calm me down. I knew there was no hope of escape. So I approached him. He looked friendly. I discovered he was a Slovakian and on our side, and breathed a huge sigh of relief."

Günther's new friend pointed out where the German army headquarters were, and Rall set off. There, he was given a jeep and by late evening was back with his squadron. Another pilot wasn't so lucky. He landed in a field of sunflowers, saw Russians walking towards him and shot himself rather than face the fate of a cruel death at Russian hands. It turned out the Russians were actually prisoners of the Germans and were being led to a nearby prisoner of war camp.

The Germans took Kiev on September 19 capturing half a million Soviet soldiers and almost nine hundred Russian tanks. Over one hundred thousand German men were killed, while Soviet casualty estimates reached half a million.

"It was a decisive battle, but terribly costly for both sides," said Rall.

Operation Typhoon

Against his General Staff's advice, Hitler launched his attack on Moscow on the final day of September, 1941. Code-named Operation Typhoon it came as great a surprise to the Russians as Operation Barbarossa. They were unable to comprehend that the Germans would begin what would undoubtedly prove to be a prolonged battle so close to winter. But the Wehrmacht moved its divisions fast, taking in quick succession Orel, Bryansk, and Kaluga. Rall's wing now found itself setting up temporary airbases one after another. Over the next two years, from 1941 to 1943, the nine squadrons would move forty-four times in difficult conditions, laying out hastily-constructed landing strips as they followed the course of the war and pilots were supplied with maps that showed the locations of partisan-held areas that were fighting for the Russians, indicating the minimum height it was safe to fly over.

However, the heavy rains became a factor. The "Rasputitsa" is the muddy season, and occurs as summer gives way to winter. Most Soviet roads were built without adequate sub-base and base courses. Moreover they were poorly drained so that harsh weather together with extraordinary war-time traffic quickly led to their utter deterioration and they became almost impassable. Thus the German advance on Moscow was bogged down first in rivers of mud and sleet that sucked everything into their depths. Then the ground froze.

The most bitter winter in more than one hundred years was about to engulf the region. Hitler's plan to penetrate deep into Russia and crush it with a summer and early autumn campaign well before the cold weather set in was thwarted when snow arrived far earlier than usual. The sudden onslaught of freezing weather, constant snow, and biting frost affected Rall's unit's moods, attitudes, and morale. They had never experienced such cold or its effect on their operations. They had not been supplied with winter uniforms. Clothing, bedding, and tents were pathetically inadequate.

"We had lived happily and comfortably in tents since March but now, with the freezing winds and frost it was quite a different situation psychologically as well as physically. We were in the barren south. There were no roads. Only mud and frozen ruts." Plagued by respiratory ailments and frostbite many pilots succumbed to illnesses for which they were ill-prepared. Little medical assistance was available and the crushing cold was unrelenting.

When the generators failed small fires were lit in containers and placed beneath the fuselages to keep the planes' engines warm enough at night for instant scramble. "The oil in the engine would freeze overnight so we kept it viscous by warming it up. That was an old Russian trick we learned." The Russians had developed cold-weather flying techniques that allowed them to land even in the Arctic, which they did in the mid-1930s near the North Pole. The following winter the Luftwaffe would be supplied with covers to wrap around the engines.

"We envied those stationed near Leningrad with better conditions, and those on the Western Front. We slept on straw in tents stretched over trenches we dug. Flying under these conditions was extremely difficult. We were forced to send our heavy trucks back to Poland since they couldn't be used in that terrain so we had to rely solely on air transport. When I got the orders at night to move once more I always asked, 'How many Ju 52's can I get?' The usual answer was three, far fewer than needed. The German air force," said Rall, "had neglected to establish a comprehensive transport command for their offensive operations on the Eastern Front and many Ju 52 aircraft were lost during the battle of Crete and over Malta while supplying Germans in North Africa. This lack of air transportation dealt a heavy blow to the Luftwaffe. We never recovered from the losses. We had to move our men and materials in a series of flights each time, with the result it cut in to the number of combat missions we needed to fly."

After the overwhelming success of the start of Operation Barbarossa, Germany's newspapers had trumpeted Hitler's message: When the first snow falls, the war in Russia will be over! "But when that first snow fell in October we were shivering in our tents in Poltaba," said Rall. "We'd repeat the joke: The snow is here. Must be time to return home. Let's go!" In reality Hitler's war against Russia had just begun. It would be three more years before the Soviets pushed the Germans back from their ravaged homeland.

For III./JG 52 the winter in the desolate Russian steppes was raw and frigid. Guards delivered wood every night so the occupants could light a fire. "We lit logs right inside the tent. No one cared if it was dangerous or not. We were horribly cold." But Günther was not to endure the cold too long. In November of that year, on a mission that took him between Taganrog and Rostov, Rall crashed, breaking his back. While he lay in hospital, the Russian Army commenced a massive counter-offensive around Moscow on December 6, 1941, the day before the Japanese bombed Pearl Harbor. Rommel was on the run in North Africa and Hitler decided to take over the command of the German forces himself.

From his hospital bed Rall read in the newspaper that Mölders was ordered to return to Germany for the funeral of General Ernst Udet, who had committed suicide by shooting himself with his pistol, an event that was kept secret for years. Udet, a highly educated cosmopolitan intellectual, was depressed by both the military and political situation in Germany. Before the war he had helped many Jews escape.

Udet was the highest serving surviving German ace of World War I and in World War II was placed in charge of directing aircraft development at Hitler's prestigious Berlin headquarters. Göring forced Udet, who loved flying, to take the desk-bound assignment. It was a job for which Udet was ill-suited. It was so stressful with its enormous responsibilities and expectations of keeping the Luftwaffe supplied with aircraft and supervising production that Udet lapsed into a mental disorder. By 1941 he was on the point of suicide.

"He believed that Göring had taken Hitler's side against what was best for the Luftwaffe, embracing the Führer's senseless strategies," said Rall. Udet left a photo of Göring on his bathroom wall together with the words, "Göring, you cheated us." The SS found the note and photo and hushed it up. "My friend, an ordnance officer, told me these details," said Rall. "He was forbidden under threat of death from speaking out at the time. I am happy to say that Udet had a grand hero's funeral."

Another funeral would soon be held. Mölders and his adjutant were on their way to Berlin as passengers in a Heinkel 111 to form part of the honor guard for Udet's funeral. As the plane neared Breslau, Germany, today part of Poland, they learned

Rall in his Bf 109 cockpit, attended by his chief mechanic Broich, and ground crew

that bad weather had fogged in the Berlin airport. They decided to risk it. After all, the crew were among the Luftwaffe's finest. On final approach the plane's right wing hit a nearby factory chimney. Everyone was killed except Mölders' adjutant. Mölders was 28 years old. Another irony of war.

III./JG 52 moved its base frequently wherever they were needed for air support. Rall focused on protecting the ground troops as closely as possible, often in critical situations and at the edges of the Russian front lines, using his squadrons almost as fire brigades to douse Soviet advances.

The logistical problems of each move during the winter months were horrendous. It was a nightmare moving the group. There were no roads, only frozen mud and thigh-deep snow-drifts. The ground crews and mechanics had enormous problems transferring the supplies and equipment. It was almost impossible to travel anywhere quickly or easily.

"Once winter hit, the snow was impassable to ground transport. We had to depend strictly on Ju 52s to bring in supplies. They brought in food and took back our injured who arrived constantly from the front lines. The German Wehrmacht and Luftwaffe were completely unprepared for the hardships we had to endure."

Rall is reluctant to relive his day-to-day experiences in the freezing blizzards that he and the Luftwaffe were forced to fight under during the terrible winter of 1941, and the subsequent winters he spent there. Suffice it to say conditions were horrendous and harsh in that great uncivilized, undeveloped vastness that was southern Russia at that time. III./JG 52's daily activities blurred into one long series of take-offs, combat, landings, and bed. Each night the pilots had to fill out lengthy reports. Rall's routine was to file his, then write to his wife.

"The reports had to be so detailed," said Rall, "with witnesses in the air or on the ground, and personal accounts of the combat, the type of enemy aircraft, and what sort and how many rounds of ammunition you used. I realized how valuable these documents were, though, when Galland reminded me that Marseille's reports showed he needed only fifteen bullets per victory. That gave us all a high bar to scale."

But Günther never failed to make time to write home to Hertha. By the light of a candle or a lamp if he was in a tent, or by the dim glow cast by an electric bulb if the unit was lucky

Rall in his Bf 109 warming up for take-off. Russia, 1941

enough to find a farmhouse for temporary quarters, he penned pages and pages to Hertha. The couple numbered their letters to each other to keep tabs on their receipt. Luftwaffe personnel fighting on the front were allowed free postage and their mail was carried back by Ju 52s to a central point behind the front lines for delivery to post offices in Germany. Collections from the war zones were erratic, however, and often the letters arrived at their final destinations out of sequence.

"Of course, Hertha told me that the thought was always in the background that when I wrote her a letter I was alive, and when she received it I could be dead."

Pouring out his heart Rall wrote of the dreams he envisioned of their lives after the war ended and Germany was victorious, how they would be together always, and where they would live. Hertha wrote in return and the letters, his only tangible and crucial link with his wife, were carefully guarded as the unit moved from base to base. He often read specific parts to himself before going to sleep.

Whenever he was sent home due to an injury, or to receive an award, he brought the growing pile of Hertha's correspondence with him and stored it along with the couple's other precious belongings in a lock-up warehouse facility. Many years later when the Ralls went to Vienna to retrieve their possessions they discovered that the facility had been taken over by the Allies and then abandoned and left open. Everything was stolen, including Günther's correspondence and letters, and all of his medals except the Iron Cross, which he had worn as part of his uniform throughout his service.

"The letters were priceless to me. At a time of the terrible conditions we were fighting under in Russia, they kept my spirits up and brought Hertha into my soul," said Rall. "It was terribly disappointing to realize they were lost forever."

While based at Soldatskaya, north of the Terek River that flows from the Caspian Sea, Rall's unit flew in support of the German attacks on Grozny where the Russians were protecting their oil storage tanks in the area. For a short time during this period Rall's squadron had a prisoner of war. Rall had shot down a MiG in the Caucasus, and the pilot bailed out, parachuting into another of Russia's ubiquitous sunflower fields near Günther's base. "Our NCOs surrounded him, and he was shooting at everyone. Finally, they disarmed him, fixed up his slight injuries from the crash and brought him to me. I was sitting in my van, talking on the radio. One of my NCOs spoke fluent Russian so we communicated. I offered the prisoner, whose name was Antonov, a cigarette. He refused it. As I lit up, he relented. Then I offered him some tea which we kept in our fuel containers. Antonov obviously thought

JG 52's Russian POW Antonov, shot down in his MiG in the Caucuasus

we were trying to poison him because he refused the tea, too, but after he saw me drink out of my canteen he then drank from it. It was obvious he didn't trust me."

With little inclination or time to guard a prisoner of war the ground crew mostly left Antonov to his own devices until a Ju 52 arrived to transfer injured Germans. Antonov joined the group and boarded the plane. Rall learned later that, not surprisingly, he disappeared after arriving at one of the temporary medical centers.

In Soldatskaya, Cossack and Tartar tribesmen rode in on horseback to German camps and offered their services to the Wehrmacht. The tribes traveled with the German forces but remained as a family group and included wives, children, and horses as well as camels to pull their sleds over the snow. They were sympathizers and fought fiercely alongside German troops against the Red Army until the Allies triumphed. Then the Tartars were exiled by the Soviets as German collaborators and sent to Uzbekistan. "Those tribesmen were excellent fighters, tough, resolute. They had a good sense of humor, and loved music."

The cold of the frozen Soviet soil seeped through the thickest of blankets that the pilots slept upon. Orders to relocate came frequently as the fortunes of battle waxed and waned for the Germans. Moving constantly from place to place wherever they could find a strip of land suitable for a runway the unit set up primitive base after primitive base, carrying only essential equipment. Cots were not considered a priority. Personnel and pilots alike, wrapped in thin blankets and wearing every piece of clothing they could find, slept on the snow-crusted soil inside wind-battered tents. At one point Rall was luckier than most.

"I had found a rusty iron bedstead somewhere and hauled it into my tent. It was better than sleeping on the ground but how I envied the Luftwaffe pilots stationed in Norway, or even at our northern Russia bases, where they had barracks and an officer's mess."

The continual transfers from place to place were particularly dangerous when there were no intelligence reports of where the Russian army was on the march. One incident occurred when Rall, away from the Russian Front and in East Prussia meeting with Hitler, received a first-hand report of it upon his return to Russia.

"My unit was camped in a field near Malaja Wiski, east of Uman," recounted Rall. "They were awakened one night by the rumble of wide-track T-34 tanks. Before anyone could move, the Russians ploughed right through, crushing the tents under their tracks where our men were sleeping. We lost eighty airmen. It was carnage."

Tested by both battle and weather conditions, the squadron found it difficult to survive, let alone fly and fight.

"I love a challenge, but a positive, not a negative challenge." Rall and his fellow pilots hoped day after day for a diplomatic or political agreement to end the war. "When we kept retreating morale was almost impossible to maintain. I knew it was hopeless."

Grozny was the extent of III./JG 52's advance through Russia. From this point on, the unit would be in constant retreat to dozens of temporary air strips. Almost sixty years later Günther can recall each of those locations, the Russian names rolling off his tongue as if it were yesterday, among them: Charkow-Rogan, Gontschakowska, Ivanovka, Perescririno, Makejewka, Zaporoszhe, Kirovograd, Dnjepropetrowski, Nikol, Kamenez Podolsk, Krim Chersonaise, and so many more.

Rall Returns to the Eastern Front–1942

Eight months after his almost fatal crash Rall limped out of the hospital in Vienna and into a military transport that took him to the Franz Josef train station, on his way to Krakow. He was on the first leg of the journey back to his squadron. At the station he left a teary-eyed Hertha.

"Actually, she began crying eight days before I left," said Rall, smiling at the memory. "It was very emotional for both of us. We were so in love but didn't know if we'd ever see each other again. I was determined I would do everything in my power to come back and marry her someday."

The young pilot had overcome what doctors had told him were insurmountable odds. He was walking again after breaking his back in three places and suffering from a partially-paralyzed right side. By sheer force of will he had conquered the disabilities. Although the muscles in his right leg had atrophied, he trained the leg to respond and eventually walked without a limp. Indeed, in his later years he hiked mountainous terrain and skied some of the steepest runs in Tyrol and the Bavarian mountains.

As the train, packed with soldiers and airmen, pulled out of the station and the young couple had waved their last, frantic goodbye, Rall called out, "Don't worry. I will come back. I promise you!"

He tried to settle into his seat. The back injuries still bothered him and questions raced through his mind. Could he handle a Bf 109 again? Would pain distract him in combat? Was it possible he'd be sidelined after all his efforts to recover?

In Krakow Rall was met and driven to a German air base. Here, he boarded an He 111 and was flown to III./JG 52's current base in Rostov in the Caucasus.

Once more with his unit Rall was anxious to take a look at the front lines and check out the terrain. He was also eager to test himself after so many months away from flying. He asked Otto Decker to accompany him as his wingman on the flight.

The emotion Günther felt as he approached the Bf 109 assigned to him was almost indescribable. With the help of the ground crew, his back still bothering him, Rall clambered into the cockpit and settled into the familiar seat. Instantly all the glorious sensations of flying came back to his five senses. He knew he could have been blindfolded and still found his way to a Bf 109. The smell of the fuel after the mechanics filled the tank, the feel of the cold, hard edges of the cramped aluminum cockpit, the taste of the smoke from the wood fire lit beneath the fuselage to help the engine warm up, the view through the 90-mm armored-glass windscreeen. And the high, distinctive whining of the engine as he went though the start-up procedure.

"But wait a minute! What's going on here? The controls are different!"

Puzzled, he checked out the instrument panel, staring at the compass, the manifold pressure gauge, the altimeter, tachometer, and the fuel and oil pressure gauges. He gazed around at the canopy release, the circuit breakers, the radiator flaps switch, and the oxygen regulator. Nothing was out of place. Everything appeared normal but something still bothered him.

Fighter pilot talk, May, 1940. l to r: unknown, Decker, Rall, unknown

"Then it hit me. Because of my back injury I'd placed a thick cushion on the seat and under my legs. This pitched me farther forward than usual."

Günther's new cockpit position was a sight that was to be-

Lfd. Nr.	Typ	Datum	Uhrzeit	Ort	Höhe	I. Abschüsse Zeugen		Be
20	R 10	4.10.41	12,37	SO Walki	1000	Fw.Köppen	8.St.	Aufschl
21	R 10	5.10.41	12,44	O Sudrenkow	2000	" "	8."	"
22	R 10	5.10.41	16,32	W Mertschik	900	" "	8."	"
23	IL 2	14.10.41	15,45	N Poltawa	700	Lt.Burk	8."	"
24	I 26	15.10.41	07,37	O Bogoduchow	1200	Uffz.Wachowiak	8."	"
25	I 26	17.10.41	07,25	S Kolomak	1000	" "	8."	"
26	I 61	23.10.41	13,32	S Alexandrowa	1200	" "	8."	"
27	I 15	24.10.41	12,45	NO Takyl	15.	" "	8."	"
28	I 16	24.10.41	16,17	SW Takyl	800	" Steffen	8."	"
29	I 153	31.10.41	11,25	NW Alma-Tamak	1000	" "	8."	ins Meer
30	I 61	8.11.41	11,44	SO Asow	1500	" Wachowiak	8."	Aufschl
31	I 16	9.11.41	13,52	SO Djakowi	1000	" "	8."	"
32	I 61	22.11.41	13,50	SO Agrafenowka	1200	" Kirschenlohr	8."	"
33	IL 2	23.11.41	13,35	SO Rostow	150	Lt.Graf	9."	"
34	I 16	27.11.41	14,06	NO Agrafenowka	250	Uffz.Wachowiak	8."	"
35	I 61	28.11.41	10,27	NW Rostow	500	" "	8."	"
36	I 16	28.11.41	15,05	N Rostow	1000	Fw.Steffen	8."	"
37	I 153	2.8.42	09,35	S Ssalsk	1000	Uffz.Ermisch	8."	"
38	Mig 1	2.8.42	13,10	S Gorkaja-Balka	1200	Lt.Funcke	8."	"

Rall's logbook showing victories 37 and 38, barely a week after he returned to active duty

come familiar and famous to all who saw him fly: a pilot who sat closer to the windshield than any other. Whenever his fellow pilots saw that silhouette in a Bf 109 they knew it was Major Günther Rall. The loss of weight while in the cast, in spite of his rehabilitation gymnastics, reminded the twenty-four year old Rall that flying a Bf 109 again was going to be a challenge.

"I was as keen as ever to return to combat duty but the G forces in a 109 are much higher than they are in the BJ I took my medical test in," he said, "and after so many months in the hospital I wasn't sure of my resistance."

Fall, 1942. Rall in Gonchakifka on the Terek River, Russian Front, enjoying a cigarette with his chief mechanic, Schinka

That remark was tested on the first mission he undertook the next day and it didn't take him long to get back into the groove and notch up more victories. In fact, over the course of the next three weeks he tallied a total of twenty-four planes shot down.

On August 2, 1942, barely a week after he returned to active duty, he bagged an I-153 and a MiG-1. On August 3, another MiG. The small, poorly-handling Soviet MiG-1 fighter was a new addition to the VVS, first coming into service in April, 1941. On August 6 Günther recorded four victories: two Il-2s and two Lavochkin LaGGs. The Ilyushin Il-2 was a close support ground

Lfd. Nr.	Typ	Datum	Uhrzeit	Ort	Höhe	Zeugen	Bemerku
39	Mig 1	3. 8.42	16,17	W Armawir 16774	800	Uffz.Ermisch 8.St.	Aufschlag
40	Lagg	4. 8.42	17,47	SW Armawir 15112	1700	" " 8. "	verbrannt
41	IL 2	6. 8.42	09,45	SW Armawir 15112	800	Oblt.Decker 8. "	"
42I	IL 2	6. 8.42	09,49	SW Armawir 05253	300	Uffz.Ermisch 8. "	Aufschlag
43	Lagg	6. 8.42	18,06	N Kurgannaja 06813	2600	Oblt.Decker 8. "	"
44	Lagg	6. 8.42	18,09	N Kurgannaja 06644	2000	" 8. "	"
45	Lagg	9.8. 42	07,36	SW Kurgannaja 05194	50	Fw.Wachowiak 8. "	"
46	Lagg	10. 8.42	06,09	S Krasnodar 85232	1800	Uffz.Hohenberg 8. "	"
47	Lagg	13. 8.42	16,11	SO Pjatigorsk 34132	800	Oblt.Dickfeld III./52	zerschellt
48	Boston	13. 8.42	18,17	S Mineralny-Wody 35741	2100	Uffz.Lotzmann 8. "	Aufschlag
49	Boston	14. 8.42	09,52	N Kragatsch 34232	2300	" " 8. "	"
50	I 16	15. 8.42	10,23	N Hochun 34462	900	Lt.Funcke 8. "	Aufschlag
51	Lagg	16. 8.42	10,04	N Kuba 34134	1300	Oblt.Dickfeld III./52	Aufschlag
52	Lagg	16. 8.42	10,07	N Kuba 34134	1200	" "	"

Rall's logbook listing victories 39 through 52, all claimed the month he returned to active duty

attack dive bomber and was one of the most worthy of Russia's combat aircraft, as it was almost single-handedly responsible for defeating German armor on the Eastern Front. It was known in the West as the Shturmovik, or armored attacker.

Unlike the maneuverable Yakovlev Yak-7 or LaGG fighter, the well-armored Shturmovik tipped the scales at twice the 6,600 pounds of its hangar-mates but they were also slower at 270 miles an hour compared to more than 375 miles an hour of the Yak-7 and LaGG. While a Yak could match speed with the best of Germany's fighters, the Il-2 was a heavily-armed ground-attack plane the Russians used against German tanks, and were often sent on missions that were likely to be suicidal.

"Because of their armor they were extremely difficult to shoot down," said Rall, who was to bag fourteen of them on the Eastern Front.

During the next few days Günther shot down several more LaGGs and MiGs, a couple of Bostons, and a Pe-2. On August 15 he hit a Polikarpov I-16, known by its nickname Rata, bringing his total to more than fifty enemy planes downed. Rall's largest victories would be, by far, Lavochkin fighters (LaGG-3 through La-7), of which he downed a total of 183. The LaGG, mainly constructed of wood, was supplied to the Soviet air force in March, 1940, and, like the MiG, revealed serious handling and performance flaws until they were modified in 1942 and their horsepower increased from 1210 to 1850.

Still moving from one temporary air strip to another, from Rostov to Armivir and then to Mineralnyye Vody, Rall received an order from his group commander to seek out a site for an airfield in the Terek River area near where the German army was planning an attack. His unit was needed for air cover. The small town was isolated but renowned for its mineral waters. However, health cures were not among the pilots' priorities.

"I flew with a two-ship formation into unknown territory. The landscape was wild and primitive. I was looking for enough length for a landing strip. As we reconnoitered we encountered some Russian LaGGs and we turned and fought with them. It was really a nuisance because I wanted to find a field, not bother with victories at that moment. After a short skirmish, the Russian aircraft left, there were no casualties on either side, and we continued our search."

Spotting a likely area Rall told his wingman to protect him as he went in to land.

"It could have been swampy down there and there was no

sense both of us getting stuck in the mud," said Rall. Günther landed, fixed his throttle and jumped out of the cockpit. He marked the place, well outside the tiny village of Gontschakowska that consisted of five or six stone cottages, with a piece of white fabric. Three days later the squadron moved to their new base.

"It took us a long time to find it again because there were no landmarks and the fabric I'd left was barely visible and dirty. We parked our planes under the trees, and settled in."

At dawn the next morning, the first to scramble and flying solo, Rall took off on his mission as usual. At 19,000 feet his eyes searched the skies and caught sight of a fine but formidable target: a twin-engined Petlyakov Pe-2, one of the Soviet air force's multi-role bomber, ground attack, reconnaissance and fighter-bomber aircraft that was the backbone of the VVS. Armed with machine guns in the nose, rear cockpit and rear fuselage the Pe-2 was flying at 26,000 feet. As Rall continued to climb to challenge it a movement on the instrument panel caught his eye. A tiny field mouse was peeking out at him from the empty socket where the clock would normally be situated. The clock had been damaged and not yet replaced. Knowing that mice could chew through an aircraft's electrical wires, Rall, smiling with delight, reached out to catch the mouse but it quickly turned tail and disappeared back behind the panel.

"I was touched to see that little creature twitching his whiskers and staring straight at me. I didn't plan to kill it, just catch it and bring it back to base. Imagine, there was a living animal with me in the cockpit at 19,000 feet. I was not alone. I had a partner up there. It was an illuminating feeling, quite emotional. But I wondered how the mouse could survive at such an altitude. I had my oxygen mask on and at times it could

Typ	Datum	Uhrzeit	Ort	Höhe	Zeugen	Bemerkungen
5	19.10.42	1303	S Elchotowo 44721	100	Lt.Funcke	Aufschlagbrand
3	22.10.42	1432	O W.-Kurp 44531	1200	"	"
5	22.10.42	1433	N Nishnij-Kurp 44363	1200	"	"
5	22.10.42	1436	W W.-Atschaluki 44651	tief	"	Bruchlandung
1	30.10.42	1036	N Ssalugardan 44752	2205	"	Aufschlagbrand
5	21.3.43	0730	N Sslawianskaja 86512	4000	Markhoff	"
5	21.3.43	0743	N Sslawianskaja 86514	4200	"	"
5	24.3.43	1142	NW Anastasiews-kaja 76682	600	Uffz.Hohenberg	zerschellt
5	24.3.43	1143	NW Anastasiews-kaja 76682	600	"	auseinander gebrochen
5	26.3.43	1122	SO Krymskaja 85174	2500	"	zerschellt
3	26.3.43	1124	SO Krymskaja 85321	800	"	Aufschlagbrand
cobra	2713.43	1431	S Anastasiews-kaja 76833	3000	"	"
5	9.4.43	0827	NW Cholmskaja 85161	500	Lt.Funcke	zerschellt
cobra	10.4.43	0833	NNO Cholmskaja 85132	6000	Markhoff	Aufschlagbrand
5	12.4.43	0834	O Sslawianskaja 86672	2000	"	"

Rall's logbook listing his 100th victory, earning him the Knight's Cross to the Iron Cross.

freeze to my face so the mouse must have been in difficulties with its breathing. I admired it."

Distracted by the incident, and anxious to find the mouse again before it could short out the cables Rall broke off his ascent towards the Pe-2 and returned to base. In spite of a prolonged search by several mechanics no one was able to find the small mouse and it was declared a war casualty.

On September 2, 1942, Rall gained his sixty-fifth aerial victory, a LaGG, which earned him the *Ritterkreuz*, the Knight's Cross to the Iron Cross. On October 22, he bagged his 100th kill, one of three LaGGs he shot down that day and all within an incredible five minutes. The first was shot at 2:32 p.m. and the third at 2:36 p.m., earning him the *Eichenlaub*, the Oak Leaves to the Knight's Cross.

By now the VVS was equipped with better American and British planes, including P-39 Airacobras and Spitfires. The P-39's radical mid-fuselage rear engine layout enabled its huge 37-mm canon to be fired through the propeller hub, a world first. This less-than successful design, however, required a long extension shaft that passed under the pilot's seat – a development that has never been duplicated. Britain's spunky little Spitfire was so maneuverable in aerial combat it was a fine match for the Bf 109. It was the only Allied fighter to be continually developed and produced before, during and after the war.

The Battle of Stalingrad now took front and center and was to become one of the bloodiest battles of the war, where more than a million Russian solders were killed. III./JG 52 flew in support of the German advance but soon found itself helping to cover the retreat.

Towards the end of March, 1943 III./JG 52 moved to Kertsch, the eastern-most point of the Crimean Peninsula. By now Russia had resuscitated its air force so completely it was able to inflict great damage on the Luftwaffe, courtesy of the Allies' Lend-Lease program to Russia. The VVS was now fully equipped with P-39 Airacobras, A-20 Havoc bombers, and B-25 Mitchell bombers. The B-25 twin-engined medium bomber had become famous with General Doolittle's Tokyo raid a year earlier. The fast attack bomber fought successfully in every theater of World War II.

The P-39 was regarded as obsolete by the British and Americans by 1943 and was replaced in 1944 with the P-63 Kingcobra. Dimitriy Loza points out in his 2001 book on Airacobras that the 5000 P-39s provided to Russia were primarily used for air interception. The plane was built for short range and relatively low altitudes because most dogfights were fought below 15,000 feet. The P-39 VVS aces Alexandr Pokryshkin and Grigoriy Rechkalov shot down seventy Bf 109s between them in their P-39s. In addition, the Airacobras were equipped with sophisticated radio communication, enabling the Red Air Force and the Red Army to coordinate their operations far more effectively than the Germans.

At Taman, near the Kuban bridgehead in the northern Caucasus where III./JG 52 was now based, Rall's pilots confronted this new Russian air force with little surprise.

"We knew that a high percentage of the aircraft the Soviets were flying now were British and American planes. The VVS had also changed their tactics so it was a far more effective air force. In fact, superb," admitted Rall. "We were now being challenged as never before." Directives from headquarters came tumbling one on top of the other, often just hours apart, forcing the unit, at times, to backtrack as the German forces gave way to the Russians. At one stop near Sebastopol in the Crimean Peninsula, a macabre sight greeted the unit when it came across a bunker they planned to occupy. It was stacked high with skeletons still clothed in their Wehrmacht uniforms, casualties of Lt. General von Manstein's effort to take Sebastopol in December, 1941.

Now that they could no longer rely on German ground transport to take their mechanics and equipment to their next base, Rall issued an order that in case of emergency each pilot was to somehow fit a mechanic into his aircraft, accommodating him anywhere in the small, cramped Bf 109 to ensure that no one was left behind to be captured.

"It was a hopeless situation on the Crimean Peninsula. The cavalry was killing its horses. The ocean was filled with blood. Every thirty minutes we were attacked. We had no supplies, no spare equipment, nothing." If a plane crashed on landing the chief mechanics would no longer assess its damage and repair it ready for combat again. Instead, they'd swarm over it like wasps, stripping it for parts.

The winter months of 1942 brought more misery and although Günther had almost fully recovered from his spinal injury except for some painful twinges he was still vulnerable to illness. Sleeping on the ground and surviving in damp, draughty tents during the Russian winters caused several III./JG 52 airmen to come down with flu and respiratory ailments. Worse was Rall's virulent attack of a malaria-type fever, which laid him low for several days in his tent.

Rall Makes
a Lifelong Friend

"We celebrated Christmas in 1942 but it was a miserable, merciless one."

There was one bright spot for III./JG 52 before the calendar ran out. A newly-commissioned fighter pilot, Lt. Friedrich "Fritz" Obleser, joined the 8th Staffel III./JG 52 on New Year's Eve of that year. The fair-haired, cheerful young man, still in his teens, had received orders at his base in occupied France to transfer to Rall's unit.

The journey was arduous and took almost eight weeks as he had to wait days for military trains and a seat on a Ju 52 transport plane. When he finally landed in a snowstorm at his new squadron in Gigant he was minus his luggage, which had been lost in transit. Obleser wasn't worried. His previous base had stockpiles of spare equipment and clothing. Dressed in summer uniform and carrying his oxygen face mask, Obleser expected nothing less than full replacements when he arrived on the frozen Eastern Front and ran shivering in foot-deep snow from the cockpit to the command center. There, he was mortified to discover that the only extra gear that could be found for him was a pair of well-used overalls. He was also surprised to find that open farmland was currently serving as JG 52's temporary airfield.

"It was very different to the circumstances we enjoyed in France," said Obleser. "Here, there was one small stone hut where

Rall with a dog on the wing of a Bf 109

the farmer lived with his goat and chickens and Rall had set up his HQ in the hut's only other room. There were no hangars and only tents for the men. Snow covered everything but I was thrilled to be serving with one of Germany's great heroes. Günther Rall was famous. His name was mentioned almost every day on the newscasts along with those of Galland, Ösau and Mölders."

Obleser had requested to be posted to Russia and, specifically, to serve with Major Günther Rall.

"I knew that the best combat for a fighter pilot was there,

where I could score the most victories and get fast promotions," he said. "The Russians presented a large quantity of targets and Luftwaffe missions on the Eastern Front were famous for their frequency. Also, I knew that the risk to our pilots wasn't high because at least in the beginning the Russians had no Spitfires, which, along the coast of the Western Front, were a good match for our Bf 109s. To us young pilots Rall was already a phenomenon, he was one of the greatest and it was a huge honor to get into his Wing."

The young pilot's arrival was a fortunate occasion for JG 52. Because of a shortage of generators needed to keep the planes warmed up round the clock the unit's technical officer was having trouble ensuring that the aircraft were ready for take-off by 6 a.m. every morning. A nearby squadron had "borrowed" two of JG 52's generators and refused to return them. Rall was furious with the situation and spent most of Obleser's introductory dinner in the mess tent castigating the technical officer.

"I was seated at a rough wooden table with twelve or so other pilots, as well as the captain, the squadron leader, and the first lieutenant, many of them already decorated with the Iron Cross and Knight's Cross," said Obleser. "At the time it was the most highly decorated squadron in the Wing, and as the youngest one there, barely 18, I was tremendously impressed."

The crew ate by the flickering light of emergency generators.

Obleser wondered how he would make his mark among such exalted company. The answer came almost immediately although it was not, initially, in combat.

"Günther was the most well-organized commander I've ever met and the technical officer's failure to get Rall's plane ready in time drove him nuts," said Obleser. "He demanded punctuality even in the worst of circumstances. He wanted to be up and away, hunting the enemy. If he couldn't take off as soon as he jumped into the cockpit, it became an impossible situation for him. Patience wasn't his strong point."

Obleser, who in spite of his youth demonstrated great initiative, took it upon himself to solve the problem. After making inquiries that evening after dinner he found a JG 52 ground personnel driver who knew exactly where the missing generators were but who lacked the authority to repossess them.

"We drove to the nearby squadron in the middle of the night. I told the guard posted there that I had an urgent order to pick up the generators immediately because we were now flying night missions. The guard showed us where the machines were and we took them back to our unit."

At dawn the next morning, Rall's aircraft was primed and ready on the dot at 6 a.m. He was pleased to see that the generators were back doing their job. When he returned from his mission he sought out his technical officer to thank him for securing the return of the precious generators.

"Oh, it wasn't me, sir," said the corporal. "It was that new pilot."

"Which new pilot?"

"That one over there, sir."

Günther strode across to the youth with the irrepressible grin who looked barely old enough to ride a bike let alone pilot a Bf 109.

"Congratulations! You are now the technical officer!" declared Rall. Obleser was put in charge of maintenance for each of JG 52's Bf 109s, which varied in number between 12 and 16 aircraft depending on crashes and repairs. Often, the unit had only six or seven operational aircraft. It wasn't exactly a plum job.

"I had to be the first one outside before dawn in that terrible cold weather. It was truly miserable. I had to check on every mechanic to make sure the aircraft were ready for take-off. Then I jumped into my own plane. After we'd all returned I spent the evenings overseeing repairs. The other pilots were in their warm bunkers playing cards. Every time I came inside and told Captain Rall I'd checked the planes, he'd say, 'Hey, isn't there anything else you have to do outside? The aircraft must be perfect.' But my new duties brought me into greater contact with him and we soon became firm friends because we respected each other highly." In fact, flying on Rall's wing became a habit both enjoyed.

"I always felt safer flying as Günther's wingman than at any other time in the air, even though he was a tough pilot to keep up with, always changing direction, chasing opponents far into the hinterland," said Obleser. "I knew that nothing would happen to me if I stuck close to this amazing squadron leader. He was a superb teacher and within two months I had scored sixteen victories. He told me to learn by watching him, his tactics, how to concentrate on the target, and especially deflection shooting, where his aim was incredible. He believed the best way to master the skills of aerial combat was not through lectures or diagrams on the ground but through observation in the skies on actual missions."

Within a couple of days Obleser gained enough experience to satisfy his squadron leader and, in fact, became Rall's favorite wingman. The job, however, was not an easy one.

"Most of the other pilots hated to fly on his wing because Rall was very demanding. He required strict adherence to his instructions. Some of them didn't realize that following his rules could save their lives. Since I was eager to learn I loved every order he gave me. I soaked up his words like a sponge. He had an incredible instinct for finding the proper position to score against enemy aircraft He could maneuver his 109 in a flash to gain the advantage."

In return, Rall is still at a loss for words to express his high regard for Obleser.

"Certainly he was the most technically talented. He was a genius. If you put Friedrich into the Sahara Desert with just a screw driver and returned a year later, he'd have built a factory. He was also the most reliable of pilots," said Rall. "He only left my side in battle and always immediately returned. I trusted him completely. We'd fly deep into Russian territory. I told Obleser, 'Stick with me.' He'd say, 'OK.' And he always did. The pilots were all different, but Fritz was certainly the most talented."

"We made a good team, I think," said Obleser. "He was generous in combat, always making sure he gave me lots of opportunities to score." He eventually became one of Germany's respected aces with 127 victories.

Only once did Obleser invite Rall's wrath.

"We often joined other Luftwaffe squadrons on missions. During my second mission flying with Günther I could see that one of the other units had encountered a group of LaGGs. In high excitement I broke away from my own formation and joined theirs." Günther was almost speechless at this *faux pas* and Obleser's headphones sizzled as soon as Rall found his voice. Fritz also learned quickly that this particular squadron leader preferred to score the first victory for the squadron to start his day off nicely. After that, it was open season.

"Maybe it was matter of courtesy, but we all stood back until our squadron leader had his kill, then we felt free to go in," quipped Obleser years later. The two also began an enduring friendship that has lasted throughout their lives.

The Battle of Kursk

After the turn of the year, in 1943, Rall received the order to fly in support of the retreat from Stalingrad. Despite having been denied Moscow, the German army continued its sweep across the Ukraine into the Caucasus fully expecting to overcome the enemy at Stalingrad regardless of the Soviets' strong defense. Hitler's armies surrounding the city on the river Volga at the edge of Asia were again facing a fiercely cold winter and supplies failed to arrive. The Russian counterattack was gearing up and by the end of January the Germans were all but doomed. Those who weren't under siege in Stalingrad were forced to withdraw, while bad weather grounded most of the Luftwaffe's airlifts and relief flights to the stranded troops.

The Soviets had six armies attacking in the nearby Caucasus and Günther's unit was fully engaged providing cover for General Friedrich von Paulus' besieged Sixth Army. A month earlier, Hitler had personally refused to allow von Paulus to break loose from the Soviet trap of encirclement around Stalingrad. On January 24, 1943 von Paulus asked Hitler's permission to surrender. The request was denied. Instead, he was appointed Field Marshal but the promotion came on the same day the Russians forced von Paulus to surrender.

By mid-January the Luftwaffe had lost its last air base at

JG 52 on parade in Romania as Air Force Commander General Speidel reviews the troops

Stalingrad and suffered the destruction of five hundred transport planes as the Soviets continued the battle against the Germans. A few weeks later III./JG 52 received the order to move north to Mineralnyye Vody but because of Russian advances almost immediately had to evacuate even further north to Gigant, still supporting the army retreating from the battle of Stalingrad. The battle finally ended on February 1, 1943, when the 6th Panzer Army surrendered to the Red Army. During one of the support missions Günther lost one of his closest friends, Otto Decker.

"His plane was hit over the river but he managed to fly past

General Speidel, Air Force Commander in Romania, second from right, confers with three Romanian Air Force Officers.

the river bank and belly-land. We watched as he got out of the plane and was captured by Russians. He walked away from the crash but we never saw him again."

At the Gigant base the extremely low temperatures and snow from horizon to horizon made any operation difficult for III./JG 52. Based at one of Stalin's farm collectives commandeered by the Germans, III./JG 52 flew continual daily missions. Here, the unit was ordered to Austria to take delivery of the new Bf 109G. The pilots drove by jeep to Nikolayev, in the Ukraine. From this air base they flew to the Messerschmitt factory in Wiener Neustad, Austria, to take delivery of the Gustav. Improvements on the new version included a bigger, heavier, more powerful DB 605 engine teamed with the Bf 109F's fuselage. Although the mass-produced G version accounted for almost two-thirds of all 109s built, it proved in Rall's view to be a mixed bag because of its over-development, loss of maneuverability and all the worst characteristics of the earlier version. In spite of Rall's opinion of its shortcomings it was his favorite model.

"It was very advanced and equipped with new, more sophisticated technology. Nicknamed Gustav, the Bf 109G was well-armed but not as light as the earlier E and F versions. Its more powerful engine meant higher power settings whose initial climb rate sent it soaring to 18,700 ft in six minutes but at low speed the plane was difficult to handle. Although its range was a hundred miles more than the 109F with its auxiliary tanks at the bottom of the fuselage the modifications caused a loss of maneuverability. We had to make sure we dropped the tanks when they were empty to help with maneuverability. In any event, the tanks were a limiting factor. Most of us considered the 109G over-developed. Poor landing characteristics added to its woes."

During the last few days of April, 1943, III./JG 52 flew their new aircraft back to the Crimean Peninsula to Kertsch and across the small strait to Taman on the Asian side of the Peninsula, where the Germans and Soviets were fully engaged.

Piloting his new fighter plane on May 5 Rall shot down his first Spitfire supplied to the VVS south of Krymskaya in the Caucasus Mountains. Pleased with the victory, Rall quickly filled out a report but was immediately told to keep it quiet.

"Orders were issued that same evening that we were not to reveal Spitfires were now engaged on the Eastern Front. Apparently, it would make our pilots nervous." But the following morn-

ing Spitfires appeared in a group of twenty.

"A bit difficult to hush them up after that," observed Günther. "Then we saw P-39s and B-25 bombers. Some were delivered to Russia from Iran and some through Alaska, via Montana. They changed pilots in Grozny, where the Russians took command of the planes."

The harsh winter months had taken their toll on Günther's right leg. Almost crippled again by late spring, he was sent back from Taman to Vienna for a four-week program of electrical treatments. The respite was more than welcome. It was a rare chance to see his mother in Stuttgart and Hertha in Vienna. Bomb damage on homes in Stuttgart was widespread but raids on Vienna were uncommon and Rall felt himself almost in peacetime as he approached the district where Hertha was living. Yet as he came to the corner of her street he was shocked to see only one residence remained standing. Every other house on the street lay in ruins. His mouth went dry. As he walked past the burned homes he was stunned to discover that the building standing alone was hers.

Hertha and Günther made the most of their time together, with Rall enjoying hearty, hot food and civilized accommodations. But his visit was cut short. At the end of the third week he received a telegram telling him to return to his unit in Russia immediately to assist in the Battle of Kursk. Major Hubertus von Bonin, formerly with the Condor Legion, had been transferred north and Rall was to be group commander. Bonin was newly married but his new posting was to prove fatal. After four weeks at his new air base, he was killed. As group commander it was Rall's duty to find a successor for his previous position, squadron leader. It was an easy decision.

"I had known for months that I would recommend Fritz to take over as squadron leader of the 8th Squadron. I was sure that he would be able to adapt as easily as I did. And that is exactly what happened."

Obleser didn't share his squadron leader's confidence when

told the good news.

"Oh no," he protested. "I couldn't possibly do that. I am the youngest one here! All the other pilots are heroes, not me!" Obleser had not yet celebrated his 20th birthday. "I cannot accept." But Günther was not, of course, a man to be denied, and Obleser became the squadron leader in June, 1943. Because of the speed at which he notched so many victories, Fritz had already earned the respect of the other, older pilots and the transition was smooth.

"In addition," said Obleser, "Rall had turned me from a youth into a man. When I arrived at JG 52 I was a kid. Under his example, I grew up. I watched Günther handle his pilots' problems not only in the air but their personal problems on the ground. He talked to them like a father, even though he was only in his mid-twenties himself, and he seemed so wise. He had great compassion, especially when any of the crew received news of illness at home, or when we were completely fatigued after several missions every day and we didn't seem to be making any headway. He was always available to listen, to calm us down, to offer advice. Conditions during wartime are so different from peacetime, and although we were close, like a family, we still had private issues to deal with."

Obleser, who said he had never experienced any personal family problems of his own and felt unprepared for his new duties which included counseling the crew, was so inspired by Rall that he was able to rise above his doubts.

"Günther gave every pilot that confidence, the ability to not only meet his standards but to exceed them. He was remarkable. He set the highest of standards and insisted we meet them, which, to our great surprise, we did. He brought out the very best in us, and gave me a priceless gift, that of believing I could accomplish anything."

Revered as a leader who put the welfare of his pilots above all else, engendering fierce loyalty in return, Major Rall was also respected for his modesty, recounting missions and aerial combat exactly as they occurred and never trying to cover up mistakes. In the book, *Fighter Aces of the Luftwaffe*, by Colonel Raymond F. Toliver and Trevor J. Constable, Germany's greatest ace, Erich Hartmann, recalls how Rall "took an exceedingly modest part" even in the restricted social life of his Group. "He went to bed early, and woke early, to hunt the enemy."

The Kuban air war, rarely mentioned in post-war literature and even considered insignificant except by those involved, signaled a benchmark for the VVS. Stalin's aviation factories, well beyond reach of enemy fire, were turning out thousands of new planes and by the end of 1944 close to one hundred thousand would roll off the assembly lines. With no new pilots arriving from Germany to replace their losses, and with ever-decreasing parts and supplies, the thinly-spread Luftwaffe on the Eastern Front fell easy victim to the Soviet's revitalized air power.

During the week-long battle of Kursk, the Germans lost several of their tank divisions and failed to pinch off the Soviet salient line of defense. It was almost the middle of summer and conditions on the semi-arid desert steppe were difficult, with dry winds stirring up clouds of dust. In the summer of 1943 Hitler ordered another offensive, striking first at the small town of Kursk on July 4. III./JG 52 joined the massive force of five hundred bombers, two hundred and seventy dive bombers, and four hundred and eighty fighters that pounded the sixty-six Russian air bases where most of the Soviet aircraft was concentrated.

On the ground, Kursk was the biggest tank battle in history,

Rall in the cockpit of his Bf 109.

involving two million men and more than six thousand German and Soviet tanks, with the Russians outnumbering the Germans by two to one. In the air, fighting was just as fierce, with four thousand aircraft involved. The VVS sent up planes around the clock. But the superiority of the Luftwaffe's fighter pilots was much in evidence. On the first day of battle more than four hundred Russian planes were lost, compared to less than two dozen on the German side.

"It was a huge air battle because we were trying to hold on

Rall exiting the cockpit of his Bf 109

to the bases we'd established in the area."

Nevertheless, by sheer force of numbers, superior tactics, and the grim determination of Soviet soldiers to rid their land of Germans, Hitler's armies were being driven out. After several days Hitler ordered his forces to stop fighting although he deliberately neglected to issue a directive to withdraw. The Russians continued to push forward, and by the end of July the Germans were in full retreat. "After Kursk we no longer believed in an assured victory on the Eastern Front." The lines, however, were stabilized in a matter of weeks.

While Rall's unit was in the Caucasus, in Gontschakowska during the retreat from the battle of Kursk, the Luftwaffe recruited friendly bi-lingual local tribesmen to monitor the VVS pilots' radio frequencies and listen in to their plans and tactics and to get a fix where they were. Listening in to a German unit's radio frequency Rall became very familiar with the Russian pilots' names, particularly Pokryshkin's, and picked up a lengthy vocabulary of slang and swear words.

Reporting to Rall now were three of the Luftwaffe's most outstanding and successful fighter pilots of World War II and, indeed, of all time: Erich Hartmann, Friedrich Obleser, and Walter Krupinski. Günther was to be their commander for the next several months. "All three were superb fighter pilots and we had an excellent relationship."

Krupinski, nicknamed Punski, was born in East Prussia, and flew his first missions on the Eastern Front in 1942 with III./JG 52. He was famed for waiting until the last minute, until his enemy practically filled his windshield, before firing. He later became a top ace with 197 victories: 177 on the Eastern Front, and 20 on the Western Front.

"He was a good friend of mine," said Rall. "He was not an easy guy to know on a personal level but I respected him. I was group commander and he was one of my squadron commanders. He was brilliant, simply brilliant and was swiftly promoted. I had the greatest admiration for his combat skills."

Hartmann arrived at III./JG 52 as a very young man who took, said Rall, a little time to feel the thrill of scoring his first victory but he soon became the most successful ace in history, with 352 enemy planes shot down. On two separate occasions he shot down seven enemy aircraft during the course of a single day, although it didn't match Punski's record of eleven aircraft in one day, or Marseille's 17 Allied fighters in North Africa.

Mid-Air Collision

E ngaged in the greatest tank battle in history in the offensive against the Soviet salient near Kursk from one of III./JG 52's temporary crater-pocked air strips, the recently-promoted Major Rall experienced a critical incident that could have proven fatal as the result of extraordinary and rare aerial combat.

"It was late afternoon, around five o'clock. I was flying on a westerly heading with my adjutant in a standard two-ship formation over the Russian Front at an altitude of about 19,000 feet I saw two spots coming towards us. Behind them was a huge, wide cumulus cloud. The sun was setting but still sending out bright rays from the edges of the cloud. It was dazzlingly bright.

"We approached at full power and as we got closer and closer I was able to detect what appeared to be large radial engines. But the rays distorted their image. The oncoming planes were flying in our German two-ship formation and straight, not like the Russians normally flew so I thought they might be the new Focke-Wulf 190s with the stubby nose that had arrived on the Russian Front two days earlier. The aircraft were assigned to Major Druschel's group which was stationed nearby. I'd seen photos of the Luftwaffe's new fighters on the ground but never met them in the air. So we held our fire."

Equipped with 14-cylinder, 1600-horsepower BMW radial

engines, the Fw-190 was faster than most Allied competitors. The A-series were built as fighters and fighter bombers carrying bombs, cannon, and other armament, and deployed on the Russian Front in 1943 and 1944. One of their greatest advantages was air-cooled engines that did not require radiators and pipes that presented vulnerable, easy targets in combat; another advantage was a rear-raked, almost-seamless cockpit canopy that allowed for close to 360-degree visibility. The Fw-190 F flew close-support day and night missions, replacing many of the Junkers Ju 87 Stuka dive bombers on the Northern Front, then on the Eastern Front during Germany's retreat from the Russians.

Was the aircraft in front of him an Fw-190?

"There was no haze but I was skewered by the sun," said Günther. "I couldn't see the planes' colors or emblems. All I saw were black silhouettes against this huge white cloud."

Pulling up to gain height in order to help them identify the mystery planes by observing their colors against the white snow on the ground, Rall and his wingman looked down as the aircraft flew under them. Suddenly the second airplane executed a split-S and Rall was able to distinguish the markings.

"The dark green color and red stars of the Russian air force! A LaGG! My speed was now excessive and I couldn't bypass him otherwise he would be behind me and I'd be smack in the middle of his gunsight. Now I must attack. He was only about 165 feet underneath me as I dived down at full speed."

Rall turned his 109 quickly, pumped the button and sent a full burst into the enemy's cockpit. At such close quarters Günther had to pull up again – fast. He'd attacked far too closely. But the quick ascent caused his Bf 109 to go into a high-speed stall – exactly above the LaGG he'd just hit.

"I crashed down hard sideways, right on top of him. The

noise of grinding metal as our aircraft smashed one against the other in mid-air was unbelievably loud. My propeller cut off his right wing. As my speed carried me over him his prop sliced through my undercarriage, slashing the fuselage. I shall never forget the sound or the sensation of the impact. He went into a spin and never recovered, poor guy."

The collision set up a horrendous vibration in Rall's plane.

"I thought the engine was about to break off so I adjusted the throttle for the right RPM to correct it, to smooth it out, but nothing worked. I was at 13,000 feet over Russian territory and needing to land. I knew I was seriously hit so I made my turns very gently as I prepared to come down, careful to pull no Gs so the aircraft wouldn't break apart The problem was, where was I? Down below battles raged all over the place and I had no idea if I was behind German lines or not. I was looking for our tanks so they'd see me and pick me up."

Finding a field near his base, Rall landed and brought the shuddering aircraft to a stop. "When I cut the engine and I got out to inspect the damage, my propeller looked like a limp banana skin, the blades bent forward. The fuselage had a long, six-foot gash wide enough to fit a fist through, so it was a total write-off. I felt extremely lucky and thankful to be on the ground."

A couple of days later III./JG 52 was again in retreat, from Chaikov to Makeevka. Here, a journalist arrived after hearing on German radio stations that one of the Luftwaffe's most successful fighter pilots had achieved a hundred and ninety-eight aerial victories and was about to reach his second century. Wearing the uniform of a soldier as was required of all media covering World War II, the journalist wanted to be on hand for the special event.

"It wasn't difficult to notch up high scores," said Rall, " we often went on five, six or seven missions in a single day. We were pumped up with adrenaline." Most days the pilots left at dawn, landed several times to refuel, often never left the cockpit, re-armed, and took off again. Their daily schedule was exhausting. Up at dawn, fly several missions, return when darkness fell, fall asleep.

"This was our typical routine until that journalist showed up. Then my routine was disrupted. It was unnerving to have him following me around waiting for me to shoot down two more Russian aircraft I could barely sleep," said Rall. "He put me under greater pressure than my commanders ever had. That can be dangerous."

"Well, when are you going to do it?" the journalist repeatedly asked Günther.

Lfd. Nr.	Typ.	Datum	Uhrzeit	Ort	Höhe	Zeugen		Be
						I. Abschüsse		
199	Lagg	29.8.43	0810	SO Kuibyschewo 88462	1800	Lt.Funcke	III./52	Aufsch
200	Lagg	29.8.43	0822	W Ssinjewka 88364	2500	"		
201	Lagg	1.10.43	1445	NO Saporoshje 58212	2500	Fw.Birkner	9.St.	
202	Lagg	1.10.43	1445	NOwo-Gupulowka 59791	3000	" "	"	
203	Lagg	2.10.43	1104	Krasnoarmeis-koje 58132	1500	" "	III./52	zersch
204	Lagg	3.10.43	1044	Bol.-Tokmak 58821	2000	" "	"	Aufsch
205	Lagg	4.10.43	0907	O Saporoshje 58191	2000	" "	"	
206	IL 2m.H.	4.10.43	0934	Saporoshje 58162	2000	" "	"	
207	Lagg	4.10.43	1419	Bol.-Tokmk 58644	4500	Uffz.Tenner	8.St.	
208	Lagg	7.10.43	0750	W Schulgowka 49322	4000	Fw.Birkner	III./52	
209	Lagg	7.10.43	1516	NW Mashurin-Bog 39263	1500	" "	"	
210	Lagg	9.10.45	0646	NO Kischenki 49123	1500	" "	"	
211	Lagg	9.10.43	0651	S Kischenki 49144	3000	" "	"	
212	Lagg	9.10.43	0659	Ssoloschino 39262	2000	" "	"	

Rall's logbook listing his 200th victory

200th victory, with Krupinski at right.

"I'll do it when I do it," he snapped back. "Stop making me nervous."

The press would soon have its story.

On August 29, 1943, after the retreat from Chaikov, Rall earned his 200th victory. Rall and his unit engaged a squadron of Russian fighters and shot down two LaGGs within twelve minutes of each other, the first north of the city of Samara and the

A journalist interviews Rall after his 200th victory

other a few miles south. But the Luftwaffe ace didn't escape scot-free. The fuselage of his Bf 109 sustained several bullet holes.

"I trained my sights on a Russian LaGG's underbelly, pushed the red firing buttons and saw the hail of bullets from both my guns pepper the fuselage. The plane burst into flames. I was seriously hit but nothing could detract from my joy at achieving my 200th. It was a great event, knowing I was the third man to reach 200 victories." The victory earned him the *Schwerter* (Swords) to the Knight's Cross with Oak Leaves.

Rall's second summons to the Wolf's Lair for an award would be received a few weeks later and afford Rall a few days' leave.

In addition to looking forward to the *Schwerter* ceremony, Rall had an additional ceremony in mind – marriage to Hertha. He sent her a letter explaining the circumstances and urging her to make the wedding arrangements. Wartime weddings were hasty occasions on both sides, and Günther's was no exception.

He rushed to Vienna to marry his doctor. By now Günther was a popular hero. His was a famous name on the radio, and his face was instantly recognized in the newspapers and magazines because of his victories. But on this occasion Rall wanted no publicity. He and Hertha sought to keep their marriage out of the public eye.

"It was a very quiet wedding. No fuss. In fact, it was almost secret. Just a few friends."

Rall feared Hertha might still be under surveillance by the dreaded Geheime Staatspolizei, the Gestapo, as a sympathizer with the Jews and in 1943 his fears were realized.

"My wife was close to many Jews in Vienna, where a high percentage of the professional population was Jewish. In 1938 she had traveled to England to make arrangements for her Jewish friends there to take in some Viennese Jews. When she came back from London she was put under observation by the Gestapo. In spite of that, she managed to smuggle her friends out to the Austrian Aid Committee in London. It was a horrendous risk." In fact, the event almost caused Rall to be brought to trial because of it.

After the war, in 1948, Hertha and Rall traveled to London at the invitation of the Jews she had helped and the group held a joyful reunion. Also present was a Jewish lawyer who had gained fame in Germany as a top attorney after serving as an officer in the Great War. When the Gestapo rounded up Jews he had been sent to a concentration camp but was released because the

Rall jokes with Wing Commander Dietrich Hrabak, right, in Taman, Russia

party discovered he had been awarded the Iron Cross First Class in World War I as a regimental officer. They told the war hero he must leave the Fatherland within a week. He fled to England. During the 1948 reunion, which included the lawyer's children who were studying at Oxford and Cambridge, he instructed them to speak German to their friends, Günther and Hertha, instead of English, as a mark of respect.

Newly married and after a brief honeymoon at the Worther See in Austria, Rall took the train once more back to the front. In Krakow he picked up a Bf 109, and began the twelve hundred mile flight to the Caucasus to rejoin III./JG 52.

"For the lengthy trip I had no navigation aids and the maps

Rall in Russia, right, with Hrabak, center, and Bannemann, Taman, 1943

I'd been provided were all wrong. We'd gotten hold of Russian maps, of course, and I believe they were intentionally misleading. They showed no railways or landmarks to follow, just huge expanses of land mass." Rall knew of a German-occupied air-

Major Rall in Russia, 1943

field in Uman at which to refuel and completed the flight back.

The grueling daily grind left little time for keeping up with Hitler's war on the Western Front. Relying only on field phones to receive orders from area headquarters, the Luftwaffe pilots in Russia felt totally cut-off from news of the war in Europe, much less the war's progress in their Fatherland.

"We had no contact. Occasionally a few rumors. There wasn't time, anyway. We were in retreat, tired, cold, hungry and dispirited. Our job was to cover our ground forces as they fell back. All thoughts were of survival."

Colonel Hrabak, Rall's wing commander, soon arrived to congratulate him on his 200th victory. But the arrival of Rall's commanding general to offer his own congratulations would soon prove unwelcome.

"No more flying," he told Rall.

"I'm sorry, sir. I have to keep flying."

"You are over-stressed."

"It's the journalist's fault."

"I insist," said the general.

"Sir, would it help if I took a short leave?"

The general acquiesced.

The next day Rall rode shotgun in a Bf 108 Taifun, one of Germany's small passenger aircraft, destination: Vienna.

Greeting his surprised and delighted wife, Rall told her to pack for a holiday at the Worther See, a large lake near the Italian border in south-east Austria.

"We are getting away from the fighting and everything it represents," he told Hertha. A resort famous before the war for its large luxury hotel, the lake was now almost deserted and the hotel turned into a military hospital and rehabilitation center.

"It was just the kind of solitude I was looking for but at 11 o'clock the fourth night we were there, a knock came at the door. I was in bed and Hertha was still in the sitting room."

She went to open the door. Rall groaned. Was this an urgent call back to base?

"Congratulations! I just heard that your husband has earned his Swords!"

The bearer of the glad tidings was a military officer with whom Günther and Hertha had shared lunch that day at the hospital. "It was on the radio, the last newscast of the day," he said.

For the next few days the Ralls were on tenterhooks, waiting for a further message for the summons once more to the Wolf's Lair in East Prussia. Then the order finally came: Report to Berlin, then to Hitler's headquarters.

Leaving the Worther See, Günther went north to Germany's capital, where he reported to Adolf Galland and Hannes Trautloft, a well-decorated German ace who had flown with the Condor Legion in Spain and had been a squadron leader of JG 54 in Russia. By now Germany had lost its 6th Army and had been beaten back at Kursk. Rall's second visit to Rastenburg was not a happy occasion

Final Retreat from the Russian Front

15
fünfzehn

The crew of III./JG 52 was soon on the move yet again but the Russians weren't far behind. "They continued to break through and one night they attacked us on the ground." Sleeping in tents under a small grove of trees near Orel, north of Kursk, everyone at the makeshift base was rudely awakened one night by the crunch of bombs hitting the base.

"My armament expert came running over to my tent, shouting to the others for help because he knew I was in danger. He saw my tent had collapsed on me and thought I had fallen into the huge crater caused by a bomb. I heard the men hurrying over and I started laughing even though I saw flames outside. They'd forgotten I had an iron bed and all I had to do was swing underneath it if I feared I was about to be buried." When III./JG 52 assessed the damage in the light of day they found the crater was the size of a house.

On October, 14 1943 the US Eighth Air Force sent close to three hundred B-17 bombers on a raid over the German city of Schweinfurt where a ball-bearing factory produced crucial components for Hitler's weaponry. It was an ill-fated attack that was to become known as Black Thursday. The Luftwaffe shot down sixty-five of the bombers and damaged another seventeen beyond repair during the daylight hours. On the Eastern Front Rall heard the news but didn't rejoice.

Lfd. Nr.	Typ	Datum	Uhrzeit	Ort	Höhe	Zeugen		Be...
					I. Ab	schüsse		
241	Lagg	5.11.43	1451	S Prokowkra 49711	2000	Lt. v. Treuberg	III./52	Aufsch
242	Lagg	6.11.43	0750	SO W.-Rogatschik 48734	1800	"	"	"
243	Lagg	6.11.43	0941	Pawlowka 48761	1200	"	"	"
244	Lagg	15.11.43	1350	W Annowka 39731	400	"	"	zersch
245	Lagg	22.11.43	0842	W Michailowka 58711	1200	"	"	Bruchl
246	Lagg	22.11.43	1232	SO Krinitschki 49761	2000	"	"	Aufsch
247	Lagg	27.11.43	0837	Nowo-Nikolajewka 58231	4000	"	"	zersch
248	Lagg	27.11.43	0903	Mal.-Beloserka 48691	800	"	"	Bruchl
249	Lagg	27.11.43	1126	Pokrowka 48794	1200	"	"	Staubw
250	Lagg	28.11.43	0827	S Saporoshje 58174	2000	"	"	Aufschl
251	Lagg	29.11.43	0846	S Saporoshje 58183	2000	"	"	
252	Lagg	30.11.43	1017	SO Sofijewka 39894	2000	"	"	
253	IL 2 m.H.	25.2.44	1241	W Kirowograd 19634	500	" Markhoff	"	Schneew
254	Airacobra	26.2.44	1437	Kirowograd 29522	2300	"	"	Aufschl

Rall's logbook detailing his 250th victory

"That meant six hundred and fifty men," said Rall. "It was a massacre. But the German advantage didn't last long. After the long-range P-47 Thunderbolts arrived, it was a different story. The American fighter-bombers had the advantage of speed, and the P-38 Lightnings, though lacking the quality of the others, were equipped with twin engines that vastly outdistanced our single-engine Bf 109s. But the P-51 was truly the star fighter in Europe because of its long range and maneuverability."

That autumn Rall was back with III./JG 52 on the front lines, reluctantly part of the massive, continuing German retreat. At one point, in Colomea, the pilots hid in a hut to avoid the advancing Russians.

"We were encircled, locked into a pocket of land near

Rall celebrates his 250th victory

Kamjanec-Podofski, south of Roskoff in the Ukraine, surrounded by the enemy and completely cut off. We had flown in from Proskudoff. At night the artillery was right next to us. All day, every day, wounded German soldiers were brought in. It was terrible."

Sleeping in their flight suits, always at the ready, the squadron was awakened one night at 2 a.m. at Colomea when the adjutant received an urgent telephone call from the German front lines.

"We're in final retreat. I am the last soldier here. Soviet tanks are nine miles from you. You'd better evacuate immediately."

Rall rousted the pilots, ordered the ground staff to pack up and hurried over to his Bf 109, parked about 650 feet away.

"In the dark I stumbled into a deep ditch. The top was frozen and I broke through the ice in water up to my knees. The water was freezing but I couldn't go back and change my clothes, we were about to be overrun."

In January, 1944 Rall traveled, for the third time, to the Wolf's Lair, to receive an award. His recollections of each of those visits are detailed in the following chapters.

In March, 1944 he received orders to transfer to Lemberg, and went south to Besarabia, where he received orders to help cover the German retreat in the Crimean Peninsula, where the Germans were surrounded by the Soviets. The Russians were pushing the Germans inexorably west determined to rid their country of the invaders. At dawn, the unit was ordered to fly in support of the retreat and in Lemberg III./JG 52 found itself among many other Luftwaffe wings.

"The accumulation of aircraft was astounding. It seemed as if our entire fleet was gathered at Lemberg, all of us in retreat." In spite of the grim situation Günther was delighted by the chance to be reunited with several friends from other units whom he hadn't seen in a couple of years.

The last Eastern Front battle for Rall was in Cap Chersonaise, near Sebastopol. In mid-April Colonel Hrabak contacted Rall. "Report to me tomorrow in Mamaia." Located on the Russian coast just north of the Constanta harbor, Mamaia had become a temporary Luftwaffe headquarters with a lone hangar in the middle of open farmland. To reach it Günther flew east, together with his adjutant, for 250 miles at low level over the open

Rall taxis to a stop after returning from a mission in Russia, 1943

Black Sea. Ironically, this was the point at which Germany had started its war against the Soviet Union four years earlier and Rall had his first contact with the Russians.

Each Luftwaffe group stationed on the Eastern Front was now required to send back to Germany one of their most capable, most highly-decorated pilots to be a group commander in the home defense. With the American bombers protected by P-51 Mustangs, P-47s, and P-38 long range fighters Colonel Hrabak needed the mastery of the Luftwaffe's top aces to help combat the menace. US planes were raining hundreds of thousands of bombs onto German airfields in occupied France and onto Germany's heartland, particularly its aircraft factories.

"We need you for our home defense on the Western front to engage the long-range fighters of the US Eighth Air Force," Hrabak told Rall on arrival. "You have been named commander of II./JG 11 to replace Major Specht."

Günther Specht had lost an eye in combat in 1939 but continued to fly fighters until 1945 when he joined in an attack

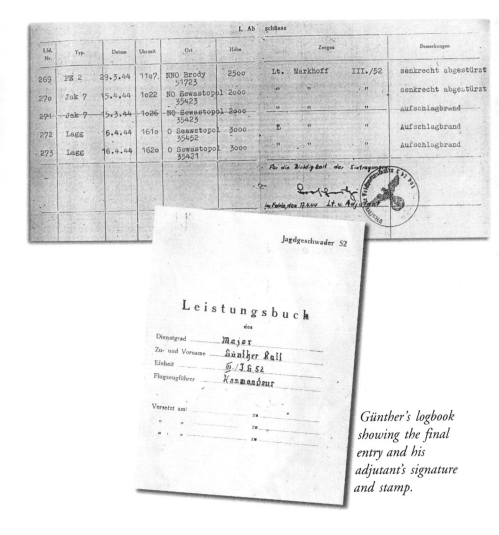

Günther's logbook showing the final entry and his adjutant's signature and stamp.

against the Allied bases in the Netherlands and Belgium and failed to return. One story had him flying his last mission in his best uniform, as if he expected to die.

Though he wasn't to know it at the time, Rall shot down his final and 273rd Soviet aircraft, a LaGG, over Sebastopol, the southernmost port of the Crimean Peninsula, on April 16, 1944. Later dubbed The Third Ace for his ranking as the fighter ace with the third greatest number of victories in world aviation history, Rall's last recorded Eastern Front victory was at 1620 hours on a spring afternoon at an altitude of 10,000 feet. Beneath the logbook's final entry on April 17, 1944 is the seal and signature of Rall's adjutant.

Before he left, Rall reminded his men to make sure they left no one behind, and transport the mechanics in their aircraft if necessary.

Part II

First Summons to Hitler

Every airman who won the Oak Leaves and higher was required to present himself to Hitler to receive a personal handshake and awards. Günther Rall received three such summonses. On November 2, 1942 Hitler presented him with the Oak Leaves to the Knight's Cross of the Iron Cross for one hundred aerial combat victories; on September 2, 1943, the Oaks Leaves and Swords for two hundred victories, and on January 11, 1944, Rall was presented with Testimonial Certificates. The ace's final tally was two hundred and seventy five victories.

These meetings, spread over a period of fourteen months, were significant to Günther because they revealed subtle changes in Hitler's behavior during three different occasions. At each successive encounter Rall became more and more alarmed as he saw first a euphoric but quiet and confident Führer, then a distracted leader, and finally a confused, indecisive man.

In 1942, the year of Rall's meeting with him, it was Hitler's custom to summon the recipients to *Wolfsschanze*, or Wolf's Lair. The extensive above-and-below-ground bunker complex was in the forests of East Prussia which at that time was part of Germany.

Chosen for its highly defensive location, the well-camouflaged complex was constructed in the summer of 1940 near the town of Rastenburg. The several buildings, resembling ancient fortresses with twenty to thirty-foot high, slab-sided concrete walls, and several wooden cabins, sprawled over more than six hundred acres and were surrounded by minefields. To conceal the garrison even more, fake trees were added to those already around the buildings. Visitors passed through two sets of security zones on the outskirts before gaining access to the bunker.

The Wolf's Lair was no hastily-built emergency shelter for the Führer. The site was carefully chosen and the bunkers designed with walls twenty-two feet thick. All of the windows faced north, and Hitler invariably sat with his back to them. The complex included water reservoirs, generators, a communications center, an airfield and a small train station where two huge diesel engines pulled the fifteen carriages, equipped with 20-mm anti-aircraft guns, that made up Hitler's special train, the Brandenburg.

Everything necessary was provided to conduct a war and at the same time live a relatively privileged life, with chefs serving venison, champagne and caviar. Although Hitler was a strict vegetarian, with his own diet chef, and a teetotaler, he didn't impose his preferences on residents or guests. He was very fond of herb teas, and made sure that each of his headquarters, whether in Germany or East Prussia, had a tearoom, which he called a casino, where, in the English custom, he had tea and cakes served to guests at 4 p.m. At Berchtesgaden his casino was next to the Berghof, and the Eagle's Nest, atop the mountain, is commonly assumed to have been one of his favorite places but in fact it was used only once by Hitler.

The innermost part of the Rastenburg complex was where Hitler and his personal staff were quartered during official conferences and meetings. His residence, a larchwood house, was where Colonel Berthold von Stauffenberg attempted to assassinate Hitler on July 20, 1944. Ironically, had that meeting been held in the concrete bunker, which at the time was being re-decorated, the full force of the blast would have been contained and thus far more deadly. Instead the bomb expended its energy by ripping off the roof of the frame house.

Cabinet members of the Third Reich High Command had headquarters on-site, including Reichsmarschall Hermann Göring, Foreign Minister Joachim von Ribbentrop, the Army High Command, and SchutzStaffeln officers. Their quarters bore such grand names as Kransberg Castle and Steinort Manor. Indeed, the complex, though no luxury resort, had wood-paneled dining rooms and mess halls, high crown-molded ceilings, arched multi-pane windows, elegant wall sconces, stone fireplaces, bronze sculptures, and damask draperies. The furnishings were those of a rural hunting lodge with ladder-back and leather-lattice chairs, comfortable sofas and an atmosphere of a well-oiled machine that called for unhurried activity.

Protection for the Führer, of course, was a priority and 12-ft thick steel doors shielded his quarters. Military vehicles were much in evidence at the Wolf's Lair but parked beside the tanks and trucks were several shiny black Mercedes-Benz sedans belonging to Hitler and members of his High Command.

When Günther arrived at Rastenburg in November, 1942 security was tight but the war on both fronts was proceeding well and there was a sense of relaxation. In fact, Günther's summons coincided with the pinnacle of the Third Reich's expansionism. Hitler's armies now occupied France, Poland, Austria, the Ukraine, Norway, Denmark, Yugoslavia, and Greece. With agreements with its Axis partners, German troops were also in Hungary, Romania, Bulgaria and Mussolini's Italy. Rommel and his Afrika Corps were inflicting heavy losses on the British Eighth Army, and Operation Barbarossa, the invasion of Russia, was currently an astounding success. Hitler's 4th and 6th panzer armies were poised to take Stalingrad. The Luftwaffe had succeeded in penetrating the north edge of that city, with the Russians forced to retreat to the River Volga.

But there were also setbacks. German forces had failed to take Moscow in 1941. The RAF was now equipped with the new lumbering but highly effective seven-crew Lancaster bombers whose 2,678-mile range and large bomb loads were wreaking great destruction on German cities. Worse, massive Allied raids on the industrial port of Cologne on the Rhine River and the chemical plants in Essen, west Germany, were overwhelming Hitler's sophisticated radar system.

Greater disasters were looming on Hitler's horizon. His juggernaut, Operation Barbarossa, would be halted by early snows in Russia and by December the invasion would grind to a standstill. Just two weeks after Rall's November 2 visit German armies around Stalingrad would find themselves in dire straits, in need of equipment and supplies, and the Soviet's encirclement tactic of surrounding Nazi troops was to pay off brilliantly. The Russians would compress the 6th Panzer Army on the Eastern Front into an area measuring a mere eighteen by twenty-five miles. Hitler's humiliating defeat in Russia, the turning point of World War II, was a matter of months away.

But when Captain Günther Rall prepared to meet his Commander-in-Chief to be decorated for his heroism he knew only excitement, pride and the taste of success.

"Hitler's high command expected to take Stalingrad. We were already at its gates and the impression I received was that in two weeks we would take it," said Rall. "Everyone's mood was upbeat."

Günther's first face-to-face meeting with Adolf Hitler was the occasion to receive the Knight's Cross with Oak Leaves for his 100th victory. Rall had been flown in a transport aircraft to the small airfield hidden deep inside the Wolf's Lair. Bristling with sentries along the perimeter fence and with guards at every building, the complex appeared to Günther as a highly-organized campus.

Along with Steinhoff, Druschel and two other pilots Rall was received on arrival by Colonel von Below, "a very fine gentleman," said Rall. Below's air force adjutant escorted the group to Hitler's bunker where entry was through a plain but armor-plated steel door. They were ushered into the Führer's private reception room.

Dressed in a field uniform, Hitler clasped each man's hand firmly as he presented each pilot with his award. When it was his turn Rall found himself taken aback by Hitler's piercing, sapphire blue eyes.

"I was totally unprepared for those strong blue eyes that seemed to burn right through you. When a man has black hair and black moustache, you don't expect such blue, blue eyes. They were hypnotic and filled with energy. We knew the Führer only from photos in the press and here we were, in his presence, just a small group of us. His charisma was so evident! I could understand why the whole nation followed him. You knew you were in the presence of a leader."

The ceremony was formal and Rall found himself almost afraid to speak.

"We were all nervous." Drinks were served after the presentations, then the group sat around the fireplace, talking.

"Where are you from?" Hitler asked each in turn. "And what are you doing? Are there any problems?"

The pilots provided respectfully short answers.

"During the conversation which soon turned into a mono-logue," Rall recounts "it was clear Hitler had every facet of the war at his fingertips. He was well informed, with details and facts and figures that astounded me. He recited statistics, logistics, the order of battle, and knowledge of every military operation and its problems. He knew production numbers, exactly how many aircraft, guns, anti-aircraft, submarines and battle-ships were being built and where they were to be deployed."

The Führer described his concept of the war against Russia, how the country would be exploited once the war was won, what Germany would build there, and how German farmers would be settled on Soviet land. It was a moment that called for insight but the opportunity slipped away without the young ace delving too deeply into its essence for meaning or motivation.

"Hitler was optimistic because at that time our armies were advancing on Stalingrad and we were anticipating taking the city within two weeks. Hitler advocated offensive operations and planned to deploy every plane in the Luftwaffe fleet towards that goal. It was also obvious he planned to focus on increased production of bombers."

One of Hitler's remarks jarred the pilots.

"I am against too many fighter pilots," Hitler told these top fighter aces, without further explanation. The remark was significant because it emphasized that Hitler was foolishly offensively oriented towards bomber strikes rather than defensive. Indeed, the Luftwaffe would pay the price for Hitler's mistake when, later in the war, there were too few fighters to defend the country.

"In fact," said Rall, "General Sperrle should have followed Galland's recommendations. He advised increasing the number of fighter pilots that year, 1942, to be ready for the British and Americans. They were building up and it was obvious they would be in a good position to attack strongly the following year." Galland's prediction went unheeded.

"We were surprised at Hitler's remark, to say the least, and I wondered for a moment if he'd mistaken us for bomber pilots, but I quickly discarded the notion because Hitler was so sharp, so knowledgeable at that time," said Rall.

"Then the Führer continued his monologue. It lasted an hour and focused on cultivating conquered lands and settling military-minded German farmers in the East and irrigating and cultivating the Nagoya snow desert to grow crops and increase trade. He told us of his intention to settle German farmers across the Ukraine and Russia, providing them with arms against marauders, much like during the era of Ghengis Khan. It sounded a little bizarre."

Hitler told the pilots of his plans to extend the railway system into other parts of Europe and the stationing of a comprehensive anti-aircraft defense on the ground so that aerial warfare could concentrate on offense. "He was extremely methodical and logical in his thinking," remarked Rall.

Günther and his fellow pilots were attentive but somewhat distracted by the fact that for the first time in months they were warm, well-fed, and away from the war. Nevertheless, Rall remembers much of Hitler's speech.

"We were all impressed at his grasp of everything. It was a lot to absorb but it boosted our morale considerably. It seemed to me he was playing the role of an elder statesman because he knew exactly the impression we, as young fighters, would take back to our units. I realized later it was intended as a message to the troops who were bound to ask about our meeting with Hitler when we returned to our squadrons."

Yet, as Hitler wound down his monologue, 24-year old Rall could not restrain himself. Germans on the Eastern Front were freezing in blizzard conditions.

"Mein Führer, may I ask how long the war on the Eastern Front will last?" The other pilots were shocked at Rall's brash question. Who would dare to question the Commander-in-Chief, especially a mere captain? But Hitler wasn't annoyed.

"Rall, I do not know," he replied, shrugging his shoulders.

There was a stunned silence. Günther was appalled at the careless response but said no more. It was the first time after listening to his speeches since 1938 that Rall had ever heard Hitler say, 'I don't know.' Disturbed by Hitler's uncertainty, he left the Wolf's Lair by night train to Berlin, then to Vienna. It marked another turning point in his life; he and Hertha were married on November 11, 1942.

Second Summons to Hitler

T en months later, on September 2, 1943, Rall was called to report to Hitler to be awarded the Knight's Cross and Oak Leaves and Swords for his 200th victory.

Ominous signs of cracks in the Wehrmacht's Panzer Divisions and a halt to their relentless march east left Hitler a different person. His health appeared to be deteriorating. A few months earlier several of Hitler's top aides and his medical specialist, Dr. Theo Morrell, had expressed concern about his mental and physical condition.

On this occasion only four pilots received honors: Major Hartmann Grasser, who had been transferred to France after commanding II./JG 51; night fighter Major Prince Heinrich Sayn zu Wittgenstein; Captain Walter Nowotny with JG 54, and Rall.

"It was obvious that circumstances had changed Hitler's personality, as well as his health," said Rall. "This was a different Hitler. Nothing that he had promised had come true. Few of his goals had been reached. It seemed he had no solution for the direction the war had taken. It appeared it was a mystery to him."

Indeed, the 6th Panzer Army had been lost in the battle of Stalingrad. The Afrika Corps was defeated and on the retreat, in the battle of Kursk the German army had lost much of their tank power, and Hitler was about to fire General Franz Halder, one of his top military strategists.

"I think Hitler knew that another diatribe would no longer be effectual, although it didn't stop him. 'Don't worry,' he said, 'we may be in a deep, dark valley now but there is a silver lining on the horizon.' He described his plans for the expansion of the Third Reich effort, basically a repeat of the talk he had given to

right: Rall receives the Oak Leaves and Swords from Adolf Hitler at the Wolf's Lair. Drüsel and Steinhoff are to Rall's right.

below: Hitler and his adjutant, von Below, right, congratulate Rall at the Oak Leaves and Swords ceremony. Grasser, von Wittgenstein are to Rall's right, and Nowotny to his left.

At the Wolf's Lair, East Prussia, 1943. l-r : Heinrich von Sayn-Wittgenstein, Hartmann Grasser, Walter Nowotny, Rall

the pilots during Rall's first visit. Rall said that the small group of pilots was unanimous in its belief that Hitler was deluding himself if he believed Germany could still win the war.

"He blustered and was no longer the leader who had firm control of things. This time, he seemed to have few facts at his command when we asked him about the progress of battle." Worried by Hitler's attitude, hesitancy, and apparent lack of leadership Rall knew in his soul it was the beginning of the end.

"At that very moment, I was beginning to feel that we were floundering," said Rall. "The Führer didn't need to say another word. Here was our leader. Our future was in his hands and he had no idea what it should be!"

Afterwards, the group were told to report to Göring at his nearby bunker headquarters. The Reichsmarshall was in a meeting with Galland and night fighter pilots, so Rall and the others cooled their heels in the reception room. "We all had to formally advise Göring that we had received our awards, stepping forward one at a time."

The group left the Wolf's Lair in a depressed state of mind. "It was not a signal for victory," said Rall.

Again spending a few days with his wife, Rall told her, "This war is finished."

Leaving the Wolf's Lair, East Preussia, 1943. Rall, far left, with Hitler's air force adjutant Colonel von Below, center

Grasser, Wiittgengstein, Rall, Nowotny after the ceremony

Between Rall's second and third meeting with Hitler, everything would change: Retreat from the Caucasus. Retreat from Stalingrad. Retreat from Kursk.

Third Summons to Hitler

Günther, now a major, went to the Wolf's Lair for the last time on January 11, 1944, to receive the Testimonial Certificates for the Oak Leaves and Swords. While other aces with fewer victories than Rall's 275 received the Knight's Cross with Oak Leaves, Swords and Diamonds, Germany's highest military award, Günther was never awarded what many considered his due, even though Hermann Graf with 212 victories, Gordon Gollob with 150, Helmut Lent with 110, Werner Mölders with 115, and Walter Nowotny did indeed receive the honor of the Diamonds.

Unofficially, it is common knowledge that the courageous actions of Rall's wife touched upon in Chapter 14 were the reasons her husband was not honored with the Diamonds, although the great Gerhard Barkhorn with 301 and Otto Kittel with 267, were similarly slighted.

Rall's Iron Cross with Oak Leaves and Swords Testimonial Certificates were impressive. Elaborately-designed in a classical style on thick parchment and encased in heavy ivory silk covers with the Third Reich's eagle symbol embossed in gold leaf, the diploma was signed by Hitler in a peculiarly small, cramped handwriting barely an inch wide and sloping downward, as if he was squeezing out the last of his energy. The extravagant flourish with which Hitler had signed his name to earlier treaties and pacts had vanished.

Sixteen pilots – eight of whom would fail to survive the war – were present to receive honors, among them Galland, Nowotny, and Ösau. After the ceremony, lunch was served.

"Around Hitler's plate at the table," said Rall, who was sitting two places away, "were all kinds of medications. He looked a lot older and somewhat confused, talking about every little thing that might create some hope for him. We all remarked later how slowly Hitler walked, how long it took him to raise his glass, how tentatively he ate his food."

Then it was time for Hitler to deliver another speech. The focus was on an invasion on the Western Front, where and when it might happen and how Germany should react. He ranted on about the British and their political problems with the Labor Party and the Conservative Party and how their differences were affecting the British people.

"He didn't realize that the British would come together, no matter which political viewpoint they held, to support a European invasion of Germany."

Hitler seemed to be grasping at any straw. As if he could conjure up hopeful signs by the sheer force of his will. But there were none. By five p.m. the ceremonies were over. Göring's adjutant ordered the pilots to take the train to Berlin so that they could visit the Reichsmarschall at his hunting lodge, Karinhall, to participate in the celebrations for Göring's 51st birthday.

"While Galland flew down because of his high rank, we all took the train from Rastenburg and arrived at the Berlin station at 7 a.m. when civilians were setting off for work. What a strange sight after being in the midst of fighting a war in a vast wasteland. It was surreal to be in a normal city setting, where daily life was going on as usual in spite of air raids." The feeling was mu-

Leaving the Wolf's Lair. l-r: Baer, Rall, Graf, Baumback, Lent

tual. The civilians were just as open-mouthed to see such highly-decorated airmen, carrying their Certificates.

The pilots were met and bused to Karinhall, where an adjutant made sure they were given a hearty breakfast.

"I can still almost taste it, it was superb after eating out of tins in the snow in Russia," said Rall. "We were given really fine cigarettes, of a much superior brand than we were used to," said Rall.

Karinhall, named after Göring's first wife who died in 1931,

Swedish-born Baroness von Rosen, was a sumptuously decorated residence situated forty miles north-east of Berlin, on the outskirts of the city.

"We stared at the richness of it all, the dimensions of the place, the decor, the statuary, the art works, it was amazing."

The birthday reception was held in the baronial Great Hall, a vast room whose split-beam ceiling soared 30-feet and windows were almost as tall. A massive stone fireplace dominated one end of the room. Scattered around the floor were bear skins and other animal pelts and on the walls hung dozens of stag racks.

Göring gave the fighter pilots an effusive welcome, obviously pleased to be surrounded and celebrated by his Luftwaffe heroes. They included Colonel Günther Lützow who was to denounce Göring to his face for calling inexperienced pilots cowards later in the war. Also present was the whole diplomatic corps plus top level generals from Prussia, one of Hitler's architects Albert Speer, the German Minister of Economic Affairs Walther Funk, and Prussia's Prince August Wilhelm and many others.

The party began at twelve o'clock.

"The family went in alone to the Grand Hall to congratulate Göring on his birthday, then the various delegations, then the ambassadors, and then the Luftwaffe pilots followed. We were led by Göring's deputy, General Erhard Milch, formerly a captain in World War I."

The tremendous hall, with its twenty-five foot high window that showed a view down to a lake, was an impressive sight.

"Göring shook hands with each of us. After lunch Funk delivered a formal speech then Göring responded, saying, We will win the war because we MUST win the war! We will fight to the end! It sounded ridiculous to us. I remembered those words towards the end of the war when I learned that the great

Reichsmarschall had begged the Americans to take him to England as a prisoner."

Rall was disgusted with the birthday celebrations, the lavish display of gifts, and the buffet tables piled high with every delicacy.

"The contrast with what we all were enduring on the front lines with their horrible conditions was repugnant to me. This pompous birthday party, the stilted speeches, the rich food, free-flowing liquor, the museum items that were probably looted and presented to Göring as gifts, the merriment, all this was unbearable. It was January, 1944. The US Fifth Army was in Italy, the Soviet forces had crossed the former Polish border, and long-range fighters escorts, P-38s and P-47s, were accompanied for the first time by P-51s. They were all over Germany."

Rall and his fellow pilots ended their day with supper at the Hotel Adlon. Once one of the most famous in Europe, the Hotel Adlon was almost a burned-out ruin from the regular pounding of Allied bombs. Located near the Tiergarten and the Reichstag, and in the shadow of the Brandenberg Gate, the seven-story hotel had been frequented by Albert Einstein and Charlie Chaplin. Today, renovated and remodeled, the hotel, in the heart of Berlin, is a five-star luxury hotel once again.

During Rall's visit there was no glass in the windows, which were covered with sheets of thick brown paper.

"The smell of smoke was everywhere."

He headed to the lobby to meet his fellow aces, Austrian-born Major Walter Nowotny who, in July, 1944 would test the Luftwaffe's Me 262, and Colonel Walter Ösau, a former Condor Legion and Battle of Britain hero who had been the commander of JG 2.

"It was a sad time. When we finished our meal and said goodbye we looked each other directly in the eyes and knew we would never see each other again." Four months after this reunion, Ösau was killed. Ten months later Nowotny was killed. And Rall had already found himself hanging from a tree after yet another bailout. Günther is convinced that had he not been on the injured list and in a hospital he would never have made it through the rest of the war alive.

After Göring's birthday party, he headed home to Vienna totally disheartened. Granted a few precious days' leave, Rall was reunited with his wife. "Hertha, the war is lost. Hitler is a confused man," Rall told her sadly. He returned to his base depressed but determined to give it his best.

"You go back to the front lines and you are faced with a new challenge every day. There's no time to dwell on what might happen. In the air you act and react. We still followed our code of honor, to fight for our country."

A year later, Karinhall was ordered destroyed by Göring as the Allies advanced on his beloved estate. According to reports, Göring asked the Americans to take him prisoner. He apparently feared for his life from angry fighter pilots after he had reproached them for behaving like cowards and brusquely refusing a technical discussion on aerial warfare offered by experienced pilots who were in the thick of the action.

Wolfsschanze was also ordered blown up by the Wehrmacht in November, 1944. Some of the buildings still exist and today are open to the public.

"Had Hitler stopped when he reached Austria, he would undoubtedly have been hailed as the greatest German in history," said Rall. "He built up the Reich and the Western Allies accepted it when he marched into Austria. If he had disciplined himself and stopped there he would have had his empire. But his limitless ambition to grab land turned the Allies against him. Now, and probably for the next century, the German people must bear the burden of what he did."

Part III

Commander of II./JG 11
in the Western Theater

On April 18, 1944 Major Günther Rall bade a fast, reluctant farewell to III./JG 52, packed his meager belongings, wished his successor well, and flew home to check in at an airbase in Wunstorf, west of Hanover. "After settling in I quickly realized that the Luftwaffe's air war strategies on the Western Front were very different to that on the Eastern Front. No longer did I go out hunting for the enemy all day, as we did for VVS aircraft, shooting down as many as we could, returning to base to refuel and re-arm, then taking off again."

Rall's new war provided a new dimension and proved in no way similar to his previous experiences as a fighter pilot in Germany in 1940. This was a far more deadly operation. The threat overhead had increased tremendously with the advent of the Eighth Air Force's long-range fighters that were escorting the bombers as they attacked one city after the other in the effort to wipe out the enemy. Against the Eighth Air Force Rall's unit was given a single designated target: the group of Allied fighter escorts that protected the Allied bombers against attack as they streamed across Europe in vast numbers. For Günther who had just spent three and a half years of his life in daily aerial combat on his own terms the order was somewhat irksome.

On the Eastern Front Rall had become accustomed to a culture built on hardship, basic survival, brutal conditions in a foreign country, and living on the edge, never knowing whether he'd return safely from a mission or not. On the Western Front living conditions were more comfortable and the combat challenges were immense but Rall met them head on and almost with happy anticipation. On the other hand, he'd already been shot down eight times before making it back to base. How much longer could this cat's luck continue?

"In the East we flew a tactical warfare, primarily from the Russian side, concentrating from air to ground, but in the West, we waged strategic warfare."

Weather presented a different scenario, too.

"Thick clouds covered most of the region much of the time, very different to the clearer and colder skies on the Eastern Front. When you're fighting above clouds you can't see any landmarks. You can't tell where you are. Another problem was the numeric relationship between our fighter attack forces and the long-range fighters. This relationship was one to ten. It was hopeless. Defenders are always outnumbered in such a situation."

By coincidence, as Rall arrived in Wunstorf, another transfer occurred on April 18 that was to affect his life forever. Colonel Hub Zemke, group commander of the 56th Fighter Group, US Eighth Air Force, was ordered to relocate his unit several miles farther south from its air base in Halesworth, England, to Boxted in Essex where a base had been built specifically for bombers near the old Roman capital of Colchester, north-east of London. Zemke guessed the move to add fighters to the airfield was in preparation for an Allied invasion of France.

At Wunstorf Rall was given command of II./JG 11 and posted to an airbase outside the medieval Saxon city of Celle,

northeast of Hanover, Germany. Known today for its historic and classical stallion parades, in Rall's time the city of Celle was more famous for its proximity to Hitler's crucial synthetic oil production facilities in Wietze.

One month after he'd taken up his new command, Rall got the usual order to scramble. The signal was relayed from German Naval ships in the North Sea, which were tuned in to the frequency of the US Eighth Air Force. Word was that an attack of eight hundred bombers, escorted by twelve hundred fighters, was imminent. II./JG 11's main mission in their Bf 109s was to engage the long-range American fighter escorts so that the Luftwaffe's well-armed but heavy Focke-Wulf Fw 190s could attack the bomber stream, a tactic that succeeded in bringing down hundreds of Fortress and Liberator bombers. Because of the weight of their extra cannon the Fw 190s were vulnerable to attack, or "bouncing," by Allied fighters. Teaming up the Fw 190s with Bf 109s meant the lighter planes could protect them.

It was 5:25 a.m. May 12, 1944. Rall was awakened by the Division Commander.

"When the American fighter escorts reach the Zuider Zee, I'll send the fifteen-minute alert, then the five-minute alert, and the cockpit alert," said the commander, "then you can scramble."

The signal came soon enough. The squadron met at a rendezvous point over Steinhudermeer, west of Hanover, with Rall's group of Bf 109s providing top cover for two groups of Fw 190s, numbering a total of fifty aircraft The heavier fighters would engage the stream of bombers and the Bf 109s would engage the fighter escort.

Before dawn that day Second Lieutenant Robert "Shorty" Rankin, a flight commander with the 56th Fighter Group of the Eighth Air Force at Boxted, was among those to receive the order to escort a group of B-17 bombers whose targets were Germany's six oil refineries.

The most victorious Allied fighter unit in Europe with more aerial victories than any other during World War II, it was known as the Wolf Pack and commanded by Colonel Hub Zemke. Rankin, a 25-year old from Washington, DC, who was to make USAAF history that day, was excited because Zemke's Fan was to be tried out for the first time and he was ready for action. Hub had perfected what was to prove one of the most successful aerial combat tactics of World War II. Dubbed the Fan, it broke up the usual group formation once the groups reached their designated area and allowed the P-47 Thunderbolts to spread out fan-wise in a 180-degree arc instead of remaining in formation. An extra section was maintained in the center of the Fan. Zemke reasoned that if his Group went out well in advance of the B-17 Fortress bombers it escorted, the unit stood a good chance of routing Luftwaffe aircraft assembled for a mass attack and would more easily be able to break them up. The tactic had gained official approval just the day before, on May 11, from Major General William Kepner's Eighth Air Force Fighter Command headquarters at Bushey Hall, north of London.

Taking off from Boxted that morning, Zemke's 56th flew in tight formation across the Channel towards Frankfurt, hoping to fool German radar into thinking the fighter group was a bomber strike.

"We needed to get there forty-five minutes before the B-17s arrived," said Rankin. "We knew the Germans would bring in fighters from several different airbases, that they'd form up into groups, climb, and head for the bomber trail. Except there would be no B-17 bombers. They'd find us instead, the fighters."

Side profile of a Bf 109E with its external fuel tank

The ruse was to work like a charm.

When Zemke's Wolf Pack set out that day each flight was given a heading for a fifteen-minute period.

"Then we were to turn and do a reciprocal and come back to the designated area," said Rankin. "When we got over Frankfurt, flying in from the north-west, our altitude was around 25,000 feet."

In the meantime, Rall and II./JG 11 were about to appear, flying in from the north-east, intent upon attack.

As the confrontation between the titans, the P-47s, the Fw 190s and the Bf 109s, drew near it was to become one of the most significant combat encounters of the air with both sides sustaining heavy losses.

More than eight hundred Allied bombers and twelve hundred escorting fighters, and two to three hundred German fighters would clash high above Nazi Germany. Over the course of the day dozens of dogfights took their toll on aircraft and men but for Günther Rall, his date with destiny had the name of one of Zemke's pilots written all over it. Wingman Captain Joseph Powers, killed later flying a P-51 in Korea, has been credited with downing Rall although in Powers' combat report it is difficult to verify. One young pilot, however, remembers many details of that day.

Cleon Thomton, barely twenty-five years old, had graduated and was commissioned at Marianna Army Air Field in Florida six months earlier. Assigned to what he called "the hottest fighter Group in the European Theater," May 12 was his first mission as a fighter pilot.

"I was flying wing to Lt. Rankin who was the flight leader of the team of four," wrote Thomton in his declassified Encounter Report. "We were designated for target support. That meant we would fly into the target area ahead of the bombers to intercept any upcoming enemy fighters. This is exactly what happened when four of us found about thirty Bf 109s assembling over a bunker station, a vertical radio beam that held German fighters in position above a cloud layer. Without hesitation Rankin busted into this group of German fighters and they scattered like a covey of quail."

Thomton's job was to protect his flight leader so he could shoot, enabling Rankin to down four enemy planes within minutes.

Rankin recalls that the Bf 109s still had their external fuel tanks attached at the beginning of the encounter.

"I decided I needed to get some of these guys," said Rankin. "I pressed the attack and they saw me coming. Then all of a sudden they dropped their tanks. I was kind of excited watching twenty or thirty tanks flopping down into space but I kept on and then they just split and the fighters took off in every direction."

Rankin latched onto two of the fighters, following them down at breakneck speed.

"I was indicating 575 [mph] and was bordering on compressibility because what happens is your controls get real tight and they can lock up on you. I noticed that the first Bf 109 I was on started to buffet. It was really severe. He was trying to pull out of it and he couldn't.

"I'd given him just a short burst, pulling the sight through him and in doing that, I'd blocked the plane so I couldn't see if I had any hits on him or not."

Following his quarry down, Rankin was able to observe the buffeting and knew the German plane was in trouble. Time to go.

"I put both hands on the stick and pulled with all my might. I was pretty strong in those days" remembers Rankin, "and we finally broke out barely brushing the treetops with the altimeter registering 1,500 feet. The Bf 109 crashed and exploded."

"Who Needs Two Thumbs?"

II./JG 11's twenty-five Bf 109s pressed towards the stream of Allied bombers that Zemke's P-47 Thunderbolts was escorting. "When I arrived at the rendezvous point with my escort fighter group," said Rall, "I radioed the Fw 190s that I was here above at my usual altitude. Then we all cruised south. I was flying at 35,000 feet and was soon able to pinpoint the bombers coming from England by their contrails. As we reached our position we went into battle formation and dropped our external tanks. The Fw 190s were at 26,000 feet. It was very unusual for Bf 109s to fly at such a high altitude because they could stall. We had no pressurization or heat, and it was darned cold."

The size of the Allied force took Rall's breath away. The eight hundred B-17 Flying Fortresses and B-24 Liberators, both long-range bombers, flew in a mainstream formation and twelve hundred fighters covered the airspace from the Hartz Mountains, the tallest in central Germany, all the way down to Stuttgart, a distance of approximately two hundred miles. The Allied aircraft seemed to form an endless canopy, as if to blot out the sun.

"I'm sure the earth below must have been trembling because the thunder from those thousands of engines was tremendous." Rall was also impressed with Allied logistics. "How did they manage to coordinate so many squadrons stationed at dozens of different bases and have them meet at the same time in the air, in the early morning darkness?" When Rall saw them coming he instructed his pilots to spread out in battle formation, keeping a good distance from each other.

Almost immediately he received a call over his earphones to take over the whole formation because the leader below had radio failure. Annoyed, Günther now to had to descend from 35,000 feet to 26,000 feet as fast as he could to take command. He immediately rescinded his order to spread out.

"Damn. OK, close in." The Bf 109s ran straight into a P-47 fighter formation. "As I dived down, I went on the attack against the first three, closing into the leading element. In a left turn I shot up the wingman. There were horrendous flames because these long-range fighters had large fuel tanks. Then I turned to jump on the other one. I aimed and fired but he went into a split-S and I lost sight of him. I learned much later it was Hub Zemke, leader of the group." Rall's wingman suffered engine failure and bailed out but the battle was far from over. "I jumped on the nearest P-47, came really close and hit him, and he went down in flames."

Now, faced with a sky filled with the enemy, Rall quickly took advantage, diving down and hitting a target, pulling up, diving again and hitting another. But when his wingman bailed out with engine problems and Rall whirled his Bf 109 in a tight split-S, he found himself face to face with four P-47s sitting abreast of his windshield. Rall was well aware that a P-47 was much faster in a dive and had much higher structural strength than a Bf 109 but he realized he had no other choice than to descend.

"If I turned left or right or pulled up I would face American guns. Then one of their wingman hit me in the engine and chased me down from 26,000 feet to treetop level. He hit my engine, hit my coolers, and then I got one more tremendous hit."

The final burst of fire from the enemy cut through the left side of the cockpit. Günther felt a sharp pain in his hand as it controlled the throttle. A bullet had sliced through his thick leather glove and severed the thumb.

With the hand useless, he thrust the stick between his knees because he needed his other hand to wipe the ice off the windshield. The ice began

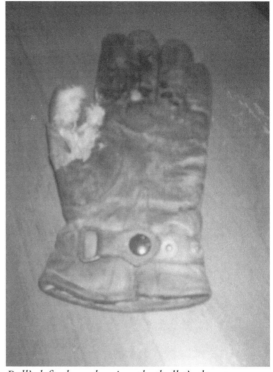

Rall's left glove showing the bullet's damage

to melt when he dived steeply down from the high cold air mass to the warmer lower one and he couldn't see through it to judge his altitude. Clearing a small patch in the windshield, all he could see was clouds.

"I saw the left wing then the right wing starting to come apart. I pulled on the stick harder and allowed the plane to stall out."

Still the P-47 followed. Later Rall was to wonder testily why the darned pilot didn't go home to England. "He knew I was finished. I was right on the edge of the 109's structural limits because when I pulled up my wings were wrinkling and the color was blistering off the fabric. I knew I had to bail out so I put the aircraft to the stalling point." The plane rolled over backwards and Rall found himself hanging upside down. He quickly jettisoned the canopy and began to bail out.

"At least the American couldn't follow me, his P-47 was no longer maneuverable at this low altitude. He could see I was half out of the cockpit trying to bail out. Finally I was able to free myself but as I jumped I got hit in the neck by the cable of my microphone. I could see the tail of my plane as I was hanging out and it reminded me of Marseille who had died by hitting the tail of his plane. Then I was tumbling in free-fall but I couldn't reach the release handle to open the parachute. I felt as if I was in a washing machine. I couldn't even figure out which way was up. But as my arms and legs swung around and around they had a stabilizing effect and I was able to pull the ring, opening the parachute at just 325 feet."

Günther's first thought as the chute billowed above was: Ah, I have cheated death once again so I can return to Hertha, as I promised her I would. His next thought was of his orthopedist in Vienna, who had told him, if you have to bail out look for a tree with plenty of branches. Luckily, Günther did just that. He landed several feet up a tree, cushioned by branches. But when he released the straps to free himself from the chute he rolled down a steep slope into a trench.

"My thumb had finally stopped bleeding but it hurt like hell. Even so, I was very, very happy!" Tucking his hand tightly under his right arm Rall followed a narrow path through the trees into an open meadow. By now his focus was off survival and on to the throbbing injury. In an instant, however, the pain was forgotten as Günther faced another threat. Before him stood a very apprehensive, very angry farmer, pitchfork at the ready. Rall, who was wearing an American-style air force jacket, greeted him and the other farmhands who came running.

"I tried to identify myself because he saw my jacket and

thought I was the enemy. I told him I was a German but he continued to glare at me, waving the pitchfork threateningly."

"Who are you?" the farmer demanded.

"Major Günther Rall, Luftwaffe."

Amazement and a broad, delighted smile instantly told Günther that his name was recognized. He mentally blessed those state radio broadcasts of his victories for saving his life. After surviving so many crash landings and injuries, how ignominious to die impaled on a pitchfork. But Rall's unbelievable luck, like a cat with nine lives, still held.

"The farmer and his helpers knew me right away. I was still in agony but very happy. They took me to the farmhouse and gave me some juice because I was dehydrated from the loss of blood, and offered me a couple of their hand-rolled cigarettes."

Günther's thumb, severed at its base, was still inside his glove. Surprisingly, he could see the thumbnail unscathed and free of blood, shining white beneath a gash in the glove where the bullet had torn through the leather. He also had a piece of shrapnel from either an enemy bullet or a piece of his own plane lodged in his elbow, where it remains to this day.

Wrapping his hand in a cloth as best they could as the Allied bombers continued to stream overhead, the farmer and his farmhands led Rall to their farmhouse where they passed the time entertaining him with stories of their service in World War I. When the raid was over the farmer called for an ambulance and Rall was taken to a hospital in nearby Nassau in the Lahn Valley.

"I told the doctor there, who needs two thumbs? It's a surplus."

Two days later an anxious Hertha arrived from Vienna. She'd been told by Günther's NCO that her husband had been shot down but was alive. She had no idea of the extent of his injuries.

With no airport close to the hospital in the Lahn Valley, she traveled by train, nervous she'd miss her stop in unfamiliar territory. She constantly asked her fellow passengers if the station she needed was coming up next. Finally, one of the passengers asked why she was so anxious.

"My husband was shot down and I'm going to the hospital to see him," she said.

"What's his name?"

"Günther Rall."

"Oh, the ace! We heard it on the radio. He's fine but he lost his thumb!"

The incident was news all over Germany. Reports of the activities of heroes such as Günther and their exploits were used as propaganda morale-boosters by Hitler's government-controlled media and broadcast daily over the radio.

A week after their reconciliation, the Ralls, accompanied by a military aide, departed for their home in Vienna, Günther's injured hand in a cast.

Unfortunately, he had left his doctor's care too soon. The wound refused to heal. It was apparent that bone fragments were still embedded inside the flesh. He needed another operation to remove the splinters. This time he went to the air force hospital in Vienna, where Hertha was able to assist in the surgery.

"Three days after I got back home after the second surgery, an ambulance arrived to return me once more to the hospital. I asked, 'What's going on?' They replied that I had contracted diphtheria. The wound had become infected and I must return for treatment and be quarantined. Our apartment had to be fumigated."

Once more in a hospital bed, Rall asked how the infection had occurred. He was told that an American pilot from a downed

Rall's thumb injury, with his mother, Minna

B-17 had broken his leg. The injury had not been attended to quickly enough and infection had set in. With no antibiotics available, the pilot's leg had to be amputated. As in all wartime hospitals, the injured came in fast and furious. Often hygiene was forsaken in favor of saving lives. Thus diphtheria, a highly-infectious disease, was passed along to Günther as he lay on the same operating table the unfortunate Allied pilot had just left.

Rall's lengthy recuperation took him through the middle of the summer, when he learned of the July 20 assassination attempt on the life of Adolf Hitler. Günther's initial reaction was indignation at those who, in difficult times, turned on their leader, weak-

Rall reading a newspaper after his thumb injury.

ening morale and thus the defense of Germany. However, when he learned after the war of the motivations of the several conspirators – to rid Germany of Hitler and negotiate an immediate surrender to the Allies – and heard their familiar names as members of Hitler's High Command he began to reconsider his opinion.

The eight schemers included Lt. Colonel Count Claus Schlenk von Stauffenburg who placed the bomb at the Wolf's Lair, General Friedrich Olbricht, and long-time Hitler-opponent General Ludwig Beck, among others. Members of the resistance who knew in advance of the plot included Field Marshal Erwin Rommel who was only marginally involved, Admiral

Wilhelm Canaris, and Field Marshall Erwin von Witzleben.

"Rommel's name, in particular, gave me pause. He was a hero. He'd fought long and hard for the Third Reich. He was a patriot of the first order, a man of great integrity. If he was involved in this plot, he must have had an urgent reason for it."

Rommel, suffering serious injuries after his car had been hit by Allied aircraft, was reported as believing it was his duty to rescue Germany from a mad Hitler but he did not agree with an assassination. Instead, he proposed arresting Hitler and bringing him to trial. Like the conspirators, he wanted his country delivered of the stubborn, irrational Führer. Troops were forced into retreat all along the Eastern Front, the situation on the Western Front was at a critical stage and it was only a matter of time before the Third Reich would topple.

Rall read of the traitors' trials, of those who weren't shot on the spot, from his hospital bed.

"The spectacle frightened me," said Rall. "Every relative of Stauffenberg was arrested, even elderly grandparents. Eight conspirators were hung on meat hooks and strangled with piano wire. It was brutal, horrible." In fact, thousands were arrested and hundreds executed. Another set of trials sure to bring the death penalty for others party to the plot was scheduled for the following January when, ironically the judge, Heisler, was himself killed in a bombing raid over Berlin.

Rall was finally judged fit to return to duty. One week after he left the hospital it was bombed, killing sixty nuns and some of the patients. The loss of Rall's thumb was to have far-reaching consequences, assuredly prolonging his life into a ripe old age because he would become commander of a fighter leader school and would no longer engage in aerial combat.

Years later the events of May 12, 1944 would be discussed many times. Rall and Colonel Francis "Gabby" Gabreski, one of Zemke's Wolf Pack who was in the same air battle that day in May, compared notes during a symposium in Montgomery, Alabama in 1977 where Rall first learned that Zemke's unit was responsible for his lost thumb. A television station had asked Rall and Gabreski to share an hour of wartime reminiscences. An interpreter was provided who, to Rall's astonishment when he recognized him, had been a general on Rall's staff at NATO. Gabby, Günther and the general spent a lively hour, answering questions back and forth. Then Rall was asked how he lost his thumb. As he described the incident Gabby said, "Hey, wait a minute! I was in that battle on May 12, 1944. There were only two P-47 units there that day, Zemke's and mine. Hub was the top cover."

"Gabreski told me he was in that dogfight," said Rall, "but he could not identify who was where. He said there were only two P-47 groups engaged in the battle that day and he headed up one and Zemke the other, so it must have been one of Zemke's pilots that shot off my thumb and I believe that person was Joe Powers."

When Rall emerged from the TV station, an American general was waiting outside for him. He told Günther he was an Air Force historian and that the archives confirmed the May 12 facts.

"We certainly made history," Zemke was to write later in his 1988 autobiography, *Zemke's Wolf Pack*. Also making history was Robert "Shorty" Rankin who modestly related that he'd "had a good day." In fact, Shorty shot down a record five enemy aircraft, ensuring his spot in aviation history.

"Hub was a marvelous man," said Rall. "I have deep feelings and unlimited respect for him. This was the thing about fighter pilots. We were all the same under the skin. We had the same mentality, the same qualities but served on opposite sides. We fought fair. It was a code of honor that isn't understood today. It's safe to say we had affection for each other even as we attacked."

Indeed, the majority of Luftwaffe pilots in World War II adhered to the principle established by Captain Manfred Baron von Richthofen, who declared, "The duty of the fighter pilot is... to shoot down any enemy fighters. Anything else is rubbish," but would not permit his pilots to strafe enemy troops in the trenches.

"Each side targeted the plane, not the pilot," said Rall. "If you saw the poor bastard bail out, you were glad. During all those dogfights there was never hate. Hub Zemke was successful for the USAF and I was successful for the Luftwaffe. We had the same orders, the same ideals, the same ideas: shoot down enemy planes. It's the same attitude you find with submariners. I don't believe that future wars will have those same conditions. But lots of World War II fighter pilots made it into middle age. Most bomber pilots did not. Those pilots took the bigger risk of putting their lives on the line and were terribly vulnerable."

Rall finally met Hub Zemke face to face in 1986 at a "Gathering of Eagles" symposium produced by Virginia Bader in Las Vegas. "It was fantastic! We spent hours, days, going over aerial battles, tactics, and logistics. Hub's a great guy."

The two became such firm friends that a few years later Hub's son, Hub Zemke Jr., who was an associate of an Austrian ski manufacturing company, called Rall when he was in Bavaria. Rall invited him to visit his home in the foothills of the Bavarian

Alps. At one point as they shared a drink, Rall stared at Hub's son for several long minutes, then couldn't resist saying, very quietly, and with a catch in his throat: "Young man, do you realize that on May 12 1944 I was one of those who tried to shoot down your father?"

Later that spring Günther received a phone call from a customs official at Munich airport.

"We have some skis here for you from Zemke." Rall drove the two-hour trip to the airport to retrieve the skis. They had been sent by Hub Jr. as a gift. "They were the best skis money could buy, top-notch quality" said Rall, who still uses them.

Fighter Leader School, Königsberg, Germany 1944

21
ein und zwanzig

As Rall recuperated from his severed thumb, a process that was to take months in the absence of penicillin, the Allies continued their advance. On June 6, 1944 the Normandy landings signaled D-Day, the invasion of France. In Rall's former stomping ground where he had racked up so many Eastern Front victories many of the Luftwaffe's units were being called back to Germany for the defense of the homeland, leaving the Soviet skies to the VVS.

In August, the German Army evacuated from another of Rall's former targets, the port city of Constanta, and scuttled their ships, and in September the Wehrmacht was sent packing from Belgium, while the Allies had reached Germany. September was also the month that the synthetic fuel that filled the Luftwaffe's tanks was in such short supply it was reported that all aircraft that came back from missions were to be towed to their hangars by horses and oxen rather than waste a single precious drop by taxiing.

Günther was finally released from the hospital. Although his thumb wound had still not healed completely, he no longer had an infection. He headed straight for Berlin to request that Colonel Hannes Trautloft send him back to command II./JG 11. He was anxious to re-enter the fray. The request was emphatically denied.

"You cannot go into battle again with that open wound. The

bone is still visible. It would be madness!" said Trautloft who was now responsible for the Luftwaffe's day fighters. In charge of a fighter leader training school at Königsberg-Neumark, northeast of Berlin, Trautloft was under constant pressure from Göring to qualify more pilots to send into battle against the Allies on both fronts.

"We need you here," Trautloft told Rall. "Do you know how many fighter pilots the Luftwaffe has left as of today? Exactly six hundred and eighty. It is critical to train more pilots to cover the North Cape of Scandinavia and Western Europe and across to the Eastern Front. We urgently need you to work with fighter pilots to become squadron commanders, to teach them how to lead their units in aerial combat," he told Rall. "We also need you to turn bomber pilots into fighter pilots. They are not used to making tight turns with high Gs. They get disoriented. They are currently trained for close formation tactics against the bomber stream but not as interceptor fighter-against-fighter pilots. The Americans have long-range fighters now and they're coming fast and furious. Our young, inexperienced pilots need to be trained for high-altitude squadrons to protect our Focke-Wolf 190s."

The directive was a blow to an ace of Rall's aggressive, quick, competitive nature that demanded several doses of daily danger. Although the order to switch from active combat to training pilots was not entirely welcome, with the new posting he'd enter a life of comparative comfort and safety. Teaching pilots to become leaders of fighter squadrons presented Rall with provocative, stimulating challenges, and, of course, the Luftwaffe had no time to lose. In fact, time was rapidly running out.

The Luftwaffe had reduced the bomber fleet to modify it to fighter force, so he found himself teaching some of Germany's most highly-decorated bomber pilots to become fighter pilots. "Some had a difficult time learning how to turn the Bf 109 because the men weren't used to the light aircraft's maneuverability. They couldn't follow."

Pilots were also training in the Luftwaffe's new jet, the Me 262, which was finally rolling off the assembly lines during the closing months of 1944. However, it was to come late to the war due to delays caused by problems with its engines and Hitler's insistence on it being modified as a bomber as well as a fighter plane. Rall's opinion at the time of the Führer's attitude towards the Me 262 was immediate and scathing.

"We were forbidden by penalty of death to discuss the stupidity of this plan, which was supposed to give us the classic defense airplane. In fact, the first 262s were given to the Luftwaffe's bomber units without even adequate equipment to carry bombs!"

Nevertheless, he regarded the world's first operational jet fighter as an excellent machine, able to carry two dozen rockets beneath its wings. Rall believes that had the Luftwaffe been supplied with masses of 262s a year or two earlier it would have relieved their immediate situation and saved a few cities although not enough to change the outcome of the war.

"At that stage we knew we were inferior in spite of the new jets because we were outnumbered by the sheer mass of enemy aircraft. There was nothing that could save us." In spite of training enough pilots in 1944 and producing the greatest number ever of new Bf 109s while Allied bombs rained down on Germany's aircraft factories, the writing was on the wall. The sheer weight of Germany's opponents would destroy her.

The directive to train veteran pilots presented Rall with a demanding goal because he was working with experienced airmen, and he liked nothing more than a challenge. He approached the program with gusto, pleased to be able to share his expertise learned during his own years of leadership on the front.

"We were forced to send newly-trained commanders out barely ready because we were on the defensive now. The Allies were at our gates and Germany was getting clobbered."

Günther continued to train pilots but as the Russians advanced the Luftwaffe was forced to relocate the school to Bad Wörishofen, southern Bavaria. Here, in addition to enjoying teaching new pilots, Günther had the most fun from the job when he flew captured enemy planes – Spitfires, P-51 Mustangs, P-38 Lightnings and P-47 Thunderbolts – as mock targets for his students.

"We repaired these aircraft and used them as trainers. I was eager to fly them against my own aircraft so I could compare them. How different these American planes were to our 109s! They could fly seven hours; the Bf 109 just one hour and twenty minutes. But what really broke us during the war were the American long-range fighter escorts, P-51 Mustangs, P-47 Thunderbolts and P-38 Lightnings. Once they were fitted with auxiliary fuel tanks they could fly for about eight hours. I could really detect the tactical differences between the German, British and American planes. This gave me the greatest respect for the P-51 Mustang and its extremely comfortable cockpit, good rear visibility, long-range, maneuverability, and an electrical starting system.

"The P-38 was a little strange because the control column was yoke-shaped instead of a stick. One very fascinating characteristic was the power ailerons that controlled the rolling movements of the aircraft. If you flicked a switch you could bank the plane with just one finger. The Spitfire, too, was a very maneuverable aircraft, very good in the cockpit. All these aircraft had a stable undercarriage. The Bf 109 did not. For young pilots, sometimes, the undercarriage of the 109 gave them problems because it was very narrow and relatively high."

Rall's students would chase him through the skies looking for vulnerabilities he'd told them to pinpoint. With his vast experience in combat tactics, dogfights, deflection shooting, belly landings, and bail-outs he quickly became a favorite of the airmen who were being trained at a frantic pace to bolster the Luftwaffe's losses. Dozens of Germany's finest pilots were being killed day after day as the Eighth Air Force became more and more proficient and deadly.

Rall continued to fly captured aircraft but also took the opportunity to check out the Me 262. His friend and fellow ace, Lt. Colonel Heinz Baer, was now commander of the Me 262 outfit located at Lechfeld, south of Augsberg, where, along with factories at Regensberg, hundreds of the aircraft were being hammered out as fast as the workers could complete them. Rall had a high opinion of Baer, whom he considered a very fine, straight-forward man who was among the most trustworthy Rall had ever encountered.

"He was honest through and through. Whatever he told you was the truth. He never tried to cover things up as some pilots did."

Rall made several visits to see his friend. Baer, who was to die in 1957 in an air show crash after surviving sixteen bail-outs during World War II, was elated that Rall was in the area, at Bad Wörishofen, and was eager to test Germany's much-heralded turbojet. Astonished by this new dimension in aviation, Rall readily jumped into the cockpit.

"The first thing I became aware of was how comfortable the cockpit was. It felt like sitting in a roomy taxicab," said Rall. "Secondly, I noticed that the radio transmission was as clear as a bell, without any interference. Then, I saw that one of the greatest advantages of the Me 262 over the Bf 109 was its visibility. You could see straight down the line, direct sight. It was also quiet, very quiet. There was no interruption or loud piston engine noise because of its turbo jet engine."

In spite of all its early shortcomings, Rall was fascinated with the new plane but expressed a personal criticism. "Due to the revolutionary new jet engine during the take-off you had to advance the throttle very, very slowly otherwise at 8,000 rpm the exhaust could catch fire." Initially this careful monitoring of engine temperatures presented a significant problem for the impatient Günther who was accustomed to firing up, thrusting the throttle forward in one quick movement, and zooming off. He found the Me 262 was sluggish during take-off because the throttles had to be advanced slowly. Rall quickly realized that tactics had to change.

"You no longer turned in while in a dogfight, instead you had to come in and out, and the enemy was the one who couldn't follow. Sometimes the 262 was too fast. Since the plane was so heavy it took time to get up to speed. Therefore, the 262 squadrons always used the protection of Focke-Wulf 190 D-9 fighters when they took off from the airfield to provide top cover, and again when they landed, because the Americans had discovered these were the only times they could destroy them. But once you were up to speed, you were superior to everything in the sky. The 262 wasn't invincible, of course, but it was the first jet and the Americans had tremendous respect for it."

Rall also took a turn in an Fw-190 D-9. Unlike earlier versions of the Fw 190, which were powered by BMW air-cooled radial engines, the D-9 version was equipped with a Junkers Jumo 213 liquid-cooled inline engine. It was regarded as among the finest German fighter planes in service at the time. Developed just six months earlier it was used to cover the Me 262 air bases.

Final Wartime Command.
Wing Commander of JG 300

In February, 1945, Günther was named wing commander of JG 300 based in Plattling, northeast of Munich. Warfare raged all around the area. Although he wasn't to know it at the time Rall's promotion would have validity for just three months.

Upon arrival at the airfield in Plattling he was witness to a low-level enemy attack on sixteen German planes. "It was chaos. As we approached the base in a military vehicle my driver told me to get out and take cover in the ditch. Flames were everywhere. I knew then and there that Germany was without hope."

The next day JG 300 abandoned the bombed airfield and retreated farther south. However, Rall was glad to be back in the thick of things once more and flying missions. But times had changed. The Luftwaffe no longer received priority for fuel supplies or other equipment.

"Our sorties were severely curtailed and communications and information about the daily status of the war were just about non-existent. We received no orders. I couldn't find out where our division, the Seventh, had gone and finally found out it was sent elsewhere. I never knew where." Indeed, the general staff leadership had already broken down. Now it was a matter of survival not in the air but on the ground.

"We did hear rumors, and we all knew them to be true, that

the Allied ground troops were steadily advancing from the West, were close by, and had joined up with the advancing Soviet armies." In fact, the Western Allies had reached the Elbe River and were now with the Russians.

Forced to relocate JG 300 after yet more shelling, Rall transferred the unit to a small foothill area in Ainring, near Salzburg, Austria, ironically not far from the town where he would eventually make his home decades later. But JG 300's move to its final base brought little relief.

"We landed on rough terrain and damaged a couple of our planes. Our main problem was how to get fuel supplies and food. There was no organization any more, we had no communication with our units, no information at all. We weren't even sure where the enemy was." He had one final contact with his group commander, who instructed him to "fold up his wings" when the crunch came. At one point Rall heard that a nearby Luftwaffe unit had disbanded.

"By April it appeared that our entire division staff had deserted us. So I and my adjutant took a jeep to try to find them. As we drove through a mountain pass there was snow on the ground still, and abandoned German anti-aircraft cannons scattered all over the place. I'd heard that there was a telecommunications unit in the vicinity but we couldn't find it, or any sign of our division headquarters or its commander."

In a stroke of fate that would have been humorous were it not during such tragic circumstances, Rall encountered a major of the Luftwaffe's general staff who was also driving around trying to find JG 300 to deliver an order to transfer to Prague. Transfer to Prague when this major didn't even know where the squadrons were located? Rall felt the directive was ludicrous and refused to obey it. He knew World War II in Europe was over for JG 300. During the last week of April the RAF Bomber Command flew its final raid of note over Germany, targeting Hitler's mountain refuge at Obersalzburg. Berlin was encircled by ground troops, Mussolini was hanged in Italy, and Germany's unconditional surrender was just days away.

On May 1 Rall tuned in his radio for early morning news and heard a report by the German High Command that Hitler had been killed during the final hours of the battle for Berlin, defending the city. Hours earlier the Russians had smashed their way in to Germany's proud parliament headquarters, the Reichstag, which was located half a mile from Hitler's underground bunker.

"Hitler's death was not altogether a shock to us," said Rall. "We accepted it. The interesting part is that there was no collapse of the nation. We were in dire straits because we had lost the war but the death of Hitler made no difference to us at that point," said Rall.

He and his adjutant made one final reconnaissance, again by ground transport. They headed for the Bavarian Alps to gain a high vantage point.

"We observed long lines of cars streaming over the Stein Pass." The mile-long caravan originated in Italy and headed west, followed by hundreds of Italian and German troops in retreat from Tyrol. The southern front in Italy had capitulated to the Allies long before and they thus had secured an armistice but the northern regions had not, and continued to fight.

"What's going on, do you think?" Rall asked the adjutant.

"Retreat. I heard that the Brenner Pass is jammed, too, and that the Americans are right in front us." Depressed, the pilots returned to base.

In a curious way Rall was relieved that the fighting was finished and that the next stage would begin, whatever it was. A pragmatist, Rall realized that his most pressing problem would be how to help his men keep body and soul together. He knew that the British and the Americans treated prisoners of war with more concern than did the Russians, who were notorious for brutality and revengeful massacres, ignoring accepted codes of conduct. Rall also needed to keep his pilots safe from the Third Reich's SS who were searching the countryside for those intending to surrender, and executing them.

In his biography the Luftwaffe's most famous ace, Adolf Galland, reported that the SS would hang from a tree everyone they found planning to become a "deserter." Galland would be in imminent danger of such an outcome himself when he offered to deliver JV 44, the so-called Squadron of Experts, intact to the Allies, in the hope they would prevent the Soviets from occupying Germany. The offer was declined because the Allies did not plan to take on the Russians. Among the aces assigned to JV 44 were Steinhoff, Lützow, Barkhorn, Baer, Rudorffer, Krupinski and Schnell. Galland immediately issued orders for the 262s to be destroyed.

Returning from a final reconnaissance mission, Rall landed and gathered his JG 300 family around him.

"Gentlemen, that's it," the 27-year old Rall told his pilots and ground personnel. "We cannot be taken by the Russians. It is better to surrender to the Americans, if we must. You will be remembered by your country for a hundred years. You have given everything you possibly could, and it's time to go home."

At that moment a German captain from an army reconnaissance unit drove up to the air base and warned Rall he'd seen a line of fifteen American tanks and infantry coming down the autobahn. Near the Stein Pass, west of Berchtesgaden, Rall came to a bridge that was the only means of crossing the river. German soldiers were guarding the bridge and planned to blow it up.

"Excuse me," Rall protested to the soldiers, "but we need to cross it first."

After Rall and his men reached the other side explosives ripped through the bridge.

"It was a stupid, senseless thing to do. The Allies were two or three miles away. What was the good of taking away the local farmers' only means of getting from one side of the river to the other?"

That evening the crew of JG 300 came across an abandoned restaurant on the side of a hill. The captain of an army group told Rall he would post a sentry while the pilots slept inside but when the pilots awoke the next morning the place was deserted.

"The Americans were all over the highways. I saw a jeep coming up the hill and I told my officers, 'Gentlemen, we must disappear.' We ran into the woods. We watched the Americans enter the empty restaurant. After half an hour the jeep turned around and went back down the hill. At the side of a road we saw a group of German soldiers discussing the rumor they'd heard over their short-wave radio that Hitler had committed suicide."

In the evening the news of the Führer's demise was confirmed. "The announcer said, 'The Grand Leader has committed suicide.' That was a surprise. We didn't expect anything like that. We were split between our orders and what our brains told us to do. For the first time in my life I wondered which path to follow, my duty or my common sense."

Günther divided up the base's money and food between each man and told the mechanics and NCOs to help themselves to the tools and special equipment that were used to repair the planes. Perhaps in civilian life the tools would prove useful in finding work. He advised everyone to remove all military insignia.

"This wasn't hard because we'd been wearing anything we could lay our hands on for the past few months. We were almost in tatters under our greatcoats."

Rall separated the airmen into two groups. He suggested one should start walking north and the other group, with himself, west, headed for their respective cities, not knowing what they would find. Those of the unit's injured who were unable to walk sought sanctuary with any nearby farmers who would take them in.

The farewells were poignant. Stoic to the end, the men of JG 300 held back their tears not only because of the turn of events and their imminent surrender but because of the apparent breaking of the bond that had held them together throughout the horrors of war, that spiritual tie with those who have shared the same unspeakable experiences and which is never truly severed.

The men shook hands and saluted their commander for the last time. It was a wretched parting that was repeated all over the Eastern and Western Front as the Third Reich's defeat was fully realized. Each man knew he would probably never meet his comrades again. Many would die. And some would spend years in Russian prison camps.

Günther and his small group set their sights on Lake Chiemsee. From there Rall planned to head for Bad Wörishofen, Germany, where Hertha had fled from Vienna shortly before the arrival of the Russians. She was several months pregnant and this knowledge gave Günther extra impetus to find her.

"It gave me peace and strength and was now the most important goal of my life, to be reunited with my wife."

As they traveled by night, hiding by day in barns and concealing themselves under bales of hay, they usually discovered that American soldiers were staying at the main farmhouse. Other times, it was obvious that the US soldiers knew the Germans were there, but left them alone.

"There were so many of us, moving west, trying to get home."

As Rall and his pilots passed through a small river town they watched German civilians entering abandoned stores and homes and making off with as many goods as they could carry.

"I didn't blame them, poor devils. There was little left to take. We all needed food and blankets."

After another night in the forest Rall and the remnants of his staff straggled west along the road towards Lake Chiemsee. Here they ran into an American blockade.

"The Americans told us that in order to proceed we needed a stamped pass before we could go through. We waited, and a truck came. But instead of a pass we were informed that we were prisoners of war."

Prisoner of War

23
drei und zwanzig

D uring his first days as a POW in May, 1945 Rall was moved from place to place until finally Rall and his companions arrived at a camp in Heilbronn. They were among thousands of prisoners. Conditions were terrible and every day, said Rall, at least twelve died.

"We were bunched together in the middle of a huge field with a barbed wire fence around us. Food was at a minimum and many of the older prisoners starved to death. We had to clear places on the ground so we could sleep. The camp was terrible, primitive," said Rall, shuddering, "a seething mass of humanity, all of us in rags, our morale totally destroyed." The hot summer sun had baked the soil solid and was trodden as hard as concrete by the prisoners crowded within its barbed-wire fences.

"We had no food and little water. We slept in the open on the bare ground like sardines in a tin." Those prisoners able-bodied enough to dig had bloodied fingers and ripped nails by the time they had scooped out a depression in which to rest and find some private space from the hordes of humanity. "If you had a shallow trench, that space was considered inviolate. I had no argument with our political situation," reflected Rall. "It was to be expected. Germany was once again a conquered nation, brought to her knees a second time, and we had to make the best we could of it. But we were thankful we weren't in the hands of the Red Army."

With no contact with the outside the prisoners had no idea of how their families and, indeed, the German nation, were faring. Militarily, Rall and his fellow prisoners knew how the Third Reich had ended its war and that Germany was forced into an unconditional surrender but news of civilian life was unavailable.

After a few days an American officer made an announcement.

"All Luftwaffe officers step forward! Line up here!" Hundreds obeyed the command. Then specific names were called out.

"Krupinski. Rall. Barkhorn..."

Rall instantly realized that the Americans were pinpointing pilots who had flown the Me 262, the most technically-developed fighter at that time. As the familiar names were reeled off and some of their owners failed to appear Günther wondered if they had been killed or, as he was to learn later, like Hartmann, were prisoners of the Russians. Many of those who stepped forward had sustained war wounds. Rall nursed the hand missing its thumb, throbbing in the cold morning air. The cream of the crop of the Luftwaffe's fighter aces, six or seven in all that answered the call that day, were unceremoniously packed into a jeep and driven under guard to a US Army campground in Wiesbaden where VIP prisoners were held.

"We were separated," said Rall, "and interrogated by a man who called himself Mr. Reid. This was a pseudonym because it was common knowledge he was in the secret service."

Mr. Reid made it clear to Rall that he was familiar with every aspect of Günther's military life, his Luftwaffe career, his victories, and the visits with Hitler at the Wolf's Lair.

"He knew every victory in my logbook, where I came from

and what I did. I think he knew more about me than I did myself. I was queried about the Me 262, my opinion as to its capabilities and its technology. They were as familiar with it as I was, since they had captured several downed aircraft I saw no reason to hold back any answers."

"Did you fly the Me 262?" Rall was asked.

"Yes."

"Would you be willing to help the Allies build up a jet air force?"

Günther didn't hesitate.

"Yes." He wanted to do all he could to prevent the Russians from controlling Germany and surmised that the Americans wanted to create a jet fighter fleet in Central Europe as a preventative.

"Where would you like to help us, in England or the United States?" asked Reid.

"The United States."

"One last question. Are you willing to join us in our war against the Japanese?"

"No, sir," responded Rall. "They have been our loyal allies and I could not, in good conscience, fight them." The interrogator didn't press him. Günther learned later that the interrogator was not authorized to raise the issue.

"As we left our comrades, who were waving goodbye to us through the camp fence, it was very sad." After driving two miles, the driver pulled over, got out, and uncovered a cache of food in the back. "He gave us bread, meat, tomato juice and other wonderful things."

Rall's interrogation sessions were just beginning. In late May he and a handful of pilots were flown to England in a C-47 Dakota transport plane, its windows blacked-out. Their destination was Camp 7, the Combined Services Detailed Interrogation Center on Lord Chesham's country estate in Latimer, north of London. The administrators were British but the interrogators American officers. They included members of the secret intelligence organization, the Office of Strategic Services, the OSS.

Adolf Galland and Field Marshal Erhard Milch, Göring's second in command and thus very nervous, were also at the same camp but in separate quarters. Galland, in the dusty, rumpled uniform of a major-general and toting his last box of cigars, had a cast covering his right knee due to an injury he'd sustained during his final mission in April when a P-47 had sent a hail of bullets through his cockpit. Krupinski and Baer had already been flown in.

Again, the Allies had culled the Luftwaffe's top fighter aces with experience in Me 262s. Unlike Galland who feared he might be indicted for war crimes and sent to the trials at Nuremburg, Günther had faith that he and his fellow pilots would be treated fairly.

On arrival the German pilots were told to remove their shirts and raise their arms high. Rall was puzzled. He learned that the Brits were looking for the tell-tale tattoo that members of the Schutzstaffel, the dreaded SS, had engraved in their skin to record their blood type. "I knew nothing of these marks but I complied." The airmen passed muster.

"It was a pretty nice set-up. I shared a room with two other prisoners and our treatment was friendly and respectful."

The next day the questioning began.

"At first, the interrogators tried to set us one against the other, saying things to provoke us, as if it were a personal vendetta," said Günther. "I didn't mind talking about the characteristics and technology of the Me 262, and how we fought the war in the

East, tactics, arms systems and such but not personal politics."

Most of the sessions were conducted separately, one on one, during walks through the estate's extensive grounds. The German aces were permitted to meet only once during this period, when one of the Allied officers had a birthday party. Günther believes that the reason behind the group gathering was the Americans wanting to observe the Luftwaffe airmen's reactions to each other and their generals.

The small group was next sent to another POW camp, Morton, for two days, and from there by train to Portsmouth, England's premier Naval port and submarine base, for the return trip to a French POW camp. The pilots boarded a Liberty ship already packed to the gunnels with Italians, Hungarians and other prisoners. Many were on stretchers. Designed to carry freight and troops, or modified as floating hospitals, Liberty transport vessels were built in the United States and supplied to Britain under the Lend-Lease program.

"We weren't quite sure whether to be pleased or not that we were on our way back to France," said Rall.

Notorious for its perennially choppy waters the English Channel took its toll on most of the passengers jammed together in the crowded hold as the ship crossed to Cherbourg on the French coast. When it docked the prisoners were faced with a mob of trigger-happy young French soldiers patrolling the port.

"We were worried they'd shoot us all and be heroes and I knew it was going to be tricky just walking past them. The scene was riotous, with thousands of people milling about all over the place, prisoners, guards, soldiers, civilians. All mixed together, families looking for relatives, and the French armed to the teeth."

As it turned out, Günther was ordered to bring ashore a large box of medical reports and thus, as part of a group of hospital orderlies, escaped challenge by the French. Krupinski wasn't as lucky.

"I loaded the box into the back of a jeep," said Rall, "and we drove off to the POW camp about five miles away. I was fortunate because the medical reports were needed quickly so I rode but the other prisoners had to march on foot. As we entered the camp another jeep came driving by us and the driver threw out a bloodied flight jacket with the insignia of a German captain's rank. We were all lieutenants, majors and lieutenant colonels. There was only one captain. I knew it was Krupinski."

Rall wondered if the famous ace was dead.

"Then Heinz Brücker joined us at the hospital. He was weeping. It seemed that Krupinski was wearing his Knight's Cross at his throat which provoked a French guard wielding a rifle to knock him down as the prisoners were being marched to the camp. Krupinski suffered a severe head injury. It was nine months before he recovered."

By July, 1945 Rall was being held by the US Army at Foncanville on the coast of northern France, along with a hundred and fifty thousand other prisoners of war. The crowded camp, spread haphazardly over a portion of the Cherbourg peninsula that jutted past the Channel Islands of Jersey and Guernsey, was filled with a motley crowd from all three services of the various nations who had fought for the Third Reich, including Hungarians and Austrians. Hundreds wore filthy bandages wrapped around their wounds; dozens had lost a foot, an arm, a leg, and several were sightless.

From the eastern side of the camp the POWs could gaze across to Omaha Beach, still littered with the First US Infantry Division's military equipment, landing craft and supplies left over from Operation Overlord, the Normandy invasion the Allies launched successfully a year previously.

Günther's deepest, most anguished feelings were for his wife. Was Hertha still alive? Would he ever find her again? It took immense effort for Rall not to dwell too long on those questions.

"We were all going crazy with nothing to do all day. Some prisoners walked the perimeter of the fence to where a few trees overhung their branches. They made cigarettes out of the spring blossoms and soon stripped the trees of their leaves as well as their flowers."

One mid-morning, on the fourth day of Rall's incarceration, an eerie silence came over the camp. Dozens of copies of the US military newspaper, the *Stars and Stripes*, had been flung over the fence for the prisoners to read.

What brought on this magnanimous gesture?

Splashed over the front page were the first photographs of Hitler's death camps and their pitiful piles of human bones, walking skeletons, and mountains of gold teeth, spectacles, and other items seized from the Jews.

"I grabbed one of the newspapers and couldn't believe it. I knew of the persecution of the Jews but I thought anything else was merely propaganda. Of course," he added, "it is easy to plead ignorance now, and I must live with that."

As he continued to read the newspaper, Rall sank to his knees.

"To see those horrifying pictures brought home to me how utterly and unbelievably cruel and inhuman some of my compatriots had become in our nationalistic fervor to support Hitler's goals."

The atrocities were beyond his comprehension.

"Fighting for four years against Russia on the Eastern Front was brutal and sometimes involved massacres, but nothing on this scale. It's easy to understand why the rest of the world feels as it does about us. After my service in France, Romania, Greece, Crete Island and Russia, where we heard nothing of death camps, then to come home to your beloved country and find out some of your own people did this, well, it was beyond words."

Although propaganda and hours of Hitler ranting against the Jews were broadcast over the airwaves in Germany during World War II, Rall said that it didn't reach those engaged on the Eastern Front, cut off from civilization thousands of miles away, and there was no mention of the creation of death camps.

"We knew that political prisoners had been detained at Dachau, north of Munich, since its establishment in 1935, but we didn't know about camps outside Germany. I heard that those at Dachau were held for a couple of weeks, then released. But as far as systematic death camps were concerned, I learned of those in the *Stars and Stripes* newspaper. During the war it was all we could do to survive under Soviet blizzard conditions and the massive Russian assaults as we were driven back. We were in full retreat. There was little talked about between ourselves and our regional headquarters aside from strategic and tactical discussions and our next orders," said Rall.

Interrogations in England

G ünther's imprisonment at Foncanville lasted only three weeks.

"Rall? Step forward!" shouted a US Army lieutenant.

The fighter ace did as instructed. Then he was ordered to pack his belongings and be at the main gate in five minutes.

"That amused me. What belongings? I was destitute. I had nothing. As for the guards giving me five minutes to get to the main gate, I made it in five seconds. I figured I was going somewhere, out of this hellhole, and I wasn't about to hold anyone up."

Then Rall saw he was to be joined by Colonel Hans Ulrich Rudel who had been brought from the hospital and was on crutches. Rudel was the leading tank-busting Stuka ace who had fought on the Eastern Front. Rall had escorted him many times in his Bf 109 when Rudel had been commander of III./St G 2. The Stuka pilot was credited with destroying more than five hundred tanks, eight hundred combat vehicles and a battleship in his Junkers Ju 87 dive-bomber. One of those feats cost him dear. Part of his right leg had to be amputated after a crash just before the end of the war. Fitted with an artificial limb, he often carried it in a backpack, using crutches to get around. He managed to hang on to the prosthesis when he was captured by the Americans.

"Amazingly, he still had the small backpack with his wooden

leg sticking out of it," said Rall. "He guarded it with his life, and we made jokes about it."

The two prisoners took their seats in an army jeep and were driven a few miles north to an airfield east of the port of Cherbourg where several small planes with the insignia of the Royal Air Force were parked. The two were then escorted to a mess tent where German prisoners of war served them a meal of meatballs.

"Can you imagine! Meatballs!" But as soon as Rudel caught sight of the whitecaps of the English Channel nearby, he groaned in despair.

"Oh God, the Americans are going to hand us over to the Russians!" Rudel said. As the most famous Stuka pilot who had fought so successfully against the Russians on the Eastern Front, his capture by the Soviets would have been a grand coup and a tremendous propaganda tool.

"Are you crazy?" said Rall. "It would be much too expensive to get a cruiser here from Russia just to pick the two of us up. The Allies want to pick our brains but I am sure they don't want the Russians to get their hands on us."

Rall's guess was right. The Americans and British well knew the value and scope of the German aces' expertise and experiences. According to the archives the Russians knew Rudel and Rall were POWs and asked for them to be handed over after the Americans had completed their interrogations. Fortunately, the request was ignored.

The two were led over to a Beechcraft that sat on a side runway and flown to Tangmere, the base for the RAF's crack No. 1 fighter squadron, in pastoral Sussex, southern England. Today, models of British, French and German aircraft are displayed in the Tangmere museum. Many of Britain's famous pilots had flown from Tangmere at one time or another during World War II in their Spitfires and Hurricanes, including Sir Douglas Bader, Group Captain Peter Townsend, Group Captain Hugh Dundas, Group Captain (later Air Vice Marshal) Johnny Johnson, and Commander-in-Chief of Fighter Command Sir Frederick Rosier, who would later become Deputy Chief of NATO.

Among the targets for another aircraft that flew out of Tangmere, the Blenheim bomber, had been German-occupied Cherbourg. Now, here came two of Germany's top fighter pilots making the trip from Cherbourg to Tangmere, on the reverse journey. It was Rall's second visit to England as a prisoner of war.

The British, eager for information, had an agreement with the US forces that permitted them to transfer any high-level Luftwaffe personnel to England for a period of interrogation. The Royal Air Force wanted to access the Eastern Front pilots' vast knowledge and strategic skills, particularly with regard to the Red air force, the VVS.

"We saw no reason not to cooperate," said Rall. "The war was over. We were treated extremely well, like VIPs" said Rall. "From the moment we stepped from the Beechcraft the Tangmere staff were as gentlemanly as the British are reputed to be."

The German pilots were settled in to a temporary base prison, basically a hut. But it had one great advantage. No locks.

"They left the door open. That's a good sign," Günther assured Rudel.

A British wing commander, Robert Stanford Tuck, appeared. A legendary Spitfire pilot and one of the RAF's top-scoring aces, he had been shot down over France in 1942 and spent the rest of World War II as a POW. "Gentlemen, I'm so sorry," said Tuck. "We didn't expect you so early. Would you like a cigarette?" Günther was captivated by his impeccable English accent and graciousness after the more informal and less hospitable manner of their American captors. "It was the first time we had been addressed as gentlemen. Ever since we'd been captured most of us, as officers, had been treated with disrespect. Tuck's greeting was a refreshing change."

Rall and Rudel were quick to take him up on his offer of cigarettes.

"Yes, wing commander, we'd appreciate a cigarette. In fact, ten, if you have them," said Rall.

"And have you had lunch?" asked the solicitous wing commander.

"Not for the past three months," said Rall.

After that, nothing was too much trouble, whether it was keeping the aces' beer mugs filled in the officer's mess, ensuring the comfort of their beds, or providing the much-welcomed, wonderful food. There were clean white sheets on the cots and hot water in the showers. Paradise to the Luftwaffe aces.

"It was all so civilized. So English," said Rall, who was later to be as impressed with Stanford Tuck's two sons who were among the mourners at Adolf Galland's funeral in 1996.

"You could spot them immediately. They stood out as perfect, perfect examples of English gentlemen," said Rall.

The Germans spent the next three weeks undergoing intense but friendly interrogation sessions. The RAF was avidly interested in the Soviet air force, its strengths and weaknesses, its expertise, and equipment. Rudel and Rall were happy to oblige with their assessments, opinions, and knowledge. The interrogations were conducted in civil tones.

At one point Wing Commander Sir Douglas Bader arrived from London to talk to the German pilots. The famous British ace had lost both his legs in a flying accident in 1931 but in spite of the handicap he became one of the RAF's top fighter pilots during World War II. In 1941 his Spitfire was shot down over the Pas de Calais, France and Bader was captured by the Germans.

During a meeting with the prisoner, Galland promised to allow the RAF to parachute down a replacement limb for Bader whose left artificial leg was damaged in the crash. Galland also assured the Brits that their aircraft would not be fired upon in this instance while making the drop. But then, along with the new leg, down came a couple of bombs.

"That was not very agreeable," remarked Rall.

Now, with the tables turned at Tangmere with the German prisoners, Bader expressed a great interest in Rudel's artificial leg and the metal it was made from. He wanted to compare notes and had brought his orthopedist with him.

"This was really very odd to us, but understandable," said Rall.

The doctor advised Rudel that he could improve his walking movements by obtaining an updated aluminum version of his prosthesis and Bader offered to get it for him, but the base commander stepped in and reminded the Brits they were not supposed to be fraternizing at such length with the prisoners.

"This is not a medical center for the Germans," said the commander.

"Bader was a bit annoyed at that," said Rall, "but we realized there had to be limitations."

Another surprise awaited the two fighter pilots during the weekend of their stay in England. Almost everyone at the base took off every Saturday and Sunday to have a good time in London. Tangmere virtually emptied out on weekends. Wing commander Stanford Tuck came to Rall's quonset hut.

"Gentlemen," said Tuck, "your weekend here is free, you are at leisure, though there's nothing for you to do. Just don't forget that if you need anything, ask the guards." Tuck was gracious enough not to point out that the guards were armed with machine guns.

During another visit by Stanford Tuck, Rall and Rudel were offered a demonstration of the RAF's new Hawker Tempest fighter bomber that took on Hitler's flying bombs so successfully in 1944. Tuck, Bader, Rall and Rudel spent hours discussing all aspects of warfare, range of aircraft, and comparisons of German versus Russian fighters and bombers.

By the time Rall and Rudel were returned to the POW camp in France three weeks later they were fatter and happier. Rall estimates he put on more than fifteen pounds during his time in England. The problem arose, how to settle back in with their starving fellow prisoners? To assuage their guilt they took back to the POW camp as many meatballs as they could carry after landing at the airbase near Cherbourg where they again lunched at the RAF mess tent.

A few weeks later, many of the prisoners were freed. They were driven to a German release camp in Bamberg, a small town on the Main River, where they were supplied with appropriate release documents.

"The Americans didn't really want to take care of us, there was not enough food, and what was the point? It became a matter of economics."

However, in order to ensure his freedom Rall applied to the medical center for a special pass because of his spine and thumb injuries.

"I was given two days' worth of food, which I ate all at once, and taken to the train station." Loaded onto open freight cars and wearing POW markings imprinted on their clothes, the freed prisoners traveled south, spat upon by the French and shouted at as they progressed along the tracks as the train traveled through France to Augsberg, Germany.

"People threw stones at us. We needed to retaliate. The floor of our carriage had metal slats so we pulled those up and threw them at the French. It wasn't a pretty sight."

Leaving the train at Augsburg in Germany Rall walked for more than twenty miles, headed for Bad Wörishofen, Bavaria, where he hoped to find Hertha.

Free to Find Hertha–1946

25
fünf und zwanzig

Accompanied by a fellow officer Rall completed the journey hitchhiking whenever possible. He finally arrived in Bad Wörishofen, wondering if his wife was still renting their apartment located on the upper floor of a home for the elderly. Outside the building Rall looked up at her second floor window and was surprised to see a huge American flag hanging from it.

"I went in and was told by neighbors that an army air force chaplain had thrown Hertha out and taken possession of her apartment. A chaplain! I didn't think that was a very Christian thing to do!"

Günther inquired if anyone knew where Hertha had gone, and was directed to one of the town's ancient buildings where many senior citizens were living in the upper apartments.

"She was living in a tiny room. It was like a dungeon." It was so small Günther claimed he could reach everything in the room and perform all necessary actions while sitting on a chair. "But when she saw me, well, it was a shock. as well as a joy. I was in terribly poor health, thin, with painful stomach problems because of the bad food. But there are no words to describe our emotions at being reunited. She'd had no idea where I was or if I was even alive. We were both so overcome with emotion we wept for days. Neither of us could believe the other had survived the war and was safe."

It was a thankful time for the Ralls. One cloud marred their reunion. Hertha had just lost the boy child she'd carried during the time Günther was a prisoner of war. It was her second premature birth that, like the first, had come almost to term.

"The Russians were advancing quickly in Austria but I had managed to get word to some aides to get her away before the Red Army overran the country. She boarded the last train to the West but it was attacked by British Mosquito bombers." The bombers were famed for ruining one of Reichsmarshall Göring's parades in 1943 and a rally for Hermann Göbbels held the same day. "Hertha and the other passengers had to get off the train hurriedly and run for shelter from one spot to another. There were no buildings and they had to run down steep embankments, causing the misscarriage. She had the baby baptized with the name of Axel before he died within a few hours of delivery."

It was time to return to civilian life. But what kind of jobs were available? How would Rall earn a living? The German economy was bankrupt, the country occupied by the Americans, the French, the Russians and the British. In fact, as far as most Germans were concerned their country no longer existed. The entire continent seemed like one big, foreign military camp. And no one wanted to even acknowledge knowing a German officer, let alone hiring one. Time after time Rall was rebuffed when applying for even the most menial of jobs.

Hertha had been earning a meager salary ironing clothes in a laundry at an American army base. The base commander had learned that she was the wife of Major Günther Rall and had given her a job. Having any kind of job was considered extremely fortunate for a civilian male and even more so for a woman. But Hertha's luck continued. She had two doctor friends who were able to find the funds to set up a provisional medical clinic. Hertha joined them, once more ministering to the sick and needy, many of them Jews released from Hitler's camps.

The Bad Wörishofen region was under the control of French forces. Living under a strict 10 p.m. curfew Günther and his neighbors met secretly at night, stealing out of their homes to talk and discuss their future as they collected firewood in the nearby forest. Where to find work? How to reorganize and plan for the rest of their lives? The outlook was bleak. Then Günther heard a rumor that the British were looking for pilots. He contacted Heinz Baer and the two traveled to Hamburg to check out the rumor. It proved false, and the men returned home, highly disappointed, riding a coal train.

Hertha soon received an offer to join the medical staff at the University Hospital, where she had originally earned a degree. Here she would be able to practice medicine as well study for an advanced degree. Most of her fellow physicians were female because many of the male doctors had been casualties on the Western and Eastern fronts, or were still prisoners of war.

The constant demands for his wife's services convinced Günther that he, too, should become a doctor. He believed he had the intelligence and the will to apply himself to the serious scholarship the field demanded. He knew that special permission was now needed to enter a university but with his educational background Günther assumed it would be no problem. To his astonishment he was turned down by local universities. Finally, he managed to make an appointment to meet with a friend, one of Germany's most reputable governors, the Counselor of Wurttemberg-Hohenzollern, to try to find an answer to the rejection.

"Günther," the professor said, "you are one of Germany's most famous heroes. Everyone knows who you are. You are covered in military glory. Consequently, no school wants to have you on campus. The attitude is that you would cause great unrest." Regardless of which political party he favored he was told that he would be the focal point of politically unstable, seditious students, polarizing the student body.

Rall didn't take the news calmly. He was incensed that loyal soldiers, sailors and airmen who had fought for their country under the most extreme conditions were denied the chance to create new careers for themselves. It was not unlike the situation American GIs found themselves in upon their return from the Vietnam War. No one wanted them around. They were an embarrassment. The more decorated the soldier, the less desirable the man, Rall realized. Rudel, the most highly decorated pilot in history, is said to have turned to teaching skiing in Austria because of Germany's aversion to employing war heroes.

Although this attitude changed to a certain extent in Germany after several years, it was too late for Günther to become a doctor. To earn a wage he must take a different path. The professor had recommended that Rall become a craftsman, like his own son, but Rall believed he could scale the ladders of the professionals.

"Although jobs were scarce, the years immediately after the war were decisive. I had to get on with my life. I needed to be clear about where I was going, what I would do," he said. The Ralls settled in Reutlingen, in southern Germany. Departing the train on their arrival there Hertha realized she had left the only coat she possessed in the carriage. She hurried back to retrieve it but the train was already rolling away.

In 1946 Günther's first job was as a trainee in a weaving company in Metzingen, 15 miles from his home. Then he applied for employment as a commercial clerk. The pay was extremely low.

In 1947 the Ralls moved to Stuttgart when Hertha was offered a position as a pediatrician at the Olgastift Hospital, a highly respected children's hospital. Günther finally figured out a way to survive. To improve his financial situation, Rall had worked as an agent for the Willy Burkle Lumber Company, supervising tree-felling operations. He and a friend now put two elements together: a tree disease was attacking thousands of oaks; lumber was in great demand by the occupying French army. Rall's entrepreneurial spirit devised a plan that would both erase the disease and supply the French with the wood they needed.

"My friends and I became brokers for the loggers. They cut down trees twenty-four hours a day. It was hectic. But we made a lot of money." Enough to soon buy a prized Volkswagen. Rall's luck increased further four months later when the Deutsche mark solidified, increasing his financial worth. He presented the car to Hertha, who made a point of parking it a few blocks away from the hospital to avoid an appearance of wealth in those early days after the war when Germany's economy was non-existent.

The transportation was welcome. Hertha's daily rounds took her up and down several flights of stairs throughout her shift because the hospital elevators had long since ceased to function due to war damage. When she finally came down the stairs for the last time each evening she thankfully sank into the Volkswagen's driver's seat. No more need to walk the three miles home. Günther took a job in industry, working as a salesman for Siemens, the electrical conductor giant whose empire stretched into several different countries. He was thrilled to be back in his childhood hometown, and his contacts soon led to a job as head of the field service department with Kreuz-Verlag, a publishing company.

From July 1947 to May 1948 he honed his skills as an organizer and negotiator in various fields. On January 16, 1950, Günther began work as a traveling salesman for radios and their accessories with the Siemens & Halske company. There, he finally broke through the ranks into the company's middle management level and became the manager for the southern region. He and Hertha felt it was time to start a family but after two miscarriages during the war, the couple wondered if they would ever be blessed with children.

The Ralls lived in Stuttgart for three years, until once again Hertha's fine medical skills brought an offer of a new position, as resident director of physicians of the famous Salem School near Lake Constance, an exclusive boarding school founded after World War I whose campus included a magnificent 17th century monastery. Spread over many acres the Salem School housed four other facilities and among the students were children from European aristocratic families and royalty. Indeed, the school was owned by the Duke of Baden who was married to a Greek princess, the sister of Prince Philip the Duke of Edinburgh, the husband of Queen Elizabeth II. Philip had been a student at the school himself before World War II. Prince Georg-Wilhelm of Hannover was dean.

The Ralls took up residence at Salem in late summer, 1951. The previous September 28, 1950 in Stuttgart, they had welcomed their first child, Franziska, finally dispelling any doubts about Hertha being able to carry a pregnancy to full term. Her new job was to prove a fortuitous decision for the family when, three years later, Günther resigned from Siemens. The Duke of Baden had been insistently offering Rall a position as personal aide to the dean, Prince Georg-Wilhelm, and Günther finally acquiesced. "I told the Duke of Baden that I would be honored to accept the post but that if a call ever came for me to go back to the Luftwaffe, I would go."

The Salem School offer was the perfect chance for the Ralls to be permanently together in one place. Günther's job with Siemens had meant traveling all around Germany and he welcomed the opportunity to give up constantly having to leave Hertha and his daughter. Now the Ralls could consider having another baby and their children would be accepted as students at the one of Europe's finest schools.

Yet, as Günther settled in to his new job, he still longed to be airborne once more. After World War II Germans were forbidden to fly which meant he hadn't sat in a cockpit in years but his passion raged, hidden but unabated. Every time he heard an aircraft overhead he'd listen to its engine to guess at its identity and often watch till it disappeared over the horizon. His heart was with his wife but his soul had long been pledged to the open skies.

Part IV

Civilian Life

The Ralls lived a harmonious, quiet, and stable life. He and Hertha had another daughter, Feli, born on March 17, 1955. They sailed on the lake, took camping trips in the woods, and spent winter holidays skiing in the Swiss and Austrian Alps. Kurt Hahn, the founder of the school, brought them a puppy, a springer spaniel, from England.

"It was not the most obedient of animals," said Feli, smiling. "We had a difficult time training him. Even my father, who had been a Wing Commander, couldn't make any headway."

Feli remembers her childhood at the lakeside as "wondrous," playing with her sister Franzi in the Salem School's park-like gardens, woods, and forests. When the girls reached the age of fourteen years old they were sent to Salem's boarding school, twenty miles away but still part of the campus. The change was difficult.

"I was always terribly homesick but I was permitted to come home on weekends for violin lessons so that helped a lot," said Feli.

Hertha's medical duties were many and included advising and counseling the Salem students with their personal problems, acting as a surrogate mother and psychologist.

"She was passionate about her work, she just loved it, she loved every one of the students," said Feli. "She had a very strong, bright and positive personality but was much quieter than my father. She loved to dance and ski, she was very active, full of energy. On one visit to my father's mother, who could be very stern and ran her household in the traditional, old-fashioned way and couldn't understand women who worked, grandma was scandalized by my mother because she smoked, played music, was obviously a free spirit and didn't care much for cooking. My mother was artistic and very cultured. She painted, loved museums and took us to musical concerts. We attended the Salzburg Musical Festival every year." During her reminiscences Feli was also to unknowingly echo the words of Rall's wartime crew: he brought out the best in people, and raised their standards higher than they thought possible.

At social events Rall was occasionally surprised to come across people connected to his past. At a birthday party for the Duke of Baden, a guest was ex-King Michael of Romania, of which Rall had fonder memories than of Russia. Old friends came to visit, among them Fritz Obleser, who had become a highly successful businessman.

"We spoke of flying every time we got together, and how we missed it. We discussed Germany's lack of a national air force. Many of our talks were sad."

Rall finally decided to apply for a civilian pilot's license so he could at least enjoy flying if the opportunity arose. He had no idea what the Allies planned for Germany's disbanded Luftwaffe, but, were it to be re-established, was he too advanced in age to make a useful contribution?

He was eager to prove to himself he could still fly a plane. Was it like a bicycle, or a horse, where everything came back once you were in the saddle?

Forbidden to fly even civilian sport planes, Germans had to travel outside the country if they wanted to take lessons or re-apply for a pilot's license, and even then, travel permits were necessary. Günther knew that his old flight instructor, from 1939, was now an instructor at a small airport in Basel, Switzerland.

"I applied for a travel permit and went to see my friend and rented a small and rather old Cessna. Any other kind of plane was much too expensive."

As he sat in a cockpit after an absence of ten years he was overwhelmed by such great emotion he felt dizzy. Although this moment couldn't come close to the sensation of strapping himself into a Bf 109, it was nevertheless a flying experience and he drained its joys to the very last drop. After three weeks it was obvious to Rall's test instructor that he'd lost none of his skills.

"My flight instructor made it very easy. He told me after just a few maneuvers, 'Yep, you've passed. Let's go and celebrate.'"

Rall felt immeasurably proud that he had proven he could fly again. He had secretly wondered if the old skills were still there. But while Günther frequently felt the pangs of passion that urged him to jump into a plane and take off, he knew circumstances were not in his favor. Besides, he was happy with his life. Circumstances were to change sooner than he thought. In 1953 talk of a new German air force had surfaced but it was only mild speculation. Then, in 1954, the Western Allies floated the suggestion that West Germany should join the North Atlantic Treaty Organization, NATO, established in 1949, by contributing troops to the joint European forces.

West Germany's Chancellor Konrad Adenauer, who had been imprisoned by Hitler for his opposition to the Nazi regime, took up the cause and agreed. Rearmament was a favored foreign policy objective and, as an extension, with the approval of the United States, reunification with East Germany. America did, indeed, endorse the reunification of a democratic Germany within the Atlantic alliance, especially to restore the West's balance of power with the Soviet Union, but as a peaceful transition, not as a military option.

The Chancellor realized that a national German army was out of the question but re-establishing a military presence as part of a worldwide force would be a great morale-booster for his people. Not only would the plan give them back some pride, the Allies could benefit by the thousands of military experts still alive after World War II who were willing to share their knowledge. Not the least among them were Luftwaffe aces with some of the greatest jet flight-testing experiences on the planet. However, Adenauer faced strong opposition by German Social Democrats leader, Kurt Schumacher,who claimed that only neutrality and demilitarization would lead to uniting the two halves of the split Germany.

Twelve of the thirteen original NATO members — Belgium, Canada, Denmark, the US, the UK, Iceland, Italy, Luxembourg, the Netherlands, Norway, Portugal and Turkey — approved of Adenauer's suggestion to join the organization. France's prime minister, Pierre Mendes-France, not surprisingly, was vehemently against the idea in spite of the fact that France was America's oldest ally. With visions of a Fourth Reich emerging and threatening once again to wage war on its neighbors, Mendes-France fought tooth and nail to scuttle any talk of Germany having official standing with the Allies. The containment of Germany still played an important role to both the British and the French. Fired up with the idea of the offer, however, Adenauer approached each member of NATO and lobbied to join. Among the various questions to be answered by rearming West Germany was that of the Luftwaffe and it was decided to appoint a NATO parliamentary commission to study the effect that a new German air force might have.

Krupinski and Hrabak, working as civilians, were asked to put their heads together and come up with a plan to work within the Bundeswehr, the newly-created Federal Armed Forces, which Steinhoff confidently expected to give birth to a revived Luftwaffe. Although there was no official announcement, Steinhoff came on board as their leader and he was soon on the phone to his old colleague Günther, urging him to sign on.

"How can we have a Luftwaffe without you?" Steinhoff said. Günther indicated his interest, inwardly exultant, and Steinhoff said he'd put his old comrade's name forward.

In spite of his new pilot's license Rall had doubts about returning to active duty. Was he too rusty to be of use training new pilots? What about the new jets the Americans were developing? Could his flight time in Me 262s be of use or was he out of the mainstream? Would the skills and instincts return or would the memory of his eight crashes and severe injuries prevent his total commitment to the job?

"It took forever for the process to crawl along," recalls Rall. "It was bureaucracy at its finest but eventually I was sent an official letter asking if I would be interested in helping to build up a new German air force." Faced with the prospect of his dream coming true, Günther hesitated. It would mean working with organizations known for their slow pace. Endless deliberations. Did he really want to start all over again in the world of political infighting, egotistical superiors, and incompetent, bureaucratic military planners? He thought back to his differences of opinions with the high command of the Third Reich.

He recalled the absurd decisions Hitler made, the blunders, the refusal to accept advice from the field, and worst of all, the fawning members of the Führer's cabinet who rather than tell him the truth acquiesced in his terrible campaign to continue

World War II to the death. Was Rall really ready to re-enter the fray? He knew there were tensions among the Allies and that the French would forever be Germany's enemy. It would also mean time away from his family.

"I was satisfied with my position at the Salem School, it was a wonderful place to live, and I thought long and hard before coming to a decision," said Rall. One of the highlights was being presented to Queen Elizabeth II, who visited the school during her first state visit to Germany. She and her husband, Prince Phillip, stayed for the weekend at Salem. The Duchess invited Günther and Hertha to meet them in a private informal visit and once again Rall was fascinated to find himself shaking hands with someone who had dark hair and brilliant blue eyes.

In his heart of hearts, though, he knew he would sweep aside all doubts. There was no question that Günther Rall would, once again, answer the call to serve his country.

"I realized that this was the way to go for Germany if we wanted to be accepted in the club of European countries, and, indeed, worldwide. Adenauer was building up a democratic state and I believed we needed to make our contribution at this time. Perhaps I could help other nations respect Germany once more."

Although he understood those who were opposed to even the slightest hint of German re-armament after two devastating wars, Rall was also aware of the necessity of a national army because of the East-West confrontation with the Soviet Empire and the Cold War. In his opinion, re-establishing the Bundeswehr was the only way for West Germany to secure a position alongside the Allies opposed to Russian control of East Germany.

He discussed it at length with Hertha, who well knew where his secret desire lay and understood it would torment him forever if he declined. Confident that he could now train pilots and that his expertise had not deserted him, Günther went to Bonn to formally accept a position in the new Bundeswehr. He took an exam, whose results read, in part: "Mr. Rall shows self-confidence and good manners. He is open to the problems of our times, is a warm-hearted, tactful man and a scholar. He has a reliable and humorous personality and his openness and sincerity are impressive."

Before initialing the contract he was questioned closely by the NATO staff about the reasons for his decision.

"I want to be part of our new air force, and fly again," said Rall simply. The answer was good enough. He returned to Salem to prepare to leave for Bonn as a Bundeswehr major. All Luftwaffe personnel who joined the new forces would come in holding their previous ranks.

Rall contacted some of his old pals to discuss the momentous turn of events as he embarked on his next adventure.

"Some were skeptical, wondering if it was wise to serve again, to re-establish a military presence. I myself was uncertain of the future. But I also believed that a country must have the means to defend itself or, in a larger union, be prepared to defend its neighbors and allies. I would not have joined in if it were simply a new national air force, just for Germany. Never. I felt we needed to make a larger contribution than that."

With the Warsaw Pact between the USSR and its fellow Communist states threatening Europe in response to West Germany's admission into NATO, Günther was anxious that this new political challenge be met head-on, with West Germany participating as a military partner.

"And, then, how could I turn down the possibility of flying again? It was in my blood. There was no way to resist." Aside from Rall's passion to re-enter the profession he knew and loved was his determination to serve his country once more. He would take up a position with the military as opposed to the political side of NATO, whose formation was necessitated, according to Britain's General Hastings Lionel (Lord) Ismay, NATO's first Secretary-General, "to keep the Americans in, the Russians out, and the Germans down." In truth, the military and political issues were necessarily inexorably entwined and in the coming years Rall's military duties and decisions would have a direct effect on NATO's political agenda, and vice versa.

On January 2, Günther, an airman once more, was again on a train saying goodbye to Hertha and his two small daughters. The occasion brought back so many sad memories to his wife that she wept. It reminded her of all the times she'd stood on station platforms waving goodbye to Günther in wartime, wondering if she'd ever see him again.

"There's no fighting any more," Günther said this time to comfort his wife. "I'll be back soon. Our home is here in Salem and nothing will change that."

Günther asked Fritz Obleser to visit him and discuss joining too. Fritz, Rall's longtime friend from the Eastern Front, was making a living as an engineer, and had married Anna, whom he had met just before the end of war when she was training as a Luftwaffe navigator. Obleser was happy in his civilian life and wasn't sure he wanted to go back into the armed forces.

"Fritz, we have to serve again. Let's show them how good we are."

"Alright. If you say so, then I will." Rall's leadership was, once more, difficult to ignore in spite of the fact that Obleser had lost three fingers during the war when a captured Russian weapon he was loading exploded. Günther, too, was concerned about his friend's ability to fly again. How will Fritz fly with that crippled hand? wondered Rall. He called Dieter Hrabak in Bonn.

"I am sending Obleser to the air base at Furstenfeldbruck," said Rall. "Please arrange for him to take a flight test. Make sure there is an F-84F available and a US flight surgeon to observe." More than 1,200 F-84F Thunderstreaks had been delivered to NATO forces in Europe as a ground support aircraft. Its predecessor, the F-84 was the US Air Force's first post-war fighter and the first jet fighter to be armed with a tactical atomic weapon.

Obleser acquitted himself well. Once in the cockpit he proved he could handle the F-84F jet as competently as he did his old Bf 109.

"The F-84F was really good," said Obleser. "I enjoyed its speed, twice that of the 109. Its wing span was comparable, too, so I felt comfortable in it, though the F-84F was much longer and taller than the 109. It wasn't a true fighter. I think we've seen the last of those, the Bf 109, the Spitfire, and the Mustang P-51. Today, combat aircraft are developed to be 80 percent bomber and 20 percent fighter. You just fire away and let the rocket do its job."

In addition to Obleser, Hartmann, Hrabak and several other World War II aces would also be tapped to join the new air force. Fritz himself would carve out a successful career and in years to come became NATO's project manager for the Multirole Combat Aircraft, the MRCA, a low-level, supersonic Tornado attack aircraft that was a joint venture with Britain, Italy and Germany. Operational in five variations – counter air attack, strike for air support, defense, reconnaissance and long range defense – the Tornado was considered in 1999 by the United States Department of Defense as "[contributing] to the foreign policy and national security of the United States by improving the military capabilities of Germany and enhancing standardization and interoperability of this important NATO ally."

For the second time Rall was serving his country with the same zeal, honor, and patriotism he had given the Third Reich. But this time he would have a far greater voice in Germany's future.

Jets in Peacetime

In August, 1956, Rall and a small group spent time at the US air base in Landsberg/Lech, Germany, flying T-6s, the hardy Texan/Harvard two-seater training aircraft the US Air Force and US Navy had used during World War II. One former fighter pilot of Rall's JG 300 unit who had answered the call to join the new Luftwaffe was Captain Waldermar Radener who had become a successful businessman in the fashion world and who was married to an acclaimed artist. Radener, however, was soon to become the first victim of the new Luftwaffe in a crash while training in a T-6 at Landsberg/Lech. Rall, his former commander, delivered the eulogy at Radener's funeral in Dusseldorf.

Günther himself was almost as unlucky. Due to an engine failure one day he came down hard on the runway, jolting his old back injury but not requiring medical care. It was one crash he never revealed to Hertha.

The group was next sent to Furstenfeldbruck, west of Munich, where they soon mastered the characteristics of T-33s, a two-seat trainer developed from the single-seat P-80 jet, America's first combat jet. Dieter Hrabak, Rall's former JG 52 wing commander, was now the base commander working alongside an American colonel. Once or twice Rall managed to persuade the USAF instructor that his pilots at times needed less structured training sessions.

"Fighter pilots have their own personal flying style and prefer the freedom of the skies. We love to roam, although we all knew that was not what we were there for," said Rall. "At times it was difficult to rein ourselves in but we stayed with the American system of training, which was based on normal and emergency procedures. This system turned out to be an excellent one."

The US Air Force soon decided that the German pilots were ready to be sent to Lackland Air Force Base, seven miles outside San Antonio, Texas for language and systems training. Rall and fourteen of his comrades were to take refresher courses in the US and return to Germany as Wing Commanders. Hrabak, Steinhoff and Kuhlmey were already in the US as civilians but training as airmen. Rall's group included Obleser and Hartmann, who had been released from a Soviet prison two years earlier. Magic names from the past. Forgotten German war heroes. But pilots of great distinction whose collective expertise, technical knowledge, and experience was unmatched. However, before taking on any new recruits the group had to take refresher courses themselves and then learn how to fly the new jets. The group were to train in F-84s for their fighter-bomber wing and F-86s for their fighter wing. The F-84 and F-86 were the planes that the US would supply free to the new German air force, with the Germans paying only for spare parts.

The first stop for the pilots, who included Obleser, was New York, a journey that in 1957 took thirteen hours from Brussels on Sabena Air Lines' four-engined aircraft

"As soon as we hit New York, we did the town. What a marvelous, magical place! It was amazing to us, so vibrant, everyone so energetic, the pulse of the city throbbing night and day. We were enthralled. We stayed at a hotel near Times Square where

Johannes Steinhoff

the rooms cost $3 a night because we were NATO officials."

Four days later the group flew to Lackland and got their first look at the extent of the territory of the United States. Among Günther's impressions was his puzzlement at overhead power

303

and telephone lines.

"We drove into rural areas outside San Antonio at one point where the only sign of habitation was these tall telephone poles that stretched for miles. They looked very primitive to me and were in great contrast to what we'd seen of modern, cosmopolitan New York where electric and other cables are underground. I thought every state would be the same across the country but when I realized the vastness of America and its many different regions and climates, it was understandable."

Four weeks into their stay at Lackland Günther and three others pooled their funds and bought a second-hand Chevrolet sedan. Each weekend they visited different places and became expert tourists. They went to bullfights in Mexico, rodeos in Arizona, and Indian reservations in New Mexico.

Rall particularly marveled at the Grand Canyon and the variety of landscapes. "They are endless, and magnificent. Just amazing. The East so different from the West, the mid-West and the Southern states. What an incredible country."

Known as the Gateway to the Air Force because all their recruits are processed and trained here, Lackland was home to the 37th Training Wing and various Wing organizations. However, the arrival of the first Germans they'd ever hosted on the base was a cultural curiosity for both sides. Rall and his fifteen pilots changed from civilian clothes into German uniforms. Although the war had ended twelve years earlier memories were still fresh and Rall guessed that seeing the insignia and hearing the Luftwaffe pilots speaking in their native tongue must have sent shivers up some of the Americans' spines. But the pilots and instructors on both sides admired each other professionally and the welcome Rall and the others received was extremely kind and understanding.

"A pilot is a pilot, whatever his nationality, and we all respected that," said Rall.

The editor at the local newspaper wasn't so enamored. The day after the NATO group arrived, banner headlines on the front page announced: "GOERING'S FINEST FLY AGAIN!" Accompanying the article was a photo of Rall, Hartmann and a third German pilot standing in front of a P-51 Mustang.

"We all laughed. It wasn't a big deal."

Rall and his World War II veterans began further training at Luke Field, later renamed Luke Air Force Base, west of Glendale, Arizona. During World War II Luke was a center for advanced flight training for Army Air Corps pilots in P-38 Lightning fighter-bombers. Also trained at Luke were many of General Claire Chenault's Chinese pilots known as the "Flying Tigers" in P-40 Warhawks (called Tomahawks by the RAF) and by the end of the war Luke had become the largest, single-engine advance training base in the world.

Rall trained in T-33s again as well as in the just-under-Mach I F-84 fighter bomber. Under constant development, its wings varied from straight in the F-84 Thunderjet to swept in the F-84F Thunderstreak in order to try to boost the top speed by an extra 60 mph. Rall discovered that it was the big brother to the captured P-47 he flew to train Germany's young pilots during his tenure as commander of the fighter leader school in the latter days of World War II.

"We were really challenged," said Rall. "Not only were the training protocols different, we spoke little English so reading the manuals and understanding our instructors was often difficult. Fortunately, many words used in flying are international so it didn't take us long to figure the rest out."

The German pilots found American training systems differed considerably from their Luftwaffe days. The rules and procedures were set up uniformly for airmen of each intellectual level, Rall discovered, making it much easier to grasp the basic concepts of flying the new jets.

"It was an excellent training structure with exacting standards, especially for emergency procedures that had to be followed. There was one for every situation. It was very different to what we were used to but it worked, and worked remarkably well. I particularly like the checklists pilots had to adhere to. I also was pleased that our day fighter pilots were taught night and instrument flying because this was a serious lack in our World War II Luftwaffe. We paid a high price for this deficiency during our homeland defense towards the end of the war because when our young, inexperienced pilots flew into dark clouds they became disoriented, and we lost a of lot of them. Certainly, we had special night fighters but the day fighters did not get such training. Today, pilots must be able to fly around the clock."

Rall's group was fascinated with the US supersonic jets' complex instrument panels filled with dozens of navigation, armament and engine controls.

"In the old days a fighter pilot had his eyes outside the cockpit, looking for the enemy. Once you spotted him you would check the instrument panel for only a split second for time, heading and speed and pick your position, look at your airspace to decide where to come in from and engage in a dogfight. Now, pilots tend to keep their eyes inside the cockpit, watching the panel to check the data because everything is electronic and automatic. Missiles are launched without the pilot physically seeing the target. One thing I insisted on, when I brought my pilots to the US for training, was to remind them to look outside. Get oriented. Find landmarks. Don't rely completely on the instruments. This is a safer way to fly and fight."

Rall obviously missed the good old dogfight days and lamented they have gone forever.

"Strategies and tactics have changed dramatically. We'll never have the quantity of planes as we did when carpet bombing was the norm during the last war. One aircraft today can inflict as much damage as one hundred before, we saw that proved in the Gulf War. That war was won by Tornados and guided self-seeking missiles. But the expense, of course, is phenomenal. On the other hand during the war in Afghanistan we relied on good old-fashioned bombing with B-52 so you have to adjust to the circumstances you are presented with."

Another difference the German pilots had to get used to was the youthful age of their American counterparts and instructors who were mostly in their mid-twenties. Günther and his colleagues hovered near the forty-year mark.

After four months the group was considered ready to return to Germany and begin training their own student pilots. Günther was transferred in February 1958 to Germany's Arms School 10 as operational staff officer and detached to the Allgemagne Luftwaffenamt, the General Office of the German Air Force. When they were back in Germany most of the group of World War II pilots were promoted to Commanders or Wing Commanders of the newly-established flying group. Rall joined Kuhlmey's fighter wing staff . The general was with the Ministry of Defense. To keep current with new advances in aviation Rall flew F-84s every other weekend with Krupinski, while others flew for their own practice and to gain flight hours to maintain their licenses.

As part of a team that studied the various Swedish, US and French aircraft that the new Luftwaffe was considering accepting from foreign countries, Günther knew that the American F-104 fighter-interceptor was the prize that each pilot wanted to win. In November 1958, officially ordered to head up the F-104 project, Rall left once more for California. With him were a group of engineers, auditors, and lawyers, all civilians, from Germany's Ministry of Defense who worked with the German Armed Forces. They were to assess the F-104's handling, maneuverability, financial considerations, and logistics. Modifications were to be incorporated to include a stabilizer fin under the tail, different electronic systems, and an inertial navigation system.

The engineers were the cream of the crop in their profession and Günther, the only one in the group to wear a uniform, was extremely pleased and relieved to have the benefit of their input. The F-104 was to play a different role in Germany than in the US, where the aircraft played a less significant role. In Germany, the fighter was the main aircraft for the new Luftwaffe, as it would be for the Belgians, the Dutch, the Canadians, the Greeks, the Turks, the Taiwanese, the Pakistanis and the Italians.

After inspecting the F-104's manufacturing facilities at Lockheed Corporation, in Los Angeles, a series of six test flights was agreed upon, paid for by the German government. Leaving the civilians in Burbank to discuss the project Rall drove eighty miles north to Palmdale, California, in the Mojave Desert, to conduct lengthy flights in both the F-104A and the dual-seat F-104B. He returned home with a coveted F-104 Pilot's Certificate which he framed and hung in his study at home. It reads:

Certificate of Supersonic Recognition

Signifying membership in the enviable and exclusive
ORDER OF STARFIGHTERS
NOTICE TO ALL ENGAGED
IN THE PRACTICE OF MACH-BUSTING
Col. Günther Rall
PILOT EXEMPLARY AND TIGER EXTRAORDINARY

Among the breed known as the "fighter type,"
having passed all qualifications of membership
by flying the world's fastest fighter airplane
USAF – LOCKHEED F-104A STARFIGHTER

Is recognized as one of the swiftest humans
and is entitled to all the privileges such speed implies.

Captain Keith Phillips was one of the first to test the F-104 for the USAF and help write its training manuals. He would later assist in establishing the German training programs at Luke Air Force Base.

"Six of us at the weapons school got to know F-104 designer Kelly Johnson pretty well," said Phillips, "and worked with him on changes. One problem was the USAF was stuck in an F-86 mentality with a jet that was trapped in slower speeds. It would turn out well but this F-104 was barely flying at F-86 speeds and to be effective you had to fly it very fast."

When he heard that veteran World War II Luftwaffe fighter pilots were coming to the US to test the F-104 Phillips was tremendously excited, especially when he was once given the opportunity to fly with Rall in the supersonic F-104.

"Rall had already checked out the plane, he flew it real well.

We were on our way to the gunnery range with some students to practice bombing, this was before the weapons school was all set up. I realized that Rall, like all the veterans, was a great navigator as well as flier. I guess when you cut your teeth on war combat it gives you an edge."

Phillips came to respect all of the German airmen. "They were willing to jump into the plane and fly off in the worst of weather and in the early days the plane was unforgiving, not the kind of aircraft you want to have trouble with in poor weather conditions. A group of German pilots came over," said Phillips, "and that is when I met General Rall. I was a young captain at the time so I was really impressed with meeting Rall and all these World War II aces famous everywhere for their incredible victories."

Phillips was forced to take a break in 1966 from the F-104 training sessions he ran in order to serve a tour of duty in Vietnam. When he returned he helped set up a cadre of people at an official fighter weapons school at Luke in 1968.

"The new weapons school was the original 'top gun' academy set up long before the US Navy had theirs that was the subject of the movie, *Top Gun*. I was a graduate of the school at Nellis Air Force Base and the Germans wanted us to establish the same thing for them at Luke. I stayed on until the mid-1980s. Rall and Steinhoff used to like to test us a lot, using the 'What if...' war games strategies. It was challenging and we all learned a lot and enjoyed it."

During his time with them, Phillips discovered that the senior German pilots possessed two significant traits. "They were not only great aviators, they were great leaders. Those two traits don't necessarily always go together, but the veterans of World War II all had them. The F-104 crashes they had later in Germany weren't all human error," maintains Phillips. "After they got over those initials losses in the Widow-maker, we found out that the loss rate was a combination of things, the most significant was that many of the German air force pilots hadn't flown for years, as Rall agrees, and that has a big impact not only on operational procedures but also maintenance and support."

The USAF test pilot pointed out that the F-86 and F-84 helped with the transition. "But when they brought the F-104 over there to Germany, brand new, right off the shelf, it was unlike anything they had flown or maintained before."

Keith tested the F-104 until 1972. "I was the Last of the Mohicans with that plane," he joked. But it didn't mean an end to his friendship with Rall. Phillips now lives in an exclusive Daytona Beach residential community where many private pilots have not only a garage attached to their homes but also a hangar. Whenever Günther is in the area he stops by to see him and often stays with another friend and pilot, Dave Cummock, who participates in the annual Gaggle Flight. The last time Rall joined this customarily loose formation of twenty small aircraft was in April, 2001 when Phillips invited him to be his co-pilot. in his Great Lakes two-seat bi-plane. The event was not without incident. The flight plan was to fly to Titusville for lunch with Rall at the controls.

"On the way he remarked it was his first flight in an open cockpit bi-plane in 40 years," said Phillips. "In spite of all that time elapsing he was unbelievably smooth. He was instantly right at home. About midway into the trip one of the other planes had to make an emergency landing at a small airport, and Rall brought my bi-plane in to land without a single wobble." Phillips then took over for the remainder of the flight. "On the way back we made a pass by Cape Canaveral which is always a thrill for all of us."

Handling NATO's F-104s

In the late 1950's Germany, Holland, Belgium and Italy officially formed a consortium to acquire more than 1200 supersonic strike aircraft for their national air forces. Each country was led by a team of air force officers and civil servants, who reported directly to their respective Air Force Chief of Staff and Minister of Defense. In Germany Rall was not only the leader of his country's F-104 project he was also responsible for coordinating the involvement of the three other nations' teams. He was now the project officer responsible for the coordination of the most ambitious weapons project of the new Luftwaffe. Germany's Minister of Defence and Kammhuber saw an opportunity to play on an equal aviation field with the Western Allies.

The *Air & Space Magazine* indicates in its April/May issue, 2001, that were it not for Günther Rall and NATO the F-104 might have disappeared in ignominy. The G model was selected as their main platform to deliver tactical nuclear weapons against the Warsaw Pact. The new version could carry 8,000 lbs of external stores and was equipped with the avionics for all-weather capacity and was a high performance versatile airplane with a proven airframe-engine performance history by the United States Air Force.

The general public, and to a certain extent Rall himself, believed that the F-104 Starfighter problems had been solved. Unfortunately, that was not the case. Too many pilots died in the hot-rod F-104 Starfighter. German pilots crashed twenty-eight in 1965 and several others in preceding years.

Rall and NATO were determined to discover the reasons for the accidents. They instituted new regulations that included rigorous discipline, meticulous attention to detail, firm enforcement of the rules, strict control over operations, and an analysis of reports. There were also production problems regarding spare parts and parallel production schedules and the configuration seemed to be changing every week..

"Being selected to head the F-104 project was a great, great privilege," said Rall. "I was very excited about getting our hands on the fantastic new jets we had heard so much about. The designer, Kelly Johnson, was a genius. It was a great plane for certain tactical missions. I had a lot of discussions with him about his one-engine or two-engine philosophy. He said that it was proven one engine was better than two because it meant that there were twice as many engines to fail, but I pointed out that statistically, this was incorrect, that two engines are more successful because if one goes the other can probably get you home.

"The crashes that subsequently marred the F-104's reputation were mainly eighty percent human error, not the airplane, and many of those accidents were by European pilots. When pilots have four to five hundred hours, they get over-confident. And in spite of its reputation, the F-104 at that time, had its limits. There are some aircraft, like the F-104, that want to fly, you can almost feel it straining at the leash, so to speak, while others you have to force to fly with sheer horsepower. But you have to stay within the limits."

"For the consortium version," said retired USAF Colonel

Joseph E. Andres, who was Rall's project liaison for the F-104 at the time, "the electronics and navigation subsystems were reconfigured to take advantage of latest developments. A plan was drawn up to buy fully built aircraft, but to transition the manufacture progressively from 100% U.S.-built to eventual 100% European-built over the course of several years."

The plan proved successful, with Fiat in Italy, Sabka in Belgium, Fokker in Holland, and Messerschmitt in Germany supplying parts. The resultant build-up of the air forces of the four European countries now had the capability of attack upon the Western edges of Russia and the Eastern European countries it occupied, and became a key element in Cold War diplomatic relations.

"I worked for two years at Luftwaffe headquarters near Bonn as a member of Rall's team," recalls Andres. "I found that the people in the staff group in Germany and those in counterpart groups were all outstanding technically and intellectually, and very dedicated to the program. Rall was the driving force. His boundless energy and determination, his technical understanding, and his ability to speak and convince the German parliament and foreign government members, as well as US engineers, contractors, and associates, was a major factor in this successful program."

Andres spent three years during World War II as a fighter pilot in the Mediterranean and European theaters.

"We all knew the names of the legendary Luftwaffe pilots – Barkhorn, Krupinski, and Rall, and it was a thrill to meet some of them during my time with the consortium," said Andres, who left Germany in 1963 to return to duty at the Aeronautical Systems Division of the US Air Force Systems Command at Wright Patterson Air Force base in Ohio. "I consider myself fortunate to have been a part of the consortium and the F-104 program, and to have played a small part in a significant, historical event. Rall is an outstanding gentleman, to be noted for his achievement, and I am very proud to call him my friend."

Rall returned the compliment. "What a fine man Joe Andres is. I respect him tremendously. He made all the difference to the program, with his wisdom, knowledge, and great diplomacy."

After Günther returned to Germany he was named Wing Commander of Fighter Bomber Wing 34 Allgau at Memmingen as the F-104 Starfighter originally designed as an interceptor was now being developed and modified by Germany and its European partners as a multi-purpose plane built initially in the United States and later in other countries. Although it was still considered a superb plane, the major aircraft project for the European syndicate suffered setbacks. Because produc-

Wing 34 Commander Rall ready to launch, in Memmingen, Germany

tion and development were carried out simultaneously, logistical problems surfaced. There was no longer any American production involvement. Instead, components such as the undercarriage retraction cylinders were supplied by another country. Rall was chagrined to learn that all thirty-three remaining F-104s had been grounded at his new base when he arrived to take over the Wing.

"Those were difficult first days because I had to motivate the pilots, try to figure out what was technically wrong with the planes, and keep peace among NATO members who were involved in the project." On an official visit to Wittmundhaven air base as part of his official duties to inspect aviation safety, he was on approach to the runway when an F-104 blazed in front him, spinning off to the side and exploding. The fatal accident was the first of a new series of crashes which plunged the Air Force into another serious crisis. Germany wasn't the only country to experience F-104 catastrophies. While Rall was in Italy on an official visit four F-104s crashed into the Adriatic Sea.

The World War II ace's first take-off in an F-104G was in 1958, the year Germany selected the aircraft to be transformed into an all-weather, multi-role attack fighter. Rall had earlier tested the F-104F.

"It was a glorious feeling, piloting an aircraft with such strength and speed. I put it through the most grueling tests, from low-level flights to supersonic speed, and hitting simulated targets. I flew the plane everywhere, up and down Death Valley, where the temperature hit 158 degrees Fahrenheit. I was wearing only a flight suit, the pressure suit and nothing else because of the heat, plus the helmet with all those wires. In those days if you put out 3.5 Gs you were drenched in perspiration. I came back completely wet from those missions but it was truly great. "

Enamoured of the F-104 Starfighter Rall, like Krupinski and Steinhoff who had also flown the plane, admired its design, its capabilities, its performance.

"There were some technical problems as there always are in new aircraft but it was a beauty. Stunning. It was enormous. It was fast. It was what we were looking for."

While Rall's opinion of the F-104 was positive and although he was impressed with its technical features, the jet's Mach 2 speed failed to engage his emotions.

"It was a good plane but I accepted its technology as a matter of course. Sure it was fast, but to me great speed is not emotional."

A year later Rall returned to Palmdale with four pilots to test and train day and night in the double-seat trainer. As chairman of the F-104 project for the NATO members representing Holland, Belgium, Italy, Germany and Canada, Günther held meetings on the progress of his testing of the plane every four weeks, alternating between Brussels, the Hague, and Rome. Debate raged on how best to promote and develop the aircraft and solve its technical problems. Immediately after his flights, Rall and the group recommended that the new Luftwaffe accept the F-104F as its primary fighter.

In 1961 the same group tested the F-104 combat version. The US saw NATO and Germany as the first line of defense against the 1955 Warsaw Pact signed by Russia and their Eastern European allies in response to NATO inviting Germany to join its organization. The Pact countries were equipped with such great numbers of armaments and troops, far more than NATO

Rall gives a thumbs-up in an F-104F during his first visit to Palmdale, California, 1960

member countries could command, that NATO felt it had no recourse other than resort to nuclear weapons. Thus, the F-104G would be selected as the carrier of choice and chosen by Germany to not only deliver tactical nuclear weapons against Warsaw Pact members if necessary but as a multi-role aircraft.

Rall wanted to be the first to fly the G version. He had studied the blueprints and was not convinced the pilot's safety was assured. He didn't plan to put his pilots in danger until he had tested the F-104 himself. As it turned out his test flight results prompted him to recommend a safety modification to Lockheed.

"I thought the aircraft should be more flexible with a more prompt response. There were at that time three roles that the German version of the F-104 was designed to fulfill. One was the fighter-bomber, this was the atomic concept. Secondly, in the interceptor role to find pilots in the air, and thirdly, in the reconnaissance role, which means you must reduce certain capabilities of the aircraft and make technological compromises. During the Cold War there was still an atomic role for NATO fighter bombers."

Günther flew his first F-104 bombing practice mission up to the simulated target in Death Valley, which is three hundred feet below sea level. The flight was almost fatal.

"I came into the valley below sea level, watched the targets appear on my radar, cut in the after-burner to give me full thrust, and set up the system so that the bombs would be automatically released. I came out at 27,000 feet, turned, and discovered that the exhaust nozzle was open. It should have closed but it stayed open so I had no thrust. I fiddled around but finally had to call Snake, my flight instructor at Lockheed operations." It was a May Day situation but both men were calm.

"What's happened?" asked Snake.

"I have an open nozzle."

"Damn. Read out all the instruments."

Rall read out each gauge to Snake.

"OK. If the oil pressure drops, bail out." The conversation was matter-of-fact although both men knew the seriousness of the predicament. Looking for landmarks, Günther saw he was approaching Edwards Air Force Base.

"I think I can make it to Palmdale."

Rall came down at full power to 10,000 ft and appreciated the long runway. Fortunately, his long experience handling unexpected aircraft problems, quick thinking, instant decision-making and calm nerves in times of crisis enabled him to bring the F-104G in to land. As he taxied cautiously down the runway, thankful to touch terra firma, he was met by an array of ambulances, fire trucks, and helicopters that would have equipped, he remarked, several towns in Germany. The problem proved to be an electrical device that had burned out. Günther suggested that engineers add the manual nozzle-closing device they had in their American version to the German model. The technical modification was made although it took three years to incorporate into the Germans' F-104 aircraft "Any engineering change takes time because it affects everything else."

Another modification Rall required before his country would agree to accept the plane concerned the dual timer atomic

Rall leads a group of F-104Fs over the Mojave Desert, outside Palmdale, California

bomb-release computer system. Talking to American pilots, he learned that the system was absolutely necessary if the F-104 was to be armed. Due to US military secrecy, the system was not approved for other nations' F-104s for several years. This did not sit well with Rall. When he returned to Germany he sought an immediate meeting with Kammhuber.

"We need the dual-timer system because we have nuclear weapons, too," Rall complained. "There are new tactics, new theories."

"Rall, you have everything you asked for. What's the problem?"

"General, it is now a different situation."

"No, it isn't." retorted Kammhuber. The meeting came to an end with the problem unresolved. The following Sunday Günther received a call from the American embassy.

"Sir," the caller told Rall, "please come by on Monday to sign some documents. You will have your dual timers."

"It took ages," said Rall, "a lot of work, and commitment by various US agency inspectors before we were permitted to have the system installed on our aircraft. But I knew our defenses were useless if we didn't have it."

A few days before the new planes were put into full service at Norvenich, Rall received a call from the base regarding an air show and ceremony to celebrate the F-104 arrivals and observe the first test flights at the airfield. Norvenich was a weapons school and a base for Fighter-Bomber Wing 31. The Norvenich base commander planned to include an acrobatic demonstration of the F-104 by the acrobatics team. Günther was apprehensive about the event and believed it was foolhardy but knew it was not his place to override the commander's decision. Kammhuber and Rall arrived together, unaware they would soon become witnesses to the first Starfighter catastrophe on German soil.

"As we watched, the stunt team came swooping down in diamond formation, low down on the runway and flew a 90-270 maneuver which meant they would do a diving turn 90 degrees to the left and a climbing 270 degree turn overhead back over the runway." The leader, however, came in too low which brought the team into almost vertical contact with a pile of waste deposit at a nearby coal mine. Rall discovered later that the formation leader had never led an acrobatic team before.

Rall and the chief of staff arrived by helicopter at the site. They found nothing but smoke, burning oil, and a single pilot's boot. Blame was laid on human error rather than technical problems. The shock was enormous, however, and all the more so because the air show would be only the beginning of a new series of unprecedented F-104 aerial accidents in Germany.

"I had to assume," said Rall, "the main reason for our crashes was that we'd had no air force for so many years after World War II, and that long interval of time plus learning to fly these supersonic aircraft that required new technical and aeronautical skills, meant we were not prepared to fly them as well as we should."

A Trip to Japan

In 1961 Rall learned from his aide that Japan's Commander Minoru Genda, an elite naval aviator who was a co-planner of the attack on Pearl Harbor, was scheduled to visit Germany during a trip that would include other European countries. Genda would bring with him an invitation for Rall, as the F-104 project officer, to later visit Japan. Günther spent hours preparing a forty-five minute speech about the F-104 he planned to deliver in English until one of Genda's aides called to notify Rall that the speech must be given in the German language.

"Any special reason?" asked Günther. He was a little annoyed because he had timed out the talk to allow for running translations and the switch to German meant a rewrite to keep it within the time limit.

"Genda stopped in England first," the aide explained. "When he arrived, hundreds of British journalists shouted at him, 'General, what about Pearl Harbor?' and he replied, "Ha! We should have continued!' The reply caused a sensation in the British Isles and when the Japanese Parliament was informed the members considered cutting the visit short and bringing the commander back home. Parliament relented but forbade the general to speak English during the remainder of his trip to Europe and released a statement that the unfortunate remark was due to a language misunderstanding."

The Japanese Imperial Army's air division expressed an interest in the F-104. Rall arranged to meet their representatives at Edwards Air Force Base in California, where test flights were conducted for all international air forces. After the test Rall went directly to Tokyo to brief the pilots on America's supersonic jet. He informed his supervisor, Kammhuber, that he intended to fly there on a commercial airliner.

"No, no," protested Kammhuber. "You are our only expert on the F-104. I don't want to risk sending you on a civilian airline." At the time aircraft hijackings were beginning to become prevalent. Rall flew in a military aircraft. A day after he left for Japan two German pilots had landed their F-84s in Berlin in the British zone but had been forced to fly over forbidden Russian airspace by mistake because they'd computed their compasses inaccurately. It created an international incident.

"I was glad to be away because if I had asked to go to Japan after that incident Kammhuber would have said no because he feared World War III could erupt."

On his way, Günther arranged to stop off in Hawaii for the weekend. "I wanted to see Pearl Harbor. I was tremendously moved by the memorial there." Continuing on, bad weather forced a stopover at Wake Island but Rall finally completed the trip to Tokyo as scheduled. However, the German embassy aides were annoyed.

"Where have you been?" they demanded.

"What are you talking about? I said I would be here on Monday and here I am," retorted Rall.

"But today is Tuesday!" Günther was told he had neglected to observe the crossing of the international dateline. He apologized. The three-week visit proved successful and Japan agreed to buy several of the supersonic jets. As a mark of appreciation Rall was

Rall with the F-104G, Memmingen, Germany, 1964

presented with the wings insignia of the Japanese Air Force.

Back in Bonn, in November, Rall was invited to the Japanese Embassy to attend a reception which lasted late into the evening. As a weary Rall drove the eight-hour road trip home to Salem he attempted to overtake a large truck, which swerved, sending a hail of road pebbles onto his windshield, shattering it completely. Rall decided not to stop. The weekend was just beginning and he wanted to be with Hertha, Franci and Feli. Soon, it began to snow. With the blizzard coming through the broken smashed windshield and unable to see ahead, he slowed the car to a crawl, bringing back memories of nursing his crippled Bf

109 back to base in the frozen fields of the Eastern Front. He finally arrived home at 4 a.m., exhausted and bone-chilled. The active weekend he'd envisioned playing with his children turned into two days of hot baths and bed rest. On Monday, he had to fly to a meeting in Rome with those working on the Starfighter project. This time he took the train to the airport.

In 1964, free of his duties as F-104 project manager, Rall took a six-month course at the NATO Defence College, in the Military College complex in Paris where one-third of the students came from the diplomatic corps, one-third from the armed forces, and one-third were economists. Guest lectures were given by ministers of foreign affairs, ministers of finance, and chiefs of staff in the various NATO countries that the students visited as part of the course. English was the common language. "We all spoke it except for the French, who preferred their own tongue. It was all very high-level," said Rall, "and the most interesting course I have ever attended." Upon graduation, Lt. General Count of Baudissin, the dean, testified to Rall's "excellent qualifications" to serve NATO.

Rall's supervisor, Brigadier-General Kulmey, evaluated him as "a driving force, fit to find solutions for recurring problems...skillfully negotiating with international committees...highly respected as an expert by the representatives of the different nations." Kulmey recommended that Rall be promoted to Brigadier General, which he was in due course.

Major-General Dr. Stangl, Günther's division commander at the time, regarded Rall as his best unit commander among his squadron and regiment commanders and offered his own evaluation of the ace's qualities: "Energy, initiative... as well as competence, technical knowledge and organizing abilities."

Rall prepares to pilot the F-104G, 1964

Stangl, too, recommended Rall be promoted.

Soon, Rall was granted yet another promotion. Major-General Mahlke, head of the Office of the German Air Force called attention to Günther's "fresh and youthful character... the energy and drive of his dynamic personality, his vitality, and the personal respect and confidence he has earned from his subordinates. Rall debates with great eloquence, knows how to carry his point, and always remains likeable." On June 12, 1967, the Third Ace assumed leadership of the 3rd Air Force Division in Munster.

On April 1, 1968, Rall was assigned commander of the 1st Air division in Furstenfeldbruck. But driving home from Furstenfeldbruck on a Friday afternoon he collided with another vehicle as it overtook him and pulled in front too closely. The result for Rall was a knee shattered into three pieces, several broken ribs, a pierced lung, and a smashed breastbone. In fact, he almost died. He was unconscious when others pulled him from the car. As he regained consciousness he heard a man ask, "Are you General Rall?"

"I was in civilian clothes but obviously the man recognized me. I nodded. Fifteen minutes later a helicopter arrived to airlift me to the nearest hospital and within an hour I was on the operating table. That man saved my life."

Once again, Günther found himself in a cast and weeks of convalescence but it gave Hertha and their daughters, Franzi and Feli, the opportunity to spend extra time with Günther.

"When I was small he was away a lot," said his youngest daughter, Feli, "but he was always on the television news, talking from the United States about flying and testing jets. On the day of my fifth birthday I saw him on a newscast climbing out of a cockpit in his flight suit. I was convinced that he was on the TV only to wish me a happy birthday, and I waited and waited for him to say, Hello, Feli! but of course, he didn't. When he was home he was a lot of fun, with a great sense of humor but very strict about school and homework. We were well disciplined."

While Rall was recovering from his car accident his division moved to Messtetten, north of Salem, much to the joy of Hertha and their two daughters.

Career Moves

Rall was promoted on May 1, 1969, to Chief of Staff of the 4th Allied Tactical Air Force, ATAF, and relocated to Ramstein, in West Germany. Under his command were American, Canadian and German units. Here, he was billeted in a small hotel. One of the neighbors living in the house next door was Vice Commander of the 17th US Air Force, Chuck Yeager, the first man to break the sound barrier in the Bell XS-1 in 1947.

As a fighter pilot flying his "Glamorous Glennis" P-51 Mustang during World War II Yeager had become an ace at the age of 21, downing five enemy planes in a single day. He was shot down over France but managed to make his way through Spain and finally back to England where, with General Eisenhower's personal approval, he was allowed to return to combat duty. USAF pilots were forbidden to fly again if they'd been shot down over enemy territory because underground partisans who'd helped them escape would be put at risk in case the pilot was shot down again, recaptured, and forced to reveal the names of his rescuers. However, Yeager and many other fighter pilots received permission to sidestep the rule.

"I knew Chuck in Ramstein, and was told that he flew 127 missions in Vietnam," said Rall, "but we weren't close at that time. One thing I approved of, that he often took his leave in my beloved Bavarian mountains, where he hunted for deer."

Rall and Yeager would renew their acquaintanceship in the late 1980s when both were honored guests at the annual "Gathering of Eagles" symposiums at the Air Command and Staff college at Maxwell Air Force Base in Montgomery, Alabama. The events brought wartime aces and peacetime astronauts together for debates.

When presented with the traditional red blazer in appreciation of his participation, Günther was grateful for the gesture but suggested to the organizer, Lt. Colonel David McFarland who became a friend and for whom Rall has the greatest admiration, that for Rall's next visit the jacket color be changed to a less glorious one "so that I could wear it for normal occasions." He was more than surprised to be taken up on his suggestion. The "Gathering of Eagles" blazers are now navy blue.

Günther was soon promoted even higher, close to the top of the ladder, as Division Commander. He was not to wait long for the final rung.

At an air force ball in Baden-Baden, Steinhoff took Hertha aside and had a long discussion with her. That night, she told her husband that Steinhoff was going to recommend that Rall become his successor as Chief of Air Staff. Steinhoff's suggestion was quickly followed up by his colleagues. In December, 1970, Günther became Commanding General of the Luftwaffe as Chief of Air Staff in Bonn while General Steinhoff, in turn, became Chairman of the NATO Military Committee in Brussels.

Each weekend, after a weekday filled with tense debate, negotiations, and decisions, Rall drove home to Salem to spend time with Hertha and their two daughters. The pace was exhausting. The Ralls finally decided they needed to be together

German Air Force Change of Command ceremony, 1970. General Rall becomes Chief of Air Staff, replacing General Johannes Steinhoff, center. Helmut Schmidt is at left.

in one place. Hertha resigned from her position at the Salem School and the family set up housekeeping in Bonn.

"I had needed her there for a long time because NATO wives had many duties to perform, protocol demanded it, but we had wanted to see the children through their school years in one town rather than move them constantly from place to place."

NATO wives were expected to accompany their husbands on official visits to various nations around the world, and the tri-lingual and highly-educated Dr. Hertha Rall fit right in, her diplomatic skills proving a great asset.

In the fall of 1971 Chief of Air Staff Günther Rall paid an official visit to El Paso, Texas, where General Krupinski at the time was the group commander of all the German pilots train-ing in the US. The two were subsequently invited to a high mesa range to observe a missile launch.

"We were with other Germans and Americans watching as the event took place. After the launch we went to a lounge for a drink to await the others after the completion of the launch. We waited a long time. No one showed up. Finally a colonel came to tell us that the missile went down in Chihuahua, Mexico by mistake. Another embarrassed colonel was busy calling the White House to explain."

A few days later Krupinski, now a three-star general, said to Rall, "Günther, we have to go to Flagstaff, Arizona, there's a restaurant there with the best spareribs I've ever tasted. Also, I want to see the cowboys in their hats and boots. They walk right down the streets there, just like anyone else." So the two piled into an army jeep and headed north. "It was Sunday afternoon, around 2 p.m. and we were enjoying these huge ribs. Krupinski kept chomping down and suddenly broke several of his teeth. There was no dentist available on a Sunday, so we had to drive all the way back with Krupinski trying to hold the bits of his teeth together with glue that someone had provided."

One of the most exhilarating highlights of his service in the early 1970s was when Rall received an invitation from the commander of the US 6th Fleet which was deployed in the Mediterranean.

"We went to Athens," related Rall, "with some army generals and boarded a small passenger plane and were flown out to the aircraft carrier *USS Forrestal*. We landed on the deck. I was the only pilot in the group and as a courtesy I was asked if I'd care to take a spin in one of the carrier's F-4 Phantoms. Well, it had been a while since I'd piloted a jet, and certainly I had never been at the controls of a two-seater F-4, nor taken off from an aircraft carrier." But Günther, as always, was game and could resist neither the challenge nor the opportunity to try anything new if it concerned aviation. Outfitted in a flight suit he climbed into the cockpit with an accompanying instructor pilot.

The versatile F-4 fighter bomber, interceptor, escort, and reconnaissance aircraft was the first jet fighter to fly for three US services: the Marine Corps, the Air Force, and the Navy and has flown under the insignia of ten other countries.

"Our take-off was like a cork from a bottle. There was a tremendous push, and once you got away from the deck you could get up to even more speed."

Rall's route took him between Cyprus and Crete, the island he remembered from thirty years earlier that was the scene of the bloody battle between the Allies and the Germans.

"Now Europe was engaged in another war, the Cold War with the Russians, and as we flew in the F-4 I was not surprised to see on the radar scope that a Russian destroyer was escorting, or more precisely, tracking, the carrier. It followed each turn it took." After an hour Rall and the instructor returned to the *Forrestal* and Günther prepared for the landing.

"My God, that ship looked as small as a postage stamp in the ocean. I'd never landed on an aircraft carrier before and I realized it would be slightly different than an airfield. But I'd been briefed. You come in at a speed that is just before stalling, very slowly. There were four tripwires that I could catch with the F-4's tailhook. As soon as I touched I immediately throttled to full power in case I didn't catch a tripwire and would have enough speed to take off again and make another attempt. Believe me, it was quite an experience and fortunately I was lucky enough to catch a wire on the first try." But he realized he no longer possessed the reflexes of a young pilot and decided he would decline any offers of a repeat performance.

Rall stayed overnight to observe the *Forrestal's* night operations. "It was impressive to me how those pilots could see anything, it was pitch dark. It was also darned noisy. From my cabin I could hear each jet as it boinged the wire on landing." He was also impressed with the refueling process the next morning. "A tanker came alongside, traveling at about 20 knots, and I watched with fascination as all the hoses were hooked up between the two ships."

In April, 1974 Steinhoff retired and was instrumental in introducing Rall to the Military Committee as a German member. Rall was appointed NATO's German Military Representative to the Military Committee of NATO, the highest military agency, in Brussels. While the NATO chairmanship was a rotat-

Hertha Rall

ing one and passed to each member country in turn, Günther's new command was permanent.

He took office at a time when in addition to making national decisions on behalf of his country, he was now responsible for international decisions relating to global military affairs. He was also the single aviation expert and linchpin upon which the NATO partners relied. Other air ministers also sought his advice.

"During my service I learned so much about different countries. Hertha and I traveled throughout Europe and the United States, to the Middle East, Turkey, Iran, and India on NATO business."

Rall's last journey while at NATO, although he didn't know it at the time, was early in 1975 and took him to South Africa. A German journalist, formerly a pilot in the new German Air Force, wrote to Rall telling him of a reunion of veteran airmen in South Africa. Subsequently, Rall received an invitation to attend. Although Günther knew it was an unofficial, private trip it was a visit that Rall felt comfortable enough to accept and take his wife Hertha along. It would be great to see old friends once again. The African authorities, however, managed to turn it into a semi-official occasion without Rall's knowledge.

The trip proved unwise. At the time, South Africa was embroiled in the sensitive question of apartheid. During the visit to Capetown a question was raised in the German parliament by a politician demanding to know what German generals were doing in that country. As it turned out the politician was not referring to Rall since he was on a private visit, but was referring to other Germans in South Africa.

A week later the South African embassy in Germany transferred its residence from Cologne to Bonn. During the move private documents were stolen, among them the correspondence regarding the Rall visit. One of the letters suggested that because there had been a rash of kidnappings, Ralls' tickets should be issued under a false name. This letter was leaked to the press, reinforcing the politician's claim of secret dealings. When

Germany's premier national magazine, "Stern," further sensationalized Rall's visit and reported he had talked to high military representatives of South Africa's apartheid regime, the media was in full cry. The visit was then exploited by South African activists who wrote opinion columns in the international media claiming that since the trip was official it indicated that NATO and its representative, Lt. General Günther Rall, were being exploited. During the trip Rall was invited to meet with the chief of the South African Navy, who told Günther that he had fought in the Battle of Crete.

"He said he'd been on a British destroyer in Sudha Bay. I responded," said Rall," by telling him that while he was down there on a ship I was up top in a plane."

Excoriated in the press upon his return to Germany for consorting with South Africa's pro-apartheid government amid calls for a court trial, Günther was devastated. After fighting for his country for the entire length of World War II and risking his life so many times, his colleagues and supporters believed he deserved better. He had only the interests of Germany at heart. How could a vacation trip, albeit a perk, turn his life upside down in this outrageous manner? Deciding he must avoid a scandal and protect the Defense Ministry against further political damage, Rall went to see Georg Leber, the Minister of Defense, to discuss the matter, anxious that his inadvertent action not cast upon NATO any whiff of impropriety.

Rall's resignation was reluctantly accepted and he received an honorary retirement under Section 50 of the German Military Law in December, 1975. He ended his service to NATO, where he had had US, Canadian and German personnel under his command.

"It was a very serious decision for me to make but it was

347

amicable on both sides. I wished to bring no disgrace or hint of it to NATO or my staff. Leber and I are still good friends. I have the highest respect for him and the way he ran his department, and for Helmut Schmidt, Germany's former chancellor whom I consider one of the great statesman of our time."

Rall's contributions to NATO as Chief of Air Staff were among the most progressive of the post-war period. He had overseen the introduction of new weapons systems in the form of jet fighters and bombers. Forced by his principles to end his career two years earlier than planned, Günther was nevertheless given a ceremonial finale by NATO when he retired as a three-star general.

"My father was tremendously upset by the entire episode," said his daughter, Feli. "He has such integrity it was very difficult for him to come to terms with the accusations. It hurt him very much. He actually said very little about it, but we were very close, the four of us, and we knew how he felt. It was awful. The newspapers, magazines and television stations were full of it. I was just beginning my studies in Munich and everyone asked me about it, though they offered their sympathy."

Hertha lent her strength to try to cure the deep personal wound she knew her husband had suffered. "Mother brought my father back into balance," said Feli. "But he didn't dwell on it for too long. His motto has always been to go on, not to forget, but to put it behind you."

When Rall left his NATO post he was presented with a silver plaque from his grateful United States Commander, General Randy Holzapple. The plaque reads:

Salute to Major General Günther Rall
Born to command, there never was a doubt
He would succeed in capturing his goal.
But he has shown to those who cheer him on
That to progress one need not turn his back
Ignore past help, leave loyalty behind.
Indeed it's true he's done the opposite,
For, like a flag with him his principles
Have flown on high, through pleasure and through pain
Swift to decide, when speed will have the day,
His confidence was borne in challenges
He's bravely met, and from his zest for life.
No compromise has marked the way he's gone
Dedication, humility and work
Instead are signs that he is on the job.
Yet he is not a slave to his career
Interests that soar beyond all narrowness
Mark the full man – deep drinker of life's cup.
Tomorrow's his; but so he says is now,
And toward those ends he's patterned what he does.
He's shown to us how rich can be our day
If we will share with him the world ahead.

Randy Holzapple
General, USAF
Commander 4. ATAF
Commander United States Air Force Europe

A Civilian Once More

31
ein und dreizig

Günther and Franzi

Feli and Günther

After moving in 1975 into his three hundred and twenty-year old house with Hertha, Günther Rall didn't stay idle longer than a week. His daughters were now grown, Franzi studying art in Vienna and Rome, and Feli a student in Brussels and later at the Art College of Design in Pasadena, California. The daughters would pursue their own careers, Franzi becoming a top art restorer for international museums including the Louvre in Paris, and Feli opening her own industrial advertising design studio in Munich.

Once word was out that Rall had left NATO he was inundated with offers from the private business sector. Global manufacturers wanted him on their board of directors. His reputation in the aviation industry was well-established and almost unparalleled. His knowledge and expertise had become sought after for decades.

Accepting appointments to the boards of some of Europe's top industrial multi-national corporations that included German companies in the armaments industry, and General Electric, Rall's new career took him as a consultant and advisor to the governments of Russia, Czechoslovakia, the US, the UK, and South America. He was the only civilian to represent the German military aviation industry on GE's board that included British, French, and Italian representatives.

Günther, Virginina Bader, Adolf and Heidi Galland and Johannes Steinhoff, 1986

He was also chairman of the board of a company that supplied NATO with the electronics systems for missiles, and spent many weeks conferring with foreign defense ministers, military chiefs, and air force generals, this time from the other side of the table. In constant demand by different foreign agencies he also went on assignment on the recommendation of the German Defense Ministry to advise the government of Singapore regarding air defenses and their economics.

The ensuing years saw him fulfilling duties at the top levels of international trade with the Phillippines and Hong Kong, and becoming active as a board member and advisor to Ger-

Rall, left, is a guest of honor with Colonel Hub Zemke and Air Vice Marshall Johnny Johnson, at a 1992 symposium

man armaments corporations that included MTU and Buck Chemisch-Technische Werke GmbH, where he was chairman of the advisory board. In 1989, when the Wall dividing East and West Berlin was demolished, most of the industries' military boards were eliminated.

"With the Soviet Union split up there was an entirely different political situation," said Rall. "It was thought that military threats were greatly minimized and the entire military industry

Rall, center, meets with his old adversaries at an operational air base out-side Moscow, at the invitation of Russian Air Force General Andreyev

collapsed."

In 1985 Hertha, eight years his senior, died of a rare disease that affected her nerves and muscles. "She had been skiing, fell, and broke her hip," said Feli. "Soon afterwards she developed a trembling, similar to Parkinson's Disease, but it wasn't that. We thought it was multiple sclerosis, but it wasn't that either. She went from one doctor to another, seeking a diagnosis. In the end, she just stayed home, and died there. She loved the house

Rall checks out the controls in the cockpit of a MiG-29 with General Andreyv, Moscow, 1998

in the Alps and refused to go into a hospital."

As much as the daughters missed their mother, it was a searing blow to Günther, for whom Hertha had been the mainstay of his life. Traveling all over the globe, whether on government or civilian business, he knew that, back home, his wife was the one constant he could rely on. Now she was gone. Günther has never ceased to grieve but, like everything else that has come his way, he has continued to move forward.

357

"He is that rare person," said Feli, "who takes all the trials and tribulations that are handed him, and lives through them, emerging on the other side with more fortitude than ever. It seems he is always having to start again. And he does so. He has never voiced the thought that his life is over, like many do at his age."

Günther Rall celebrated his 72nd birthday in 1990 and remained continually in demand as a speaker and consultant. At times he felt himself slowing down as the decade progressed although none of his family or friends believed it would ever happen to this human dynamo. Indeed, he continued to ski fast, hike long, and fly high. Always seeking out challenges and thriving on them, he nevertheless decided it was time for younger people to take on his work.

"When I was born hardly anyone had a car. Now everyone has at least one car and they have computers in them," he said.

Even though he was now retired and his official functions with the many corporations were ended, companies and government agencies still seek his advice and ask him to undertake missions. Indeed, Rall's opinions are sought by those interested in both what went before and what is to come. Historians constantly ask the general for his views, and he is often contacted to write White Papers and articles. He rarely refuses, still pursuing his goal of helping to ensure respect for his country.

"I believe that Germany needs to be understood, even so many years after World War II. What we experienced, why we did what we did, and why and how we overcame our history still has to be explained. I believe that neither the West nor the East fully understand what made Hitler's Germany act as it did, how we evolved into a war machine, and why we followed the Führer.

But today I think they are beginning to."

The prime mover and shaker behind Rall's efforts to accomplish his goal of explaining Germany to the world was America. He credits the US for helping Germany regain a sense of pride after being submerged in shame and humiliation.

"In addition, we will never forget President George H. Bush for his assistance in the reunification of Germany," said Rall.

Indeed, barely before the smoke had cleared from the ruins of Berlin and other German cities, American corporations and the US Government provided millions of dollars to rebuild the infrastructure, reconstruct factories, and create new neighborhoods. Duplicating its investments of the 1930s, when the New York financial district and transnational corporations subsidized much of Germany's efforts to recover from its defeat in 1918, America once more invested funds to lay the groundwork for the prosperity that Germany enjoys today. "The Luftwaffe is completely Americanized," said Rall. "With all of our pilots now trained in the US, American phrases have become part of our own language. The US, unbelievably generous, put our nation back on its feet with its Marshall Plan, rebuilding our economy and bringing us back to civilization." Germany has also built up close relationships with the rest of Europe, which Rall believes is the only way to keep peace.

"For the first time in our history my country is surrounded by friends instead of enemies," said Rall. He added with a grin, "We no longer chase the Polish, the Hungarians, the Swiss, the French, the Belgians, the Dutch, the Danish or the British."

Having lived through almost a century of German history that began with Emperor Wilhelm II on the throne, then through the Weimar Republic under Friedrich Ebert, followed by the dictatorship of Adolf Hitler, then an occupation by foreign forces, and finally, Germany's emergence as a functional democratic system, Rall feels qualified to offer his thoughts on another organization, the European Community initially known as the Common Market.

"There is no doubt that we need a European military force. We must also endeavor to retain our democracy. This means no German nationalism on the old terms and no system of government based on that outdated term. The old Germany was fiercely nationalistic. The new Germany must resist that. It is imperative that we stand as firm friends with the United States. We have a multi-cultural Europe but we must unite and cooperate, while still maintaining our own identity. This is what the United Nations organization was created for. We must stay together but respect each other's cultural differences. The coalition that President George W. Bush put together to fight the terrorists is extraordinary. He moved with lightning swiftness to bring more than forty nations into agreements of support after the September 11, 2001 attacks on the World Trade Center in New York. I find that remarkable. It was also very wise."

Rall is of the opinion

Günther Rall, 2001

that Russia no longer poses a threat to other nations, only to itself due to its continuing political instability.

Fritz Obleser in 2001

"Since the Soviet Union collapsed it has experienced so many domestic and economic problems, and today, in 2001, the younger President Bush has established what appears to be a closer relationship through his meetings with Russian president Putin. Then there is the question of China. To deal with China, the European Union must cooperate with the United States. I think that later in the 21st century China will be one of the great superpowers, but not yet. We must also be careful that decisions are not made by politicians for their own purposes, as happened with Kosovo. History has proved time and time again that peace is the only way to survive, not force. I wish those Middle Eastern countries would realize this truth."

As a man who dutifully served one of the most intolerant leaders in history, Rall believes that tolerance is the key to global unity.

"For true peace and trust there has to be learning, understanding, communication, and a willingness to accept cultural differences by the peoples of every country. Being united doesn't mean giving up your national identity, it means accepting that we are different from one another. Since World War II there have been more than a hundred and eighty wars and many are still being waged because one side wishes to bend the other to its will. But problems cannot be settled by force. That is an obsolete mentality. We have proven that time and time again. Political problems must be solved by discussion, not arms. Hitler's forces had a very aggressive attitude, it was offensive. NATO's forces take the opposite position, defensive." Comparing the different schools of thought within different nations, Rall pointed out that in his opinion the Western Alliance partners develop aircraft to last a lifetime with the British opting for twenty to twenty-five years, and the Russians for a maximum development effort over as short a period of time as possible.

Recognizing that his own generation tends to cling to the past, the general is ready to pass the torch.

"We must get out of the way and let the younger ones in. My peers have the experience but there are modern problems and modern challenges. If we cannot adjust to them, they must be left to our successors."

Acknowledging that some of the colleagues in his age bracket are stubborn, Rall says he tries as hard as he can to understand current world trends, and move forward.

Part V

Reflections on the War
on the Eastern Front

Before dawn broke on June 22, 1941 thirty Luftwaffe bomber crews in He 111s, Ju 88s and Do 17s took to the air. Their target: ten Soviet airfields. Within hours five hundred German bombers, two hundred and seventy dive bombers and four hundred and eighty fighters were to attack sixty-six other Russian air bases. The effect was not only devastating, it was a total shock to the Soviets. How could Hitler invade? He had signed a treaty with Soviet leader Joseph Stalin.

"Germany broke the treaty with Stalin, there's no arguing that," said Rall. "We didn't even declare war. We just swarmed over the border and kept going. The result was a very different war and attitude compared to the war on the Western Front."

Waged on a more personal level where an instant hatred enveloped Soviet soldiers for the traitorous act of Hitler's Operation Barbarossa, far more emotion was poured into the Red Army's determination to oust the enemy. What the Russians didn't destroy with their scorched earth policy, the Germans did, burning and destroying everything behind them as they retreated from Russia, including killing civilians who were in many cases initially sympathetic to the German cause.

"From the Russian standpoint Germany betrayed Russia. Yet no one talks about the fact that Stalin had detailed plans to invade Western Europe. He made speeches about those plans in

Leningrad. Some historians have said that Stalin used his non-aggression treaty with Hitler to allow Germany to engage the Western Allies, affording Stalin time to build up his forces, especially the Red Army which had lacked leadership after Stalin purged its officers' ranks in 1937. So it is a matter of which dictator trumped the other. We triumphed in the beginning because the Soviets were totally unable to defend themselves when we marched in, and initially they were in complete disarray. For the first few weeks of our invasion they sustained tremendous losses. We scored victory after victory on the ground and in the air because they had no strategies or tactics in place."

While the Wehrmacht's three-pronged invasion in the summer of 1941 devastated Soviet troops and the Russian Air Force, the tide was soon to turn. The Russians were a quick study. Their factories began cranking out military hardware at an astounding pace. They soon picked up German encirclement strategies on the ground, and in the air the VVS copied the Luftwaffe's tactics. Within a year Soviet air power increased and went from strength to strength. By the end of the four-year conflict Russian aircraft vastly outnumbered anything Germany could produce or pilot.

"They not only had the largest tactical air force in the world, they were also assisted by the Allies' Lend-Lease program and there's no doubt they learned how to fight us very quickly," said Rall. In Günther's opinion and most historians, the decisive battles were Moscow, Stalingrad, and Kursk and particularly the fighting in the Kuban. There were three factors that Rall believes doomed Germany's grand scheme to occupy the Soviet Union after its initially successful invasion.

"First, we failed to take Moscow in 1941 because of the winter," said Rall. "We were stopped by the terrible blizzards, yes, but we did force Stalin to move from Moscow. That was a kind of victory. Second, at Stalingrad, we lost our 6th Army and had to retreat. Third, we lost the battle of Kursk, where we had too few tanks, and most of those we had were destroyed. Kursk was mainly an army operation, and when I talked about it to the Russians after the war they considered it was one of those three decisive battles that they said had an impact on the outcome of World War II. We were indeed deep into Russian territory after Operation Barbarossa was launched but if you look at the map you'll see unbelievably vast distances that make up the Soviet Union. That was the core of the problem. We had too few troops to cover those huge expanses of land. The Wehrmacht was actually a victim of that land mass, particularly the Luftwaffe. Our pilots had to be based close to the front lines, where we covered our troops, because the Bf 109 range was so limited. There was no way our pilots could cover that airspace from the North Cape to El Alamein, because we lacked fighter aircraft as well as a transport command. We never recovered from the transport planes lost in Crete. The situation was impossible. And a terrible miscalculation. So we were focused like a fire brigade on the main fire while all the smaller fires had to be left to burn themselves out."

Regarding the Battle of Kursk, he commented: "The Russians had assembled a tremendous force of tanks because they believed an attack was imminent. The Germans weren't prepared to face this force. Our intelligence had reported resistance would be negligible. But within one week the Third Reich's armies were derailed, losing hundreds of tanks, the majority of their Panzer division, on the outskirts of Kursk."

With this success, the destruction of thousands of German tanks, which Stalin considered the turning point of the war, Stalin knew that the Western Allies could successfully launch their own invasion now that Hitler had lost so many tanks.

Günther recalled a remark made by their Soviet pilot, Antonov, who was taken prisoner by III./JG 52 in 1942. Rall, unable to resist bragging, had asked him what he thought of the German situation at the time.

"We are deep into your country," pointed out Rall.

"Yes," said Antonov, "but look at the area you are occupying. It is a mere one-tenth of Russia, which stretches all the way to Siberia. Can Germany contain it all?"

Rall never forgot that remark during his time on the Eastern Front. It had brought him up short and he realized the assessment was correct. Thereafter Rall was continually surprised and angered that Hitler and the high command had not recognized this and taken it into account.

"That was the crux of the war on the Eastern Front, the dilemma that faced our forces. It is a fact that most of the German armies in Russia were never protected by any Luftwaffe fighters or bombers because we were spread so thinly."

The fact that fighting in Soviet Russia was far different than fighting in the West is a familiar one when considering the consequences of Operation Barbarossa. The war on the Eastern Front, remembers Rall, was not only brutal and cold, it was emotional.

"We attacked with no formal declaration of war after Germany and Russia had signed their pact. That was unbelievable to the Soviets, and also to us. It was the height of folly and I knew the Russians would exact a high price for this double-cross."

Consequently, captured Luftwaffe pilots, indeed all German prisoners of war, suffered terribly at the hands of a betrayed

Russia. The Soviets were beyond furious, beyond rage, by Hitler's actions. The Third Reich's second front created for it an enemy that recognized no rules of combat. Neither did it adhere to the tenets of the Geneva Convention created in 1864 when twenty-six nations signed an agreement to abide by humanitarian rules governing prisoners of war, wounded and sick military personnel, civilians in war zones, and Red Cross neutrality. Instead, the Russians vowed to kill every breathing German they could lay their hands on. While this intention was carried out to a large degree, many German prisoners of war were spared and managed to survive through the hellish conditions of their imprisonment and eventually were released and sent home. Rall admits, however, that he has no right to protest against the Soviets, given Germany's treatment of their own prisoners, especially those in the death camps.

Away from civilized Europe and ordered to support troops in the far less populated Soviet south, Rall and III./JG 52 found themselves in a barren land that stretched for vast distances without a single building or road system.

"It was impossible for our military forces to cover this gargantuan space. Invasion wasn't the problem; occupation was. How were we to hold on to this never-ending landscape? On top of that was the terrible weather, the winter that came early that year and was rated the worst in a hundred and fifty years. Napoleon experienced the same problem in 1812. He was forced to retreat after an attack on Moscow due to the bitter cold that arrived months sooner than expected. The awful winter defeated Napoleon but we didn't learn from this history."

For Hitler's Eastern Front forces, conditions were at their worst in the south.

"In St. Petersburg, the north, our military fought a steady

war with no great troop movements," said Rall. "A couple of Luftwaffe units there had permanent quarters and air bases. They requisitioned houses, estates and farms for their use. There were towns and cities where they could buy food and supplies. In the south, where the Russian steppe was semi-arid desert, it was far more primitive and inhabited sparsely by peasant farmers. In addition, because of rapidly changing war operations our pilots were required to cover long distances. We faced enormous, empty expanses of terrain and there was a sad lack of equipment and supplies," said Günther.

"It was no surprise that we were destined to fail. Roads in the southern region were non-existent so the difficulties of moving III./JG 52 with all its ground personnel and equipment forty-four times over a two-year period as the Russians pushed us back was to be expected. We rarely knew where we'd sleep that night. Our reconnaissance planes would search out a meadow that looked unlikely to be attacked and we'd trek to it, forced to make dozens of detours when we came upon gullies, craters, and streams along the way.

"The snow was always deep so we'd spend precious daylight hours clearing a strip for a runway and space for the tents that were our sleeping and living quarters. As the Red Army advanced we continually fell back, often three days in a row. The logistical problems were almost insurmountable. We couldn't use heavy trucks because they'd get bogged down, and we were short of air transportation."

A small number of Ju 52s were available but they offered prime targets for the VVS and most were shot down. So many of the aircraft were lost that none were left for training new recruits at pilot training schools in Germany – a big mistake.

"In 1942 during the battle of Crete Island, one hundred and

seventy Ju 52s had been destroyed and never replaced, another mistake that was to slow us down." The fighter pilots of III./JG 52 found themselves having to ferry equipment in their planes as best they could. The cockpit of a Bf 109 was one of the smallest of any fighter plane, including the diminutive Spitfire whose pilot practically filled the entire space, so cargo room was scant.

By now the remnants of the forces that so successfully and definitively launched Operation Barbarossa were no longer intent on conquering Russia but trying to prevent the advance of Russian troops into central Europe. The tables were turned.

Added to these factors was the Allies' Lend-Lease program, sending the Soviets hundreds of A-20 Havoc and B-25 Mitchell medium bombers as well as other aircraft, armaments, equipment, and, of course, financial aid.

Commenting on factors affecting the Russian forces, Günther's perspective was that the Soviet Air Force's tremendous losses in the beginning of the German onslaught demonstrated that their crews were poorly trained. They had no effective aerial combat tactics and flew obsolete equipment compared to Western standards. Their mainstay in 1941 was the Polikarpov I-16 fighter, nicknamed Rata, that hadn't been modified since service in Spain in 1936. Nevertheless, the Rata was a tough little aircraft with innovative characteristics that included retractable landing gear, a variable-pitch propeller for a fast drop or rise in rpm, and cantilever wings for maneuverability. Later versions manufactured in the greatest numbers during the German invasion of Russia included the I-16/24 and the I-16/24B. The aircraft had a range of 373 miles, ten more than the Luftwaffe's Bf 109. The earlier Rata's two 20-mm machine guns were on the fuselage and were well outmatched by the 109 E's dual cannons and machine guns. However, as the Eastern Front war escalated and Russian production increased, two machine guns were added for the I-16/24s.

"At first the Soviet pilots flew using completely wrong tactics. They were like a swarm of bees, circling around instead of selecting a target, coming in, and making a kill. So in the beginning of the war on the Russian Front, they suffered tremendous aircraft losses even though they had a huge number of aircraft."

The Soviets had built up the largest fleet of bombers in the world by 1940 but between June and September 1941 they lost seven thousand planes. Structured to support the Red Army, the VVS was totally under its command, leading to anger and frustration on the part of the Russian pilots. However, they soon learned to rebuild quickly, moving their manufacturing facilities well beyond the Luftwaffe's reach behind the Ural Mountains. Here, the Soviets built more modern aircraft: the MiG, Yak and LaGG series, which proved comparable to those in Western fleets.

Adding to their airborne arsenal was the Allies' Lend-Lease program. Between 1941 and 1945 the Lend-Lease aircraft that were sent to the VVS included a mix of almost ten thousand fighters: P-39s, P-40s, P-47s, and P-63s. In addition, the Russians received close to four thousand bombers.

"This saved the Russians," said Rall. "We now found ourselves up against the B-25 bomber, the Spitfire, and the P-39 Airacobra, all on loan to the Soviets." The Airacobra, in particular, was powerful and its aerodynamics and maneuverability were admired but in Lt. General Obleser's opinion, the Airacobra had one disadvantage: it burned too easily.

The VVS pilots, too, had changed. They were a quick study and soon adopted the German's *rotte*.

"They caught on to our tactical formations and copied

them," said Rall. "It became evident to us that they soon became very confident and powerful. Their morale was unbroken. As their victories mounted they created fighter pilots like Colonel I. N. Kozhedub, Colonel Alexandr Pokryshkin, and G.A. Rechkalov, the top-scoring Soviet aces."

Pokryshkin's career started out badly. Flying a new MiG-3 on a mission to intercept German bombers, he came across a group of planes he didn't recognize. Firing an initial burst and watching his victim plummet, Pokryshkin saw the Soviet's red stars on the burning fuselage. To his horror he had fired on friendly aircraft, a new Su-2 dive bomber that his unit had never seen before. The Su-2 was the first Russian plane to house a machine gun in a rear turret.

When the Russians began equipping the LaGG 5 and 7 with radial engines Rall discovered they were impossible to catch. "I chased them full power," said Rall, "but they were always beyond range. It was frustrating.

"The Russian pilots also learned a few tactical combat lessons, picking up pointers from their enemies. They caught on to our tactical formations very fast and copied them. It became evident to us that they soon felt confident and powerful."

After the Lend-Lease program brought Western aircraft to the Soviet Union, Pokryshkin is said to have proclaimed that his favorite plane was the American-built P-39 Airacobra because of its ground-attack capability.

Reflections on the War on the Western Front

T he legacy of World War I was a yoke around the neck of Germans, including Günther Rall. He attributes much of the terrors of World War II, the Holocaust, deprivations, and faltering economies to the consequences of the Great War that began in 1914.

As a small child Rall experienced the 1918 defeat of his country through a lack of food, clothing and services although his family lived in relative comfort compared to the hundreds of thousands of displaced who were homeless and starving.

"A great deal of literature was written about the Great War after the armistice was signed in 1918," said Rall. "Year after year it was continually discussed, re-played, re-lived, and re-fought. Everyone debated the reasons for its outbreak, Germany's mobilization of its forces, our decision to invade Belgium, France, the Netherlands and Russia in 1914, and the war mushrooming."

All-consuming subjects like unemployment, inflation, and the breakdown of the German economy were often favorite discussions whenever people got together, whether at social or family gatherings. The Great War and its catastrophic consequences for the Weimar Republic were never far from German thoughts after their defeat in 1918 and marked the end of the democratic system, leaving Germans to look for a leader. There was high social unrest, political instability, a change of government every year, and extremes of viewpoints.

"However, this was not the case after World War II. By then, we were sick of our misery, tired of hearing Hitler's name, and fed up with everything that reminded us of our second crushing defeat."

Like most post-war historians Rall points to Germany's World War I loss as the reason for the establishment of so many new political parties, at least thirty-six and most of them radical – Communists, the National Socialist Workers Party, the German Workers' Party, the Working Group of Combat Organizations – all clamoring for votes as they promoted their various agendas.

"Everyone said they had the solution to the Weimar Republic's problems. Middle of the road moderates were not strong. It was the radicals who led the way, who had the loudest voices. Then, in June, 1933, all the political parties except for the National Socialist Party, the Nazis, were forced to disband. And Hitler came into power. He grabbed the reins and took off."

In Rall's view, Hitler's meteoric rise was mainly due to a vanquished Germany searching to regain its soul. "We, the German people, were like fruit ripe for the plucking. Hitler appeared to present a viable solution to all our problems. But we didn't expect another war. We were duped into trusting his claims that we were being held down by the huge monetary compensations we had to pay to the victors of World War I. In addition, all of our colonies and pieces of our land were given to the Belgians, the French, and the Polish. We did not have enough agricultural areas left to cultivate crops for food and cattle. Hitler told us he wanted to give our poor farmers and starving people more farmland. The truth is, Hitler needed more resources, oil, coal, and metals to build and fuel the military's artillery, planes, and tanks, that he needed for his war machine."

Yet Hitler and Göring were shocked when England and France declared war on Germany one day after the German Army invaded Poland. After all, Britain and France had done nothing when Czechoslovakia was overrun.

"We learned, after the war," said Rall, "that Hitler had been told, wrongfully but innocently, as it turned out, by our German ambassador to England, Joachim von Ribbentrop, that England and France would not object to Hitler's incursions upon other nations." Hitler trusted Ribbentrop's views as that of a well-traveled cosmopolitan, since Hitler himself had never left the Continent.

As Rall remembers it, the Third Reich totally believed Ribbentrop's assurances that England would never again go to war against Germany. However, the British ambassador to Germany, Sir Nevile Henderson, disputed that assertion and did all he could to persuade Hitler that Ribbentrop was wrong. "But Hitler didn't believe Henderson" said Rall. "Yet the truth was, Ribbentrop didn't know how to judge the British mentality. He spent very little time in England, he was always in Germany building up his political career. Henderson had been a true and good friend to Germany but his word in this instance held no weight."

Joachim von Ribbentrop was hardly a role model of diplomatic courtesies. He had already proved he was oblivious to the sensibilities of the British, especially its strict adherence to protocol when, upon presenting his ambassadorial credentials to King Edward VIII on October 30, 1936 at Buckingham Palace, Ribbentrop stunned the monarch with a full "Heil Hitler!" Nazi salute.

On September 3, 1939, the German nation was almost as surprised as Hitler to find itself once more in full war mode with England and France. The Führer had not envisioned the two countries declaring war against him. He had counted on his agreement with Neville Chamberlain to keep England out of war. But when Hitler invaded Poland, with which England and France had treaties, then all bets were off.

"Hitler announced to the nation that the Polish had attacked a German radio station and that therefore we must retaliate by going to war," said Rall. "We learned later this was untrue. They took a prisoner from one of the concentration camps, dressed him in the uniform of a Polish soldier and took him to the German radio station where they shot him. His body was then displayed to the press as a member of an assault party. At the time we were fired up with indignation when we read Hitler's official version of it."

The staged incident gave Germany the excuse to march in to Poland but the German people were not enthusiastic about a second war within twenty years. Every family had lost someone in World War I. For the Ralls the new development brought back memories of Günther's uncle, Ernst Heinzelmann, whose story had become part of their family history.

An artist and architect, he volunteered in 1914 as an infantryman, was promoted to captain, and two years later fought and saw his army routed in the Battle of Verdun, France. When Ernst went off to war his mother had gone to live with his sister in Essenlingen.

"One day, my grandmother was taking a midday nap, when she heard her name called, awakening her. She asked her daughter, Gustl, if she had called her," relates Rall. "The daughter said, No, I didn't. My grandmother heard her name called once again. And then a third time. For some reason, my grandmother checked the wall clock, then she again told Gustl she was sure someone had called her name. They both instinctively knew that something had happened. One week later an army aide arrived with Ernst's uniform, stained with dried blood. The aide told the women that Captain Heinzlmann had died on the day and at the exact time my grandmother heard her name called, and was buried in France." The grandmother's experience is not an uncommon occurrence. There have been numerous re-countings of such events during wartime.

"I believe it really happened," said Rall, who still treasures the brass collar buckle the aide gave Ernst's mother from her son's army jacket, and his medal, Wurttemburg's highest honor, for bravery.

Rall's new belief, his new political attitude, is that racism is outmoded. We have to live together, he insists. That is the only way, at the end. This is a great period for a potentially united world.

"There's no doubt that Germany will pay for the next one thousand years for Hitler's actions. Hitler failed because of his insane approach to the troops and the troops never forgot it. We were a grand nation at the beginning of Hitler's power. Ninety percent of the younger generation, I among them, was dedicated to a certain idea. It was all so patriotic, we were bursting with pride. How could we not be, knowing that this leader, who had come from humble beginnings, would give us back our spirit? We were so committed to his vision, which gave no hint of the horrors that were to come. When I think back, I am still angry that our nation was cheated by Hitler. That will never go away for me."

Rall, not shy about stating his strong opinions on most World War II decision-makers, is full of praise for the US Marshall Plan and the US Berlin Airlift, although he adds a caveat:

"I wish the Allies had thought through its war-ending strategy more thoroughly. They insisted on unconditional surrender. That meant the Germans were forced to fight to the death. There was no effort to work out a compromise. We wanted to save our country from further ruin. Hitler was dead. What was the sense in continuing to fight? But Eisenhower gave the [Soviet] hammer and sickle permission to destroy Germany completely. Reagan and Bush were the only US presidents to encourage East and West Germanys to finally unite. That reunification was a historical necessity. It was difficult but Bush was a wonderful diplomat and made it happen."

Reflecting on the Battle of Britain, Rall still gets irate when remembering the fate of downed Luftwaffe fighter pilots, laying the blame firmly upon the lack of planning and foresight by Reichsmarschall Göring.

"One reason we lost the air fight in England was because our pilots were shot down over that country or the Channel, taken prisoner and sent to Canada for the rest of the war. By comparison, British and American pilots who were shot down during the Battle of Britain were usually flying over friendly skies, so they could bail out and return to their nearby bases to fly missions again the next day."

Rall's service on the Western Front was relatively brief – a few months at the beginning of World War II, and a year fighting for the home defense 1944-1945.

As Germany's cities were destroyed by American aircraft by day and by the British at night, the Luftwaffe found itself faced with unending streams of bombers.

"It was an impossible contest. Both sides knew it. Why the

Allies kept on bombing our cities so fiercely is a mystery to me. It wasn't necessary. I suppose it was to terrorize the German people, but to my mind this strategic concept of Winston Churchill's was wrong. Wipe out our military, yes, but not civilians and the civilian infrastructure. Sure, we also made massive air strikes, especially over London, but we soon abandoned that tactic. It didn't work. In fact, it had the reverse effect. It made the Brits all the more determined to oppose us. The same thing happened in Kosovo when the Allies bombed, encouraging those in opposition to Milosevic to join him. In World War II we concentrated on hitting naval, air force and military installations. The air raids on Coventry in 1940 were to hit military production facilities there but we bombed the medieval cathedral and civilians as well. That was a mistake."

Churchill wrote in his post-war biography that the English knew of the impending air raid because they had broken the German code but in order to prevent the Germans from learning this, they allowed the raid to go forward. More devastating was the destruction of Hitler's refineries, communication lines and transportation systems, most notably railways. Like the rest of Europe, Germany relied heavily on trains to deliver people and goods to their destinations and during World War II virtually all trains were diverted strictly to military use. Civilians wishing to travel needed permits on both sides of the English Channel.

The manner of the ending of World War II, with the Allies forcing an unconditional surrender, is a sore spot with General Rall.

"If the American generals had agreed to discuss a surrender, we could have saved many lives. We were ready for such a discussion. Ninety percent of our population had come to hate Hitler. Look how many assassination attempts were made on his life by those of his own high command. We wanted to save our country, not have it bombed out of existence. I think this was a colossal mistake on the part of the Allies."

He paused. Then continued.

"Because of that, the Russians came in and were permitted to split the country. Yes, we are reunited now, thanks to the assistance of former President George H. Bush."

Pilot Characteristics

What makes a successful fighter pilot? And how did some German pilots manage to pile up hundreds of victories each? These are two of the most frequently asked questions that Günther encounters. Here are the definitive answers in his own words:

"There were two choices for a German pilot in World War II: an Iron Cross or a wooden one! What is their psychological make-up? It is difficult to generalize. Some men are quiet, some noisy. While an officer with a reputation for taking huge risks might be considered good potential as a fighter pilot that is not always the case. Risk must be tempered with good sense. Some scientists want to study and discover what makes them tick but it is impossible. An aggressive personality can be a help or a hindrance.

In the end it is the performance that reveals how a pilot fights. There are several factors that affect the performance of a fighter pilot even if he has perfect skills. First, the target in the air must be forced into a vulnerable position and that's not easy. You must know how to trick your opponent into making moves that you know will place him in danger.

Then, you have to calculate the capabilities and maneuverability of your plane and that of your prey in order to shoot him down, that's why pilot training includes a deep understanding of the characteristics of the enemy's aircraft as well as your own.

In addition, the duration of a dogfight comes into play, for example how long your Bf 109 can hold a turn, a dive, an ascent, and what each move means to your fuel supply. Every demand you make on the throttle is a drain on the tank.

You also have to figure out how you're going to handle the fight while you're in the midst of it. A fighter pilot has virtually no time to make decisions, it is totally an instant action-reaction moment that is today called situational-awareness but reaction must be coupled with reason. That's where experience comes in and why the Luftwaffe suffered such great losses in 1944 and 1945 when we had to call on young, untrained pilots. They were keen and knew how to fly but the difference between theory and practice in aerial combat is the difference between life and death. Actual conditions cannot be taught; you must personally live through them to come out the other side unscathed. Today, jet fighter pilots experience near-reality with sophisticated simulators but during World War II we had none of those.

In addition, it should be noted that successful fighter pilots have a natural instinct, a sixth sense, for what to do at any given moment. It's an inborn gift. An almost uncanny ability to read your opponent's mind, and know how to forestall him, to be one jump ahead and figure out which way he'll turn and when he'll shoot. Hartmann was the perfect example of having this talent.

And the last but perhaps the most important factor of what makes a successful fighter pilot is emotion. There must be the passion to fly, the agreement to put your life on the line for your country, the intense will to win, the fire in the belly, and one hundred percent unswerving self-confidence to take on all challenges.

How did Germany's air force come up with the highest scores during World War II? Every nation had a mix of excellent fighter pilots, average, and poor. What made the difference was that certain conditions had to be present. The first was to find a target in the air. For us, that was easy. We had too many targets in the air wherever we went, whether it was over Germany, Russia, France, the Ukraine, anywhere. It wasn't difficult to pick them off, there were plenty to choose from. I suppose that's because we had the most enemies.

The second condition is the duration of your tour of duty. For instance, my tour lasted five and a half years straight, except for the total of fifteen months that I spent in different hospitals. In the USAF you were sent home once you're wounded and that was the end of your service unless you requested to come back, like Chuck Yeager, but not in the Luftwaffe. I went back to the front to fight after each of my three injuries and after eight crashes. There was never any question of my not returning to my unit. If American pilots were lucky enough to survive fifty missions, they went home. Many of them never saw a German fighter plane because we were so few compared to the Allies, so fifteen victories for an American fighter pilot was a tremendous feat. The same for the British pilots. They flew two hundred hours, and that was the end of their duty. In contrast, Luftwaffe pilots never stopped flying. We flew continually from the beginning of the war to its end. I was helped into my cockpit after breaking my back, and once or twice with a concussion from a crash. Specht flew with one eye, Rudel with one leg, and Petermann, an NCO who was in my wing, flew with an artificial hand. It wasn't easy to keep driving yourself to fly as many as four or five missions a day but we kept at it. Of course, our lengthy service gave us the opportunity to rack up huge scores and the adrenaline never stopped rushing.

Thirdly, a fighter pilot has to have a certain temperament, exceptional eyesight, and quick responses. You have to have an insatiable desire to be a fighter pilot. You must be able to pick out your enemy before he spots you, and know which position puts you in the most advantageous place. We knew that if we could come in with the sun at our backs we held the trump card but this wasn't always possible.

Finally, you have to recognize that you must accept the conditions of each dogfight whatever situations are forced upon you. And they can be infinite.

HEADQUARTERS SIXTY SECOND FIGHTER SQUADRON
AAF STATION F-150, APO 637
U. S. ARMY

Personal Combat Report
VIII Fighter Command F.O. No.337

a. Combat
b. 12 May, 1944
c. 62nd Fighter Squadron
d. 1230 hours
e. Vicinity Frankfurt
f. 2/10 cloud at 6,000'
g. Me 109
h. One Me 109 claimed Destroyed.
i. "I was leading Icejug Squadron when Red Leader calle
in four bogies. I did not see them and told Red Leader, Lt. Greene, to init
an attack. He headed toward them and I saw them then. Red Leader fired at
the tail end 109 and the e/a started smoking and spun into the ground. No c
appeared. I started after one of the 109's at 22,000' and finally caught hi
on the deck. I fired a burst out of range then held my fire. I then fired
another burst at about 350 yds. hitting the 109 all over the left wingroot a
tail. The 109 started streaming glycol. I then started a long chase throug
Germany, below the tree tops. My guns were not firing too well, and sometime
only one would be firing. After about 5 minutes of this, the 109 stopped st
ing glycol and started trailing black smoke. I kept taking pictures of him
hoping he was going to hit. Finally small blue flames began to come out of
exhaust ports and the engine began to burn. The 109 crashed into a small fie
on the outskirts of a small town. He skidded along on his belly and then fl
over on his back and started burning. My wingman, F/O Vitale, who had done
wonderful job of staying with me throughout, fired at this time.
                    Since there was nothing further to shoot at, we came
home.

F/O Vitale."   I claim one Me 109 Destroyed, sharing with my wingman

                                        JOE H. POWERS, JR.,
                                        Capt., Air Corps.

Capt. Joe H. Powers, Jr.,   ARMAMENT REPORT
                                42-76363   947 rounds AP/I/T

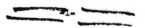

HEADQUARTERS FIFTY SIXTH FIGHTER GROUP
Office of the Commanding Officer
APO 637   U. S. ARMY

Personal Combat Report
VIII Fighter Command F.O. #337

Colonel Hubert Zemke

    a. Combat
    b. 12 May 1944
    c. 53rd Fighter Squadron, 56th Fighter Group
    d. 1145 hours
    e. 30 miles south to S.S.W. of Koblenz, Germany
    f. Clear with a bad haze layer from 12,000 feet down
    g. 1 Me 109
    h. 1 Me 109 destroyed

    i. Because of the peculiar circumstances of this mission, the narrative in my mind must begin much earlier than just the last battle and destruction of the Me 109 claimed destroyed.

    Three of us, Lt. Col. Preston Piper and 2nd Lt. W. D. Johnson and myself, had moved out to scout an area north of Frankfurt when we were bounced from above by seven Me 109's. During this engagement, my two wingmen were shot down. I have no idea of how many the two pilots may have damaged or even destroyed, but believe there were none. My escape was by outspinning and diving the enemy. As I flew westward toward home, another four Me 109's jumped me over Weisbaden and in the ensuing defensive battle, I was again just able to elude the enemy. After outrunning these aircraft, a course of 290° Magnetic was again set for England.

    South of Koblenz about four enemy aircraft were seen circling at 15,000 feet, my altitude at the time being approximately 20,000 feet. My first intention at the moment was to bounce these planes by using this superior altitude and pulling off none. I had hardly circled before several more FW 190's and Me 109's were seen to assemble with the original four. Gradually their strength built up until an estimated thirty enemy aircraft were circling below and gradually increasing their altitude as they assembled.

    I continued to circle above them calling for help to the other members of the 56th Fighter Group, who were spread in the Koblenz-Frankfurt area. The purpose being that we could pull a kill on these enemy aircraft.

    For more than fifteen minutes, I continued to circle above this concentration. As they climbed, I moved up until my final altitude was approximately 25,000 feet. At this point I was finally throwing contrails which were picked up by 2nd Lt. Rankin and his wingman, Lt. Glen C. Thornton. These two pilots moved up to within a half mile and I told them to give me top cover while I bounced the enemy circling below.

    The dive was fairly steep and a lonesome Me 109 was picked up on the outer portion of the Lufberry below. By the time I was in firing position he presented a 60 to 90 degree shot and over two rings of lead were laid off before squeezing the trigger. The fire of my tracers were well ahead of him and I allowed him to fly thru the bullet pattern. At no time did I see a terrific explosion but several hits were seen over the entire length of the fuselage.

Personal Combat Report,
VIII Fighter Command F.O. 337,
Colonel Hubert Zemke,
Page 2.

At the point where I was about to ram him, the stick was pulled back abruptly and my airplane zoomed up into a climbing turn. Looking back, the Me 109 was seen to do two sloppy flick rolls which wound up into a spin whereupon the engine burst into flames and the pilot bailed out. Because of being so elated, the fact was announced over the radio but just soon enough for me to hear Lt. Rankin announce to "break left" as there was an Me 109 on my tail. This plane was never seen for Lt. Rankin was down on top of my position and away just as I entered into combat with four more Me 109's. However, seen far below during this combat, was an airplane on fire which was spinning down. This may have been the enemy aircraft Lt. Rankin shot from my tail. My further action was to break into the four Me 109's, do a half roll to the west and out-run them. The gasoline gauge registered but one hundred and twenty-five gallons of gasoline, so after the last enemy fighters gave up, I cut everything back to the absolute minimum and moved off home by myself.

HUBERT ZEMKE,
Colonel, Air Corps,
Commanding.

HEADQUARTERS SIXTY FIRST FIGHTER SQUADRON
AAF STATION F-150, APO 637
U. S. ARMY

Encounter Report
VIII Fighter Command F.O. No. 337

1st Lt. Robert J. Rankin   Whippet Red One

a. Combat (air)
b. 12 May, 1944
c. 61st Fighter Squadron, 56th Fighter Group
d. 1200 - 1230
e. N/W of Marburg, South of Coblenz
f. CAVU
g. Me-109's
h. 5 Me-109's destroyed, 2 Me-109's damaged

i. I was leading Whippet Red flight and at 1155 Whippet White leader called in 25+ enemy fighters below him. I was about 20 miles away at the time. I started with my flight towards Whippet White leader. On the way to join him I ran into 25+ Me-109's climbing up in a left turn at approximately 19,000 ft. apparently forming up to attack the bombers. I attacked the last two of this formation. They saw our flight coming and dropped their belly tanks. I fired a short burst at 350 yards in a diving turn to the left. The Me-109 split s'd for the deck and I went with him. I fired another short burst with my nose blacking out the e/a. We continued straight down and I didn't fire again. I noticed the e/a's wings jerking violently trying to pull out. I saw he wasn't going to make it. I pulled out at 1500 ft. indicating 525 m.p.h. as the e/a crashed in flames in a small town. I claim this Me-109 destroyed. I started climbing up for altitude and when I reached 8,000 ft. I saw another Me-109 diving about 20° angle going East. I called my flight to push everything forward and we closed without any trouble. The e/a was in a slight turn left. I closed to good range, fired a very short burst and got a good concentration of hits on fuselage and engine. E/a's canopy flew back and just missed my wing man. The pilot bailed out but chute did not open. This was at 2,000 ft. The e/a crashed into the ground and exploded. I claim this Me-109 destroyed. We started climbing up again when F/O Gerick (Whippet Red 3) called in a FW-190 on the deck. He went down to attack and I lost him and Whippet Red 4 at this time. I kept climbing up and heard Fairbank leader (Col. Zemke) calling for help. I flew for 10 minutes climbing, flying on vector 240°. I joined Col. Zemke south of Coblenz. He was alone, circling above 30+ Me-109's. I called and told him I was joining him. He immediately went down to attack and I gave him cover as 30+ Me-109's pulling contrails passed directly over me and my wingman. This box of e/a kept right on course toward the bombers and didn't bother us at all. I saw Col. Zemke destroy 1 Me-109 which blew up and went down covered in flames. As Col. Zemke pulled up from his attack I called him and said I was going down to attack. I got behind 2 Me-109's and fired on the one on the left, got good hits; grayish black smoke came back and landing gear came down. I moved over on the next one. I got many hits from dead astern and this e/a smoked ladly and his landing gear also came down. I had both of these Me-109's in front of me going down in 50° angle smoking and landing gear down. I saw both e/a crash into the ground very close to each other and explode. I claim these 2 Me-109's destroyed. Altitude, 15,000 to 10,000 feet.

CONFIDENTIAL

Encounter Report
1st Lt. Robert J. Rankin
VIII Fighter Command F.O. 337
Page Two

I was coming around in a turn to the left about 15,000 ft. with many e/a still circling below. I was getting into range of 2 in formation and one ahead slightly above, when for no reason, all three pilots of these aircraft bailed out. All the chutes opened. I didn't fire, my wing man didn't fire, neither did Col. Zemke. There were no other Allied fighters in this area at all. I couldn't figure this one out for all three Me-109's seemed to be in no trouble. I make no claim on these. I was still climbing to the left when I got on 2 more Me-109's. I got in a very tight circle with them and fired a short burst at each. I was unable to observe results as deflection blacked out the e/a. I claim these 2 Me-109's damaged. Just after this I saw 1 Me-109 came up from the box of e/a and climb up underneath Col. Zemke. I called him to break and turned to get on the Me-109's tail. I managed to turn with him, fired a short burst, got a few hits and this e/a started down with a very little smoke coming back. One landing gear came down at about a 20° angle. I broke into two more Me-109's which were coming in on my wing man. As I turned I saw the pilot bail out of the e/a I had just fired on. We circled with the 2 Me-109's until my wing man had to break down and away. I kept circling with the 2 Me-109's while my wing man came up and fired at one of the e/a head on. I saw hits with glycol and smoke pouring back. The pilot bailed out as the Me-109 started down. I confirm this Me-109 as destroyed by Lt. Cleon Thornton. We circled with the one remaining Me-109. I got on his tail, fired a short burst when my tracers came and I ran out of ammunition. I closed to 50 yards dead astern and could only take a nice picture. We circled 3 or 4 times and managed to break off and head home low on gas and both of us out of oxygen. We had combat for a full 25 minutes ranging from 23,000 ft. to 1,500 ft. This was my wing men's first mission and he did the best job of flying wing I have ever seen.

I claim 5 Me-109's destroyed and 2 Me-109's damaged.

I confirm one Me-109 destroyed by Col. Hubert Zemke and one Me-109 destroyed by Lt. Cleon Thornton.

j. 1410 rds .50 cal A.R.I.

ROBERT J. RANKIN
1st Lt., Air Corps

For confirmation see Encounter Report of 2nd Lt. Cleon Thornton. Also see Encounter Reports of Col. Zemke, F/O Steven Gerick and 2nd Lt. James M. Jure.

CONFIDENTIAL

Epilogue

One of the places Günther Rall regularly visits near his home is a local cemetery that dates back to the ninth century. It belongs to the Church of St. Zeno which is famous for its basilica, the largest north of the Alps. The cemetery is where Hertha Rall is buried. Marking her grave, covered in fresh flowers even in the depths of winter, is an intricate Austrian-style wrought iron sculpture crowned with a curved gold bar rather than the flat marble or stone slab that marks most German graves.

Like those of his fellow townspeople who still remember Rall occasionally stops at another spot, this one against the wall in the cemetery, where a gravesite honors twelve Frenchmen who fought in World War II for the German side. On the anniversary of their deaths each year a wreath bearing a French tricolor ribbon is placed at the foot of the small monument which is topped with a battered German World War II helmet that belonged to one of the men.

The story of these Frenchmen is unusual. They were members of the 33. SS Waffen-Grenadier-Division der Charlemagne franzosische Number 1 that fought with Germany in World War II against the Russians and included Dutch, Danes, Norwegians, Belgians and Spanish soldiers, a little known but surprising fact. Others were from Switzerland, French Indo-China, Sweden, and

Japan. The division's men were from various collaborationist organizations that had been forced out of France and fought mainly
on the Eastern Front.

"They joined with Germany in the spirit of trying to keep
Europe free from Soviet occupation," said Rall. "None of us
wanted to be ruled under the iron fist of Stalin and these men
decided that fighting with the Germans was the best way to
prevent a Soviet occupation of Europe. But, like us, they were
misled by Hitler's idealism."

Rall related the story of the twelve Frenchmen who are buried in the St. Zeno cemetery:

"As the Allies arrived on the outskirts of town in 1945 during the final days of the war, they caught up with what remained
of the Charlemagne Division and held them captive," said Rall.
"A Frenchman wearing the uniform of an American general approached and asked if they weren't ashamed to be fighting in a
German uniform. One of them replied, 'General, do you think
you look better in an American uniform?' Whereupon the French
general told the twelve to kneel down. Then each was executed,
shot in the back of the head. We all still feel deep shame and
sorrow that their own countryman would massacre them in cold
blood, without trial, and there was nothing anyone could do to
stop it. It was a callous, unnecessary act. One of thousands of
atrocities that were committed by both sides. But these Frenchmen had fought where their conscience had led them. That's
why we honor them every year."

In addition to the gravestone in the churchyard there is another memorial at a clearing in the woods near a marble quarry
half a mile away where the executions took place. Attached to
both memorials is a grainy black and white photograph taken at
the time of the executions showing the hapless Frenchmen lined

up awaiting their fate. The photos are a stark, miserable reminder of man's inhumanity to his fellow man.

Lt. General Günther Rall's life continues to be lived to its fullest. The Third Ace receives hundreds of invitations to address military organizations all over the world. One of his favorite activities is chatting with other aviation enthusiasts. Among his most recent travels was a trip to Prague, the capital of Czechoslovakia, where he was asked to append his signature to hundreds of military books written about World War II.

"The year 2000 was the first time that these Western books were translated into the Czech language," he said. The bookstore was swamped with aviation enthusiasts eager to meet heroic World War II pilots from various sides of the battle. The event was the anniversary of a massive raid by the US 15th Air Force, stationed in Italy, on December 17,1944. Czechoslovakia at that time was under occupation by Hitler's armies. The Americans were making an assault on the Czech oil refineries and mineral mines at Silesia, on the Polish-Czech border, and were attacked by Rall's Fighter Wing 300 although he was in hospital at the time. JG 300 acquitted itself well in the unbalanced air battle, downing between fifty and sixty B-24s and B-17s but the unit lost twenty-four pilots, about one-third of its Group.

"It turned out that at the Prague book signing I was the only representative of JG 300 that the Czechs could find alive to sign the books. I was received like a king! There were eighteen Americans, some Czech pilots, and myself. It was amazing!" The mayor turned out replete with a huge gold chain of office around his neck.

Officials drove Günther around the countryside where he

was interested to see that the old German fortresses and Hapsburg castles now bore Czech names. Prague had once been part of the German empire and its university, where Hertha Rall had studied, was the oldest in Europe.

A few years earlier General Rall was at another book-signing jaunt and sat next to a Czech war hero, General Frantizek Perina, who had flown with the RAF. The store was so crowded the police were called to keep order. The Czech pilot's story intrigued Günther and he recounts it here.

"He was fighting with the Allies during World War II but when the Communists ruled Czechoslovakia he was considered an enemy of the state because he was against Communism. He eventually emigrated to the United States and lived there for twenty years. After the Communist government was thrown out of Czechoslovakia by its new president, playwright Vaclav Havel in 1989, General Perina was contacted by Havel and told, Please come home. He did and lives there still. When we spoke," said Rall, "he remarked that it continues to be a matter for debate about who fights for the East, and who fights for the West."

Indeed, Rall is a frequent debater in various countries and at US events at the National Air and Space Museum at the Smithsonian Institution, at the annual "Gathering of Eagles" meetings at Maxwell air force base in Montgomery, Alabama, and at Virginia Bader's symposiums that bring together pilots from opposing sides to re-visit their dogfights and discuss combat tactics. The symposiums give the three-star General Rall an opportunity to educate other nations on his pacifist views towards world peace, even as he describes the horrors of his own war. Still intensely engaged with the world, one of his favorite pastimes is participating in a literary group that meets monthly to discuss the works of new European authors. Diplomats, former ambassadors, and foreign dignitaries continue to seek his company at various gatherings, where he renews his friendships with them, many from ten, twenty, thirty and forty years ago.

"It's fascinating to get together with your old enemies. I've been able to meet with former American, English, and Russian rivals and have a lot of fun as well as serious discussion," said Rall. Since participating in the lively debates he has become good friends not only with Hub Zemke, his old nemesis, but also with Colonel Gabreski, America's most successful World War II fighter pilot, who died in February 2002.

One of Rall's close friends is Lute Eldridge, who gave him a wall plaque engraved with the John Gillespie Magee Jr. poem. Eldridge was a Lockheed test pilot for the F-104 whom Rall met after the war while testing the aircraft on behalf of the new German air force. The eloquent poem had been chosen to be read to the nation by President Ronald Reagan in 1986 after NASA's Challenger space shuttle exploded, killing all on board.

High Flight

"Oh, I have slipped the surly bonds of earth.
And danced the skies on laughter-silvered wings;
Sunward I've climbed, and joined the tumbling mirth
Of sun-split clouds...and done a hundred things
You have not dreamed of...wheeled and soared and swung
High in the sunlit terrace. Hov'ring there,
I've chased the shouting wind along, and flung
My eager craft through footless halls of air.
Up, up the long, delirious, burning blue
I've topped the windswept heights with easy grace
Where never lark, or even eagle flew.
And, while with silent, lifting mind I've trod

The high untrespassed sanctity of space
Put out my hand, and touched the face of God."

Acknowledgements

With grateful thanks to my editor, fighter ace Lt. Colonel Don Lopez, deputy director of the National Air and Space Museum at the Smithsonian Institute, for his unparalleled assistance, knowledge, and editing skills, and to Von Hardesty, museum curator, and Tom Dietz, museum specialist. Thanks also to historian Larry Chambers and his extensive library of military books that were of great assistance, and to Virginia Bader who deserves special thanks for her courage and confidence.

The author also wishes to thank the following for their unstinting and generous cooperation and contributions in the writing of this book:

Felizitas Rall-Wirtz; Lt. General Friedrich Obleser, Luftwaffe; 1st Lt. Kurt Schulze, Luftwaffe; Colonel Walker "Bud" Mahurin, USAF; Major Robert "Shorty" Rankin, USAF; Colonel Keith Phillips, USAF. Ret.; Colonel Joseph E. Andres, USAF Ret.; Ed Maloney, Chino Air Museum, California; Ian Smith, Imperial War Museum, London; Stephen Walton, Imperial War Museum, London; Martin Kruger, Munich; Dr. Frank D. Davis, Landesstelle fin die Nichtstaatlichen Museum, Ret., Munzinger-Archiv, Munich; Mrs. Helena von Wersebe, Hause der Geschichte der Bundesrepublik Deutschland, Bonn; Simone Mauer, Salzburg, translator; Dr. Ronald Loge; Louis C. Amadio;

Marge and Dave Cummock; Brent Hisey; Andy Zillnan; Paul Reidy; John Ryan; John Shaw; Alexander K. Smith; Stephen Craig; Dave Copnall; Steven Bader; James Pye; Joseph Chupas; Bill Hess; and Tom Underhill.

Selected Bibliography

Adolf Galland, David Baker

Adolf Hitler, John Tolland

Air Craft of World War II, Stewart Wilson

Air War Europa, Eric Hammel

Aircraft Of World War II, Stewart Wilson

Atlas Of World War II, Richard Narkiel

Attack Of The Airacobras: Soviet Aces, American P-39s, and the Air War Against Germany (Modern War Studies), Dmitriy Loza, Frank Borman, Von Hardesty (Introduction)

Beware The Thunderbolt, David R. McLaren

Blitzkrieg to Defeat: Hitler's Wartime Directives 1939-1945, H.R. Trevor-Roper

Britain, Germany And Western Nuclear Strategy, Christoph Bluth, 1995

Chronology Of World War II, Edward Davidson and Dale Manning

Cockpit, Donald Nijboer

Diplomatic History, Vol. 19, Journal of the Society for Historians of American Foreign Relations

Encyclopedia Of Weapons Of World War II, Chris Bishop

Fight For The Sky, Douglas Bader

Fighter Aces Of The Luftwaffe, Col. Raymond F. Toliver and Trevor J. Constable

Fighters/The World's Great Aces And Their Planes, Edwards Park
Fighting Aircraft Of World War II, Bill Gunston
Fighting In Hell, edited by Peter Tsouras
Fire In The Sky, Eric M. Bergerud, 2000
France, Germany And The NATO Alliance, Philip H. Gordon
In The Cockpit, Anthony Robinson
Leni Riefenstahl, Leni Riefenstahl
Luftwaffe Fighter Aircraft In Profile, Claes Sundin and Christer
    Bergstrom
Messerschmitt Bf 109, The Operational Record, Jerry Scutts
Messerschmitt Bf. 109, Jochen Prien and Peter Rodeike
*NATO: The Founding Of The Atlantic Alliance And The Integra-
    tion Of Europe*, edited by Francis H. Heller and John R.
    Gillingham
New History Of World War II, C.L. Sulzberger, Stephen E.
    Ambrose
On The Road To The Wolf's Lair, Theodore S. Hamerow
Osterfront Hitler's War On Russia 1841-45, Charles Winchester
Oxford Companion To World War II
Red Phoenix, Von Hardesty
Russia Besieged World War II, Nicholas Bethel
The Blond Knight Of Germany, Colonel Raymond F. Toliver and
    Trevor J. Constable
The Federal Republic Of Germany And NATO, edited by Emil J.
    Kirchner and James Sperling
The First And The Last, Adolf Galland
The Second World War, Martin Gilbert
The Soviet Juggernaut World War II, Earl F. Ziemke
The United States And Germany After 1945, lecture, Thomas A.
    Schwartz, 1995
The Wild Blue, Stephen Ambrose

To Kill The Devil, Herbert Molloy Mason, Jr.

Under The Bombs, Earl R. Beck

War On The Eastern Front, James Lucas

Warplanes Of The Luftwaffe, edited by David Donald

West Point Atlas For The Second World War, Thomas E. Griess

World War II Combat Aircraft, Enzo Angelucci, Paolo Matricardi, Pierluigi Pinto

World War II Day By Day, Donald Sommerville

World War II Sites In The United States, Richard E. Osborne, 1996

Zemke's Wolf Pack, Roger A. Freeman

Index